Lecture Notes in Computer Science 2133

Edited by G. Goos, J. Hartmanis, and J. van Leeuwen

T0216408

Springer
Berlin
Heidelberg
New York
Barcelona
Hong Kong
London
Milan
Paris
Tokyo

Bruce Christianson   Bruno Crispo
James A. Malcolm   Michael Roe (Eds.)

Security Protocols

8th International Workshop
Cambridge, UK, April 3-5, 2000
Revised Papers

 Springer

Series Editors

Gerhard Goos, Karlsruhe University, Germany
Juris Hartmanis, Cornell University, NY, USA
Jan van Leeuwen, Utrecht University, The Netherlands

Volume Editors

Bruce Christianson
James A. Malcolm
University of Hertfordshire, Computer Science Department
Hatfield AL10 9AB, UK
E-mail: {b.christianson/J.A.Malcolm}@herts.ac.uk

Bruno Crispo
Cryptomathic
Corso Svizzera 185, 10149 Torino, Italy
E-mail: bc201@cl.cam.ac.uk

Michael Roe
Microsoft Research Ltd.
St. George House, 1 Guildhall Street, Cambridge CB2 3NH, UK
E-mail: mroe@microsoft.com

Cataloging-in-Publication Data applied for

Die Deutsche Bibliothek - CIP-Einheitsaufnahme

Security protocols : 8th international workshop, Cambridge, UK, April 3 - 5,
2000 ; revised papers / Bruce Christianson ... (ed.). - Berlin ; Heidelberg ;
New York ; Barcelona ; Hong Kong ; London ; Milan ; Paris ; Tokyo :
Springer, 2001
  (Lecture notes in computer science ; Vol. 2133)
  ISBN 3-540-42566-7

CR Subject Classification (1998): E.3, F.2.1-2, C.2, K.6.5, J.1, K.4.1

ISSN 0302-9743
ISBN 3-540-42566-7 Springer-Verlag Berlin Heidelberg New York

Springer-Verlag Berlin Heidelberg New York
a member of BertelsmannSpringer Science+Business Media GmbH

http://www.springer.de

© Springer-Verlag Berlin Heidelberg 2001
Printed in Germany

Typesetting: Camera-ready by author, data conversion by Steingräber Satztechnik GmbH, Heidelberg
Printed on acid-free paper   SPIN: 10840096   06/3142   5 4 3 2 1 0

Preface

The Cambridge International Workshop on Security Protocols has now run for eight years. Each year we set a theme, focusing upon a specific aspect of security protocols, and invite position papers. Anybody is welcome to send us a position paper (yes, you are invited) and we don't insist they relate to the current theme in an obvious way. In our experience, the emergence of the theme as a unifying thread takes place during the discussions at the workshop itself. The only ground rule is that position papers should formulate an approach to some unresolved issues, rather than being a description of a finished piece of work.

When the participants meet, we try to focus the discussions upon the conceptual issues which emerge. Security protocols link naturally to many other areas of Computer Science, and deep water can be reached very quickly. Afterwards, we invite participants to re-draft their position papers in a way which exposes the emergent issues but leaves open the way to their further development. We also prepare written transcripts of the recorded discussions. These are edited (in some cases very heavily) to illustrate the way in which the different arguments and perspectives have interacted.

We publish these proceedings as an invitation to the research community. Although many interesting results first see the light of day in a volume of our proceedings, laying claim to these is not our primary purpose of publication. Rather, we bring our discussions and insights to a wider audience in order to suggest new lines of investigation which the community may fruitfully pursue.

This year's theme is "Broadening the Protocol Boundary". The boundary of a security protocol has traditionally been drawn very narrowly. Many security protocol "failures" involve factors that were not considered part of the protocol, such as the user interface. In addition, security protocols operate in a naturally fragile environment, and not all threats involve malice on the part of an attacker. Where did Alice get the information she sent, and what is Bob going to do with it? Who and what are the protocol end-points, and which domains are they in?

We invite you to consider these issues with us as you read these proceedings. See you next year, perhaps?

July 2001

Bruce Christianson
Bruno Crispo
James Malcolm
Michael Roe

Acknowledgements

Thanks to Professor Stewart Lee and the University of Cambridge Centre for Communications Systems Research who acted as hosts for the workshop, and to Professor Roger Needham FRS and Microsoft Research Limited (Cambridge) who provided us with the use of their meeting room and coffee machine. Plaudits of gratitude also to Dorian Addison of CCSR and to Angela Leeke and Margaret Nicell of MSRL for impeccable organization and administration, to Lori Klimaszewska of the University of Cambridge Computing Service for transcribing the audio tapes (including the static which changed a word attachment into a work of passion) and to Dr Mary Buchannan for her Procrustean editorial assistance.

Previous Proceedings in this Series

The proceedings of previous International Workshops on Security Protocols have also been published by Springer-Verlag as Lecture Notes in Computer Science, and are occasionally referred to in the text:
7th Workshop (1999), LNCS 1796, ISBN 3-540-67381-4
6th Workshop (1998), LNCS 1550, ISBN 3-540-65663-4
5th Workshop (1997), LNCS 1361, ISBN 3-540-64040-1
4th Workshop (1996), LNCS 1189, ISBN 3-540-63494-5

Table of Contents

Keynote Address:
Security Protocols and the Swiss Army Knife
(Transcript of Discussion)

Roger Needham

Microsoft Research

Keynote address is an unnecessarily grand term for what I'm about to do, and I don't particularly guarantee to go on for long — leaving more time for more interesting things. The original theme that was stated for this workshop was broadening the horizons for security protocols and (as is traditional) nobody has said anything about that topic whatever in their papers, so I thought I would see if I could say something about it now so that the theme is not totally overlooked.

Twenty years ago, or thereabouts, there was a certain amount of discussion as to what authentication protocols should actually do. You can either take a very minimalist view which says that the person you thought you were talking to was around recently, a slightly higher view that says the person you thought you were talking to was around recently and if he's still around you've got a shared secret, or you could integrate the authentication stuff into the communication protocol you were going to use in a very complete kind of way. There was a reasonable consensus you shouldn't do the latter. The practical reason put forward for this was quite simple: if your communication does not work you would like to know whether it's the physical communication that has failed or whether somebody is interfering with you, because it's a different expert you call in the two cases.

I remember having this discussion in the late 70's at Xerox PARC, because if you're signing the blocks of a message you might well say, why do we need a communications checksum as well? The answer is, because you want to know what went wrong. It was also the case — quite notoriously at that time — that security protocols were exceptionally difficult to design correctly, and I suspect as a consequence of that people felt well if we've got it right for heavens sake let's not do another one because we'll probably do it wrong.

So the things were regarded as not doing very much, you're very lucky to have got them right if you have got them right, and you tended to say here is a tool we will just use it for everything. It could be that that was the right thing to do, it could be that it *is* the right thing to do, but it also could be that because there has been some advance in knowledge over this period it becomes much more reasonable to design the security protocols fairly freely. If you've got a particular application, design a security protocol that's reasonably tailored to that application, because if the last twenty years of work has not been completely thrown away, we ought to be better at doing it now than we were then.

I don't know whether this is a sensible view or not, but if it is, or can be made to become so, I think one could assert that life will become in some ways, rather more comfortable. Perhaps what we ought to do is try to look where the edges

B. Christianson et al. (Eds.): Security Protocols, LNCS 2133, pp. 1–4, 2001.
© Springer-Verlag Berlin Heidelberg 2001

of security protocols ought to be. You can state this very briefly in the words of Butler Lampson: authentication is knowing where something came from and confidentiality is knowing where it went to. But that still gives quite a lot of space to play with. I don't have any very good ideas for how one might blur the edges but certainly it's the case that, if the authentication operation is a very large proportion of what you're trying to do, you might as well design a protocol for the whole application with the authentication in it and not separate things out. It's a bit reminiscent of discussions about layered design in communication protocols: that layered design may be a good thing, but layered implementation is foolish.

We've tended to commit the analogous sin with security protocols rather a lot, basically I would claim because we're nervous about whether we'll get it right, and we ought to have the tools available to us now to make it easier to get it right. I think that's basically all I want to say.

John Ioannidis: I've been maintaining for a while, in the context of layered design and layered protocol definitions, the attitude that for security protocols there shouldn't necessarily be a single security protocol or single "layer" where we should put security (despite my involvement in IPSec and things like that), but that for every layer into the protocol cake (conceptual layer not implementation layer) either it should be securing itself or there should be an equivalent security version and that these security versions talk to each other. So just because we have a secure network layer doesn't mean that anything above it should be oblivious to the security on the security product in the network layer. Conversely we shouldn't have 15 different security protocols each talking to the one above and to the one below without knowing what each other does.

Reply: I'm sure that's right. I think in communication protocols in general, pretending you didn't know what the neighbouring layers did has been a problem that has plagued us for a while.

Matt Blaze: Steve Bellovin, quoting someone recently, I don't remember who, pointed out that in regard to layering, we've invented this religion but we've become fundamentalists, and I think I'd subscribe to that quip with respect to communications protocols. With security protocols I'm less sure, because the way in which layers above and layers below can tend to change out from under you, is particularly acute with security protocols. For a trivial example, let's imagine designing a security protocol with the requirement that only say 2^{20} or 2^{32} bits of traffic should be allowed to go through without re-keying. The designer of the protocol knows that otherwise he'll get various types of replay attacks, or wrap around on identifiers, or what have you. The designer of the protocol knows that the application won't ever do that because it does messaging or what have you. And then suddenly someone uses precisely the same framework to send streaming video and everything falls apart in ways that are essentially invisible. I think we see that happening fairly often. Designing security protocols to have very well defined layers that have very well defined requirements, is a simple way to avoid this, and some fundamentalism might be in order there.

Reply: Yes, there's certainly a tendency among people who think about security to be fundamentalists for a variety of reasons which would be a separate discussion, but I suppose it's a question of what it costs to do it "properly". If the costs of doing it in the fundamentalist way are extremely low, I suppose most people would say, well do that. If it significantly added to the cost of the transaction then we might say, do it the other way.

Larry Paulson: I'm not entirely sure what you mean by layering, but certainly the methods I know for looking at protocols work when you have the entire protocol in front of you and don't work if you suddenly imagine you are replacing some atomic operation, say if you replace a primitive encryption operation by a one-time pad. I'm not sure that I should know how to reason about systems of protocols unless they are all being analysed at the same time.

Virgil Gligor: The problem that Matt has been pointing out is not a problem peculiar to security. Actually it occurs in other areas of systems design. For example, the major advent of database management systems in the early to mid 70's showed that many of the concurrency- control and recovery protocols in operating systems didn't really do anything for database systems. In fact they got in the way, so the database system designers had to invent those mechanisms and protocols for their own application. The lesson there is, I believe, that we should not hard-wire into lower layers, mechanisms that we could not avoid later in the higher layers.

John Ioannidis: I really like that example, because there is a direct translation of it today. The Voice-over-IP people are rolling their own security protocols for the transfer of data because IPSec is too general. Generality has a price. It may be that generality is actually what we want and we are likely to get sort of an economy of scale, but in other realms generality has a price. The example of operating systems standing in the way of databases is actually a very good one.

Reply: Yes, "the price of generality is unwanted decisions".

Ross Anderson: But if one looks at how this works in practice with banking encryption devices, we have a useful and concrete model. Firstly you've got a lot of devices out there in the field that have a command syntax of say fifty transactions, there are a couple of hundred verbs, or whatever, and it starts off by doing things like encrypt PIN, calculate MAC, and so on. Then that becomes an interface on which everybody has to build, because it's what's sold and what is approved. What happens then is that somebody goes and builds a protocol to talk ISO-8583 which handles banking transactions, and then other people implement that on top of other pieces of hardware, then other people come along and build other protocols which have to be supported on the banking hardware, and so you end up extending the banking hardware so that it will support both ISO-8583 and other stuff. So you've got this crab-wise development, up and down, up and down, and the big risk is that you end up with something so complex that you don't understand it, and you end up with trouble. So this is the real process management problem.

Audience: Seen to a hammer, everything is a nail.

Ross Anderson: It's more than that, I mean you start off with the hammer, then you invent screws and hit them in with the hammer.

John Ioannidis: Or with your wrench.

Reply: And then you end up with both implements highly unoptimised for the purpose.

John Ioannidis: Why use a hammer to pound a screw when you have a wrench?

Reply: Yes, what you're talking about is the inevitable evolution of the Swiss army knife [laughter]; and the analogue of the Swiss army knife for security protocols is even more alarming.

Tuomas Aura: One difference between protocols for the traditional data transfer and for these new applications like voice over IP, or other voice communications and video, is that their concept of integrity is different. Traditionally you would think that message integrity is protecting you so that not a single bit has been corrupted, but for voice you do want to allow bit errors. You don't want to correct them all otherwise a mobile phone would be doing error correction all the time. That is one reason why these new applications need new protocols on them.

Reply: Yes, that's an interesting point, not one that's usually made. I have tended to think that way in connection with such things as encrypting video, but it's certainly true of voice as well.

William Harbison: I'd just like to make a couple of observations about how things actually *have* changed over the years.

When we started this workshop, we deliberately chose the title "Security Protocols" rather than "Cryptographic Protocols". This was considered rather radical at the time, indeed we were often told that one could not have security protocols that did not involve cryptography. I think that there are very few people who would hold that as an absolute article of faith these days, indeed I think many of us know situations where encrypting messages can in fact reduce the security of the system rather than enhance it.

The second observation is that one sees, particularly in certain areas, protocols being designed which are very clever, very intricate, and which come (in the paper which describes them) with an associated set of assumptions, and which are then implemented in a totally different place where a totally different set of assumptions actually apply, and it's the protocol that's blamed rather than the implementation. In fact what has happened is that people have taken a solution from one framework and placed it in another, without understanding the difference between them.

Reply: I'm sure that's right. One of the serious pleas to anybody who publishes in this area is to say what you have assumed, and say it in bigger type than the rest of the paper.

Mergers and Principals

Dieter Gollmann

Microsoft Research
Cambridge, United Kingdom
diego@microsoft.com

Abstract. The term 'principal' has roots both in computer security and in communications security. We will show that in those two areas principals serve quite different purposes. We also note that the term principal is overloaded in computer security and propose a separation into three different aspects: origin of message, access control rule, and accountable entity. Furthermore, we will defend the merits of extensional security specifications and show that it is not fruitful to expect that security mechanisms can only have one 'correct' interpretation.

1 Introduction

The term 'principal' figures prominently in discussions about distributed system security, in particular in the context of authentication. Like 'authentication', the meaning of 'principal' is obvious until it is subjected to closer scrutiny. Although it would be desirable to find one accepted – or acceptable – definition of principals, we will have to settle for elaborating and separating the different usages of this term. As we will try to demonstrate, some of the ambigiuties in terminology result from different historic roots. Principals were used both in computer security (distributed system security) and in communications security. Computer security and communications security supposedly merged about a decade ago, and the two areas definitely used the same language to discuss security concerns. We will examine the effects of this merger on our understanding of principals.

In this paper, we will conduct two case studies. The first case study explores the historic roots of the term 'principal', showing that principals serve quite different purposes in computer security and communications security respectively. The second case study deals with formal semantics for SDSI name resolution. Again, it will become apparent that computer security and communications security can take contrary views of the effects of the same operation. In the light of these observations, we suggest that it is time to contemplate some kind of de-merger, i.e. to properly separate concerns of computer security and communications security and to guard ourselves against letting ideas from one area misguide our understanding of concepts in the other.

B. Christianson et al. (Eds.): Security Protocols, LNCS 2133, pp. 5–13, 2001.
© Springer-Verlag Berlin Heidelberg 2001

2   Principals

We will trace the history of the term 'principal' in attempt to answer questions like: What is a principal? Where do principals come from? What purpose do principals serve? Is there a future for principals?

2.1   Communicating Principals

A first set of quotes is collected from publications that are concerned with authentication in network communications. Publications on Kerberos figure prominently in our selection.

> Principal: A uniquely named client or server that participates in a network communication [15].

> A *principal* is the basic entity which participates in network authentication exchanges. A principal usually represents a *user* or the *instantiation of a network service* on a particular host [13].

> After authentication, two *principals (people, computers, services)* should be entitled to believe that they are communicating with each other and not with intruders [4].

> The fundamental purpose of authentication is to enable *"principals"* to identify each other in a way that allows them to communicate, with confidence that the communication originates with one principal and is destined for the other. The principals we are considering include *people, machines, organizations and network resources such as printers, databases or file systems* [2].

> In distributed computing systems and similar networks of computers, it is necessary to have procedures by which various pairs of *principals (people, computers, services)* satisfy themselves mutually about each other's identity [3].

In summary, principals are entities that communicate with each other and who can be recognized (authenticated) in a conversation. Principals are not necessarily human users. They can equally be a machine or a network service. In communication security, principals are peer entities that can run authentication protocols. They are the source of messages, but the content of these messages is irrelevant for our current considerations.

We note in passing that there exists an interpretation of entity authentication, given in International Standard ISO/IEC 9798-1, where the authenticated principal only has to show that it is alive, i.e. active during the run of the authentication protocol. This definition is not concerned with establishing secure conversations.

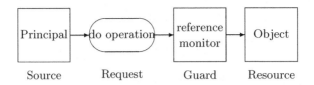

Fig. 1. A model for access control

2.2 Principals in Access Control

In computer security, we meet a scenario where messages are not being sent between equal partners, but more likely between a client and a server. Furthermore, messages are access requests and servers refer to the content of a message when making access control decisions.

> All authentication is on behalf of principals. Principals can act in two capacities, *claimant* or *verifier*. SPX recognizes the following two types of principals, *users (normally people with accounts)* and *servers* [18].

> A *principal* is an entity that can be *granted access* to objects or can make statements affecting access control decisions [7].

> Subjects operate on behalf of *human users* we call *principals*, and access is based on the principal's name bound to the subject in some unforgeable manner at authentication time. Because access control structures identify *principals*, it is important that principal names be globally unique, human-readable and memorable, *easily and reliably associated with known people* [6].

The last quote views principals in a fashion rather different from communications security. Principals are entries in access control structures. To make access control manageable they are closely associated with human users. Principals are sending messages only metaphorically, the actual work is done by subjects operating on their behalf. The following quote sums up the role of principals in access control (see also Figure 1).

> If s is a statement *authentication* answers the question "Who said s?" with a principal. Thus principals make statements; this is what they are for. Likewise, if o is an object *authorisation* answers the question "Who is trusted to access o?" with a principal [14].

Usually the access control structure is attached to the object as an *access control list (ACL)*. For each operation, the ACL specifies a set of authorized principals. To support a wider range of access control policies, the concept of 'principal' is further elaborated and [14] distinguishes between *simple* and *compound* principals. Simple principals are:

- Basic named principals: people, machines, roles
- Other named principals: services, groups
- Channels: wires, I/O ports, crypto keys, network addresses

Compound principals, helping to express policies using roles, delegation, or dual control, are built up out of other principals:

- Principals in roles: Alice **as** Manager
- Delegations: Key_13 **for** Alice
- Conjunctions: Alice $\wedge$ Bob

As a short digression, we note that principals have yet another function in computer security. Consider the Unix operating system. There, UIDs (user identities) are the principals, being an essential parameter in Unix access control. As a further feature of Unix, SUID programs run with the UID of the owner of the program, not with the UID of the user running it. For example, one may create a UID *webserver* and SUID-to-webserver programs to give users controlled access to a web server. Logging the UID of the program requesting access to a web page does not capture the identity of the user. To separate access control from auditing, Unix uses effective (logon) UIDs. We return from the digression and summarize our observations. Principals are

1. the source of messages and access requests,
2. parameters in access rules,
3. entities that can be held accountable (persons).

One term, 'principal', is used for three different purposes. In the model of Figure 1, this happens quite naturally. Principals are the sources of access requests, providing the reference monitor with the means to associate a user's privileges with a current access request. They are the glue between authentication and authorisation:

- Access control information is stored in ACLs.
- Entries in an ACL are 'human readable' principals.
- Complex access rules are captured by compound principals.
- Named principals correspond quite closely to users and roles.

Because a decision was made that access control policies ought to refer to persons (and their roles in an organisation), the access control rules are of the form 'is a given user identity contained in the object's ACL?' Because the chosen access rules refer to user identities, access requests have to be associated with user identities. Thus, we have to establish who sent an access request (authenticate an access request) in order to make an access control decision. Accountable entities must be natural or legal persons, which just happen to be our access control parameters.

From such a viewpoint, it may seem that access control by definition requires that identities (of persons) be verified. However, it is more accurate to conclude that such a view reflects the security policies distributed systems were asked to enforce a decade ago. Then, the major paradigm was still a closed user community. Computer systems controlled access to documents more than access to services. UIDs and ACLs were well suited for such an environment. Cross-domain authentication created links between closed user groups and did not fundamentally extend the scope of access control scenarios.

The changes of the last decade have made it much clearer that the three aspects of 'principal' actually refer to three separate concepts. For example, on the world wide web we can deal with parties we have never met before. Hence, their 'identity' can hardly figure in our access rules. Indeed, there is no necessity to describe or enforce access control by reference to users.

> In answering the question "is the key used to sign this request authorized to take this action?", a trust management system should not have to answer the question "whose key is it?" [5].

Other access control parameters like role, location (network address), date and time, code identity, code author, etc. will be more relevant for writing security policies. It is therefore time to divide principals into three separate concepts.

- Principal as source: 'Alice on Tuesday' is an access rule but not a proper source, not the least because the date is not provided by Alice but read from a (local) clock by the reference monitor. Code identities and code signatures complicate the picture further.
- Principal as access rule: Increasingly, access rules do not refer to users but to locations, code identities, or code signatures.
- Principal as accountable entity: The buck has to stop with a person.

To decide on an access request, it is not necessary to determine its source. An access rule has to be evaluated. The parameters used by the access rule have to be verified. We could refer to the access rule as principal and to the verification of parameters as authentication. Alternatively, we could use principal only for those parameters in a *security context* (see [9]) that we view as the source of a request. Then, authentication retains its traditional meaning of checking where a request came from. Compound principals fit better with the first interpretation.

Two quotes, separated by a decade, are further evidence for a subliminal migration from sources of requests to parameters in access rules. In the first quote, principals are the sources of access requests issued via subjects working on their behalf.

> 1989: Principals are *subjects* in the TCSEC sense, but not all subjects are principals [7].

In the second quote, principals are the collection of access control parameters associated with the subjects making access requests.

> 1999: The term principal represents a *name* associated with a subject. Since subjects may have multiple names, a subject essentially consists of a collection of principals [10].

3   Name Resolution

Our second case study investigates name resolution and PKIs. Public key infrastructures (PKIs) are currently a fashion item in security. Precise definitions are hard to come by but the common elements in a PKI are certificates, certification authorities (CAs), certificate users, and of course principals. Examples for PKIs are X.509v3, SDSI, and SPKI. Certificates are signed data structures binding names to cryptographic keys. For any given PKI, algorithms are needed to correctly interpret certificates and, in particular, to evaluate chains of certificates. Indeed, it is sometimes suggested that these algorithms together with the format of the certificates uniquely imply the true meaning of the PKI.

We will now look at principals and name resolution in the Simple Distributed Security Infrastructure (SDSI) [16]. In SDSI, certificates bind local names to principals. Principals are explained as follows.

Think of a principal as a public key, and concurrently as one who *speaks*.

This definition is quite neutral. We are not yet told how public keys will be used. Also, 'speaks' has yet to be stripped of its anthropomorphic connotations and given a meaning more congruent with cryptographic keys. Be forewarned. Speaking is an act of communication, whilst computer security uses the expression 'a channel speaks for a principal' when the channel has been associated with that principal's access rights [14].

SDSI creates linked local name spaces. A principal (cryptographic key) *Bob* assigns the local name *Alice* to a public key k by issuing a certificate binding *Alice* to k. The principal called *Alice* by *Bob* is referred to as *Bob's Alice*. In turn, there may be entries in *Alice's* name space. Name resolution answers the question: 'Who is *Bob's Alice's Mother?* SDSI includes a non-deterministic name resolution algorithm.

Given a name resolution algorithm, it is only natural to ask whether it works correctly. Hence, formal semantics for name resolution are required. In [1], this task is approached in the context of access control. A name in a local name space corresponds to an access right (a parameter in access rules). A certificate $n \rightarrow p$, binding a key (principal) p to an access right (local name) n implies that p gets the access rights associated with n. In the language of computer security, 'principal p speaks for n'.

In this language, group members speak for the group. Group members have more rights than the group, because they get all the rights given to the group in addition to those given to them individually. In this spirit, the semantics of name resolution in [1] has the relation $n \subset p$ at its core. The SDSI name resolution algorithm gives results consistent with this formal semantics, but there are derivations the semantics permits that cannot be computed by the algorithm.

To motivate the formal semantics for name resolution in [11] we refer to email as a typical application. The names in a local name space are mail aliases, principals are public keys mail may be sent to. Speaking becomes synonymous with sending mail messages. A certificate $n \rightarrow p$, binding a key p to a mail alias

n, implies that p is a member of n. The certificate is read as 'n contains p'. The semantics of name resolution in [11] is characterized by the relation $n \supset p$. Indeed, n will contain more mail addresses than p.

This second semantics of name resolution is a better match for the SDSI name resolution algorithm. There no longer exist derivations that are semantically correct but cannot be computed by the algorithm. Does this mean that the second semantics is the correct interpretation of SDSI name resolution, or is it the case that SDSI name resolution fits better into the email paradigm? In principle, the application should define the meaning of name resolution. A name resolution algorithm may or may not comply with the intentions of a given application.

4   Conclusions

The concepts dominating today's view of security were formed more than a decade ago and have to be understood in their historic context. Ten years ago, it was fashionable to announce the merging of computing and communications. Tectonic plates do not merge, they collide and create faults. Concepts sitting across fault lines are instable. Authentication, identity, principal, and certificate, are all examples for terms affected by such developments. For example, when we encounter the claim that entity authentication only applies to persons, most likely an idea from computer security has crept into communications security.

This paper carries on from our contribution to last year's workshop [9], revising the concepts at the core of distributed system security and trying to interpret these concepts in a way consistent with today's security challenges. We observe that access control does not need identities, as shown by current 'open' e-commerce systems or the security model of the original Java sandbox. Conceptually, we have to decide whether to interpret compound principals as composite sources or as composite access rules. The line separating authentication from authorisation has to be redrawn in a world where properties other than 'identity' form the basis of access control.

A high level view of security theory and practice shows that intensional specifications of security mechanisms are often substituted for extensional specifications (see [17] for more explanations), hoping to explain the true meaning of a mechanism by looking at its mechanical details. In [8], we have shown that formal intensional specifications of authentication sometimes deviate considerably from the original informal goals of authentication, thus creating their own artificial requirements.

Here, we have made a similar point about PKIs and name resolution. PKIs have no inherent meaning. In a given environment they serve a given purpose. Consider, the familiar distinction between *identity certificates* and *attribute certificates*, based on the nature of the name in a certificate. We claim that it does not matter so much whether the name refers to an identity or to an attribute. This distinction is actually dangerous because it is intuitive, correct, but still hides the 'real' difference, which lies in the intended use of the certificate. As shown above, name resolution for access control and name resolution for communications follows opposing rules.

A further instance of this problem can be found in another contribution to this workshop [12]. There, a PKI is described where a certification authority *CA1* issues identity certificates whilst another authority *CA2* issues attribute certificates relying on the identity certificates from *CA1*. These attribute certificates are used by a server when making access control decisions. When the PKI is constructed in this order, we face an awkward decision when exploring the effects of revoking an identity certificate. A number of choices for revocation policies exists, and different applications may not agree on their preferred policy. Hence, it would be dangerous to try to divine the access control policy from the PKI we have constructed. Rather, we should start from the policy and build up a PKI, considering questions of revocation at each step.

As a final thought, security is difficult when technical concepts are discussed in anthropomorphic terms. Security is difficult when discussed in the wrong framework. Unfortunately, current security discussions give ample room for confusion.

References

1. Martín Abadi. On SDSI's linked local name spaces. *Journal of Computer Security*, 6:3–21, 1998.
2. Andrew D. Birrell, Butler W. Lampson, Roger M. Needham, and Michael D. Schroeder. A global authentication service without global trust. In *Proceedings of the 1986 IEEE Symposium on Research in Security and Privacy*, pages 223–230, 1986.
3. Michael Burrows, Martín Abadi, and Roger Needham. Authentication: A practical study in belief and action. In M. Y. Vardi, editor, *Theoretical Aspects of Reasoning About Knowledge*, pages 325–342, 1988.
4. Michael Burrows, Martín Abadi, and Roger Needham. A logic of authentication. *DEC Systems Research Center*, Report 39, revised February 22 1990.
5. Joan Feigenbaum. Overview of the AT&T Labs trust-management project. In *Security Protocols*, LNCS 1550, pages 45–50. Springer Verlag, 1998.
6. M. Gasser. The role of naming in secure distributed systems. In *Proceedings of the CS'90 Symposium on Computer Security*, pages 97–109, Rome, Italy, November 1990.
7. M. Gasser, A. Goldstein, C. Kaufman, and B. Lampson. The digital distributed system security architecture. In *Proceedings of the 1989 National Computer Security Conference*, 1989.
8. Dieter Gollmann. On the verification of cryptographic protocols – a tale of two committees. In S. Schneider, editor, *ENTCS Proceedings of the DERA/RHBNC workshops on Secure Architectures and Information Flow*, 1999. Elsevier, 2000. http://www.elsevier.nl/locate/entcs/volume32.html.
9. Dieter Gollmann. Whither authentication. In M. Roe, editor, *Proceedings of the 1999 Cambridge Security Protocols Workshop*. Springer Verlag, to appear.
10. Li Gong. *Inside Java 2 Platform Security*. Addison-Wesley, Reading, MA, 1999.
11. J. Y. Halpern and R. van der Meyden. A logic for SDSI linked local name spaces. In *Proceedings of the 12th IEEE Computer Security Foundations Workshop*, pages 111–122, 1999.

12. Himanshu Khurana and Virgil D. Gligor. Review and revocation of access privileges distributed with PKI certificates. In *this proceedings*.
13. J. T. Kohl. The evolution of the kerberos authentication service. In *Spring 1991 EurOpen Conference*, Tromsø, Norway, 1991.
14. Butler Lampson, Martín Abadi, Michael Burrows, and Edward Wobber. Authentica- tion in distributed systems: Theory and practice. *ACM Transactions on Computer Systems*, 10(4):265–310, November 1992.
15. S. P. Miller, B. C. Neuman, J. I. Schiller, and J. H. Saltzer. Section E.2.1: Kerberos authentication and authorization system. Technical report, MIT Project Athena, Cam- bridge, MA, 1987.
16. Ron Rivest and Butler Lampson. SDSI – a simple distributed security infrastruc- ture. Technical report, 1996. `http://theory.lcs.mit.edu/~cis/sdsi.html`.
17. A. W. Roscoe. Intensional specifications of security protocols. In Proceedings of the 9th IEEE Computer Security Foundations Workshop, pages 28–38, 1996.
18. J. J. Tardo and K. Alagappan. SPX – global authentication using public-key cer- tificates. In *Proceedings of the 1991 IEEE Symposium on Research in Security and Privacy*, pages 232–244, 1991.

Mergers and Principals
(Transcript of Discussion)

Dieter Gollman

Microsoft Research

When the topic of the workshop was announced I found that for a change I had a paper which was relevant; maybe not broadening the horizon in itself, but pointing out some of the dangers you might encounter in this process. The relation to authentication comes through principals, and the origins of this presentation go back to Autumn last year when Ross Anderson asked me once again to give a talk at the Computer Lab and in despair I decided to find out what this term principal could really mean.

Ten years ago, not twenty as in Roger's talk, the fashionable statement was, this is the time where computing and communications are merging. What I want to start with in this talk, is to examine the effect of this merger on two case studies. One has to do, as I said, with exploring the meaning of the term principal, the other is name resolution, where I had recently been asked to review a few papers and came across observations I want to share with you. Having a read a few papers on company policies in recent times, it seems that today the management gurus tell companies to concentrate on the core business, so it's a time of de-mergers.

Case study one: what is a principal, where does this term come from, what purpose does it serve, what is it's future? Here are some quotes taken from papers around Kerberos, from a community talking about communication:

Principal: A uniquely named client or server that participates in a network communication.

A principal is the basic entity which participates in network authentication exchanges. A principal usually represents a user or the instantiation of a network service on a particular host.

After authentication, two principals (people, computers, services) should be entitled to believe that they are communicating with each other and not with intruders.

A principal is anything that can sign messages.

The fundamental purpose of authentication is to enable principals to identify each other in a way that allows them to communicate, with confidence that the communication originates with one principal and is destined for the other.

All authentication is on behalf of principals. Principals can act in two capacities, claimant or verifier. SPX recognizes the following two types of principals, users (normally people with accounts) and servers.

The principals we are considering include people, machines, organizations and network resources such as printers, databases or file systems.

B. Christianson et al. (Eds.): Security Protocols, LNCS 2133, pp. 14–19, 2001.
© Springer-Verlag Berlin Heidelberg 2001

So a principal is something that participates in a communication. A principal is something that can be authenticated. Interesting at the bottom is "A principal is anything that can sign messages". Within the same set of papers, again stressing principals are closely related to authentication, what I did not stress on the previous slide was one remark saying a principal can be a programme, a server, a person, we are quite general on this behalf. Stressed here, a principal can be a fair range of things engaging in communication, principals can be authenticated.

From about the same period, late 80s, there is a different set of papers, and they are associated with digital distributed system security architecture. Morrie Gasser happens to be one name popping up again and again as an author for the papers I'm quoting here:

> A principal is an entity that can be granted access to objects or can make statements affecting access control decisions.
> Subjects operate on behalf of human users we call principals, and access is based on the principal's name bound to the subject in some unforgeable manner at authentication time.
> Because access control structures identify principals, it is important that principal names be globally unique, human-readable and memorable, easily and reliably associated with known people.

So now a principal is something that can be granted access. There is this strong argument: you want to do access control, access control has to be understood by a human being, so the terms you should use, the principals you should use for access control, really very closely reflect human beings. Which is not what principals were on the previous line. This is history really, that is Butler Lampson's model of authentication and authorisation: the rôle of the principal is to issue access requests, the rôle of the reference monitor is to check where an access request comes from – that's called authentication – and then look up the rule and decide whether the principal actually should get access – and that step is called authorisation.

I've been saying this is history, but it's still quite important because even today (if I read papers on access control in distributed systems, authentication in distributed systems), that is the reference point I want to go back to, that's how they want to think about the world. There are simple principals like people, machines, rôles, and there are compound principals, a principal working in some rôle, delegation, conjunction of principals.

Maybe one should start to note that earlier the principal was the source of a request, whilst now principals are becoming rules, and I will elaborate this point later. There are two meanings of principal in this world and they start to deviate.

In the 1992 model of access control, principals are quite definitely the glue between authentication and authorisation: the access control information is stored in access control lists, the entries in an access control list are human readable principals, complex rules are compound principals, and if you follow this view, you might end up with the conviction that to do access control (because access control consists of authentication and authorisation, because authentication means establishing the source of a message, or of an access request), you really have to know where access requests come from. It is sort of subconsciously suggested to you if that is your frame of mind.

Question, to break the flow of argument up a bit. Some five years ago I got an e-mail from a gentleman from the ANSI Committee in charge of standardising authentication, and his request was, can you please help, I have two sets of people on my committee, one set insists that authentication only applies to persons, and the other set says, no, it's much more general. Can it be that these ideas from computer security access control have somehow made the way into the other communications security community, and you see this fault line between two worlds which haven't merged.

So, principals are both sources of messages, parameters in access rule, and (I have to acknowledge Martin Abadi on his train ride back to London) entities (people) that can be held accountable. So the question to be discussed in a short time: should we use one word, one concept for three very different types of concept in our world of computer security? And linked to that, might it be the case that the term principal we're using, and that still has a fair influence on the way we think about security in distributed systems, reflects the world as it was ten years ago?

Things have changed in the last decade. Given the mantra of electronic commerce – you can do business with people you've never met before – the identity of those people you have never met before doesn't look like a good parameter to use in access control. I heard a very nice talk last Autumn at NORDSEC'99 in Sweden by Zven Laanshon from the Swedish Defence Materiel Administration, and he was saying the old paradigm – creating your own island, protecting your data – is no longer relevant for what we're trying to do now. It is about participating in the global information infrastructure and protecting your information flow, but not in the sense of information models of the past. Matt Blaze and trust management speakers have made this point. Here there are actually two processes one could look at in terms of access control: one is finding out about the rule one wants to apply, the other is applying that rule.

Some suggestions on why I don't think principal as the source of an access request is very meaningful; Roger's favourite example that meet "him as a manager" is a fine principal but meet "him on Tuesday" isn't really a source. Access rules, I would claim, increasingly do not refer to identities but to other issues like location, code identities, code signatures. And with accountability, you are still talking to people. So, change your focus.

A reminder of last year's diagram fits a little bit in with changing your focus. I'd made the point last year, and I'm making it again, that it might be worthwhile thinking about access control by ignoring the centre and trying to find out – or trying to discount access controls in terms of – what happens at the receiver's side.

I want to go on now to my next case study: Public key infrastructures. Fashion item this year, go to any commercial event, that's what you have to have, public key infrastructures. Certificates, data structures binding principals to local names. A quote from the SDSI paper: think of a principal as a public key and concurrently it's one who speaks. So the question is, what do we mean by speak, and I claim it is symptomatic that the authors of SDSI are Ron Rivest and Butler Lampson, coming from the two worlds of access control and cryptography/communications.

In the world of access control a channel speaks for the principal using the channel. You could say the principal gets the access rights associated with the local name. The local name would be used as a parameter in an access rule. Martin Abadi has written a paper on the logic of name resolution and compared what his logic does to what the name resolution gives you. In his world, the arrow from the name to the principal matches a subset relation, and in my view of the world, that fits quite nicely. If a user speaks on a channel, or if the channel speaks with the user, the request coming on that channel gets the access rights associated with the user, maybe more. If you think in terms of groups and members of groups, then as a member of a group I get all the access rights given to the group, but I might have more individually. So again this subset relation fits nicely.

Then a couple of years ago at a computer security foundations workshop there was paper by Halpern and R. van der Meyden on getting the name resolution logic right[1] and my view (they're not very explicit about it) is when they think about speaking, they think about sending e-mail messages. If you then look at the local name as something like a mail alias – definitely they say a certificate indicates that the principal is a member of the local name, member of the group, read this as "N contains P" – then they end up with a logical name resolution that is exactly the dual of what you saw before. The local name is a superset of the principal. It makes sense with mail addresses: Microsoft contains more mail addresses than Microsoft Research Cambridge, and Microsoft Research Cambridge contains more addresses than the Security Research Group here, and so on. That's why (which is the main point really of this talk) you have two worlds – communication *and* access control — that look at the same topic, name resolution and they come up with extremely different interpretations of what the world really looks like.

So, plate tectonics, we were talking about the merger of computing and communication, and I look at it as two tectonic plates meeting. They don't merge, they create force. If you have a term like principal, or authentication, or certificate, or name resolution, that's used in both worlds, those terms are dangerous terms because they are unstable, they cross a fault line. And the reason is that you have these two worlds, they are different, and one has to be aware of the differences.

---

[1] A Logic for SDSI's Linked Local Name Spaces: J.Y Halpern and R. van der Meyden (submitted to the Journal of Computer Security)

So some remarks:

- Access control does not need identities.
- Protocols do not have inherent meanings you find out by simply looking at the protocol and analysing the messages being sent, you have to specify the environment and intention they should serve and *then* you can check whether the protocol does what it's supposed to do.

and some questions:

- Is a compound principal a complex source, or a complex access rule?
- Where is the line that separates authentication from authorisation if you do away with the concept that everything has to come from a principal?

So, de-merge IT security again. Be aware when you are talking about communications, and when you are talking about access control.

Ross Anderson: Is there any useful heritage of the era in the 1970's when communications and access control were more or less one subject?

Virgil Gligor: I personally think that there never was such a time. A lot of organisations never merged. They had two very separate groups, two very separate concerns, who didn't quite trust each other.

Ross Anderson: But at some point they talk to each other.

Matt Blaze: Let me make a really nasty comment (and then back off from it). The difference between the crypto world and the security (and protocols) world is that the crypto world has made progress and security world has regressed. Let me just backtrack and say that politely: that the requirement of encrypting is becoming much more complex wherein ...

Virgil Gligor: Our universe has expanded much more rapidly.

Matt Blaze: The requirement of a cipher has not changed, whereas the requirements of a secure computing organisation system most certainly have.

Virgil Gligor: Are you saying that the security area or that the act of controlling has regressed? Security always takes second place to application functionality, and that by the way is the way it should be.

John Ioannidis: Yes, this is another one of those perennial problems, that most people designing applications (whether communications or not) when the protocol is finished, call up Matt or me or one of us and they say, I've got this wonderful new protocol, can you make sure it's secure. They want the blessing of the security pixie dust. It's extremely hard to convince people that they shouldn't be first designing the protocol and then come to me, that it's not the way it should be done. There is a universal reply to "this doesn't work", which is "all right, so tell me how to do it". It's a lost cause, and I don't know how to respond to it, and that's another way of putting your comment.

Matt Blaze: People ask, I designed this protocol and we've just realised it had to be secure, can you please take a look at it and tell us if it's secure. Invariably my answer will be one of two things, either I can't tell because I don't even understand what you've done, let alone know whether it's secure; or there's something obviously wrong with it, like the first part of the protocol is transmit the key in the clear, and you say no it's completely insecure and broken in some fundamental way that can't be fixed. Invariably the answer then is, oh I'm sorry, you've told me something I don't want to hear, I'm going to spin the wheel again and ask someone else. And you know it sounds very cynical but the security engineering of protocols whose primary function is not security, it's something that simply doesn't happen very often.

Roger Needham: I once heard this dialogue in a large U.S. software house:

Q: Is this protocol secure?

A: Tell me what it's for.

Q: Uh, let me get back to you.

Authentication and Naming
(Transcript of Discussion)

My original title for this talk was going to be why IPSec doesn't work, and I started out writing this. Then I realised that what I was going to talk about was far more general than just fiddling about with one particular network layer encryption protocol. In fact there is a general problem that I'm starting to see in lots of protocols all over the place, which indeed is related to some of the things Dieter was talking about earlier. And so what I really want to talk about is authentication and naming.

Now it is possible to have authentication without names. If you have a point to point link, and you give the same symmetric key to both ends of the link, then they can quite happily authenticate each other. Quite clear: it matches the key, it's from the other end. I don't need any other name for it, other than it's the other end of this piece of wire. So you can have authentication without naming.

But typically you get into situations where there's more than a point to point link. You have "quote" Alice, and "quote" Bob, and the key distribution server. The key distribution server tells Alice that she is talking to Bob, and tells Bob that she is talking to Alice. Unfortunately in this picture, by calling them Alice and Bob – these nice friendly human names – we are perpetrating a great and very serious deception. These entities aren't really called things like Alice and Bob. They have various kinds of binary identifier, many of which are not human representable. We're also assuming everybody knows what Alice means, everybody knows who Alice is. But in a lot of distributed systems, it's completely unclear to some of the participants in the interaction what this identifier actually refers to.

So this is the core problem: naming is hard, and authentication protocols inevitably buy into naming problems. A lot of the reasons why our authentication protocols don't work is nothing to do with the crypto, it's not the block cipher that's the problem, it's that you're binding things to the wrong kind of name.

The example I first wanted to talk about was IPSec. There's a distinction in the Internet protocols between your name in the domain name service, or in a host, something like www.microsoft.com, and the IP address, which is this numeric dotted quad. Whenever you're designing a protocol where you've use any security protocol on top, you've got to think to yourself: which of these two things ought I to be binding the key to?

Now it turns out that in IPSec implementations, usually, long term keys get down to addresses. They get put in to certificates which have lifetimes measured in years, they get stuck in configuration files who have lifetimes measured in – well, until next time the system administrator gets round to editing the file.

B. Christianson et al. (Eds.): Security Protocols, LNCS 2133, pp. 20–23, 2001.
© Springer-Verlag Berlin Heidelberg 2001

Unfortunately IP addresses in the current Internet are not long-lived quantities. There's a thing called dynamic post-configuration protocol: you plug your machine into the network, switch it on, and some server on the network tells you what IP address you have, for some length of time, typically in hours. If you switch your machine off and come back later, you're likely to get a different one. It's even possible that, while you're running, you will be told, oh your lease has expired, sorry, you can't have that address anymore. Here's your new address. So the bottom bits of the address change because of that.

Also, because of what the people designing routers are doing, the top bits of your address can change as well. There was an assumption in the early days of the Internet that routers can have knowledge of where every network is in the world. So they can have a big table in memory, just look at the top bits of the address, and say: right, that goes out on this interface.

As the number of networks became larger – for some of the papers I was looking back on, 10,000 hosts on the Internet would be a large number, and we are now considerable orders of magnitude beyond that – as it gets bigger, it becomes harder and harder to keep up to date these big tables containing every network.

So what you do is route aggregation: you say, these several networks which are all down that same trunk over there, I am going to force them to all have the same high order bits in their network address, so that I only need one entry in my table. But this means that when you change your network topology – when you put in a new fibre optic trunk or something that changes your topology in a drastic fashion – you are then going to have to force them to change their addresses. Because if they kept the same addresses, you would have to split up separate entries in the table, and you don't have enough RAM for that, so no, you've got to renumber them.

So all in all, all the bits of your address are potentially changeable. And yet this address is the thing that IPSec is using to look up the key to work out whether you are you. This is just clearly not on, but it's really hard to fix.

The second example goes back to ten years ago, when I was working on X.400 security. (Yes, I did that.) X.400 has a nice naming architecture for users, with structured addressing, attribute values, etc. And of course it uses X.500 directory service for its certificates, which also has a nice structured form for addresses. Not the same nice, structured form for addresses. So you're asking the question: I want to send this message to a particular mailbox, which key should I use?

Well, my names for mailboxes and my names for certificates to get me keys are in completely incomparable spaces. There's no way the program can work out which one corresponds to which, other than by asking the user – who can do some kind of textual comparison possibly, or have some kind of out-of-band knowledge – and so it really fundamentally doesn't work. Because you're binding names to the wrong things.

It then got worse, when I started doing privacy enhanced mail, because then you had RFC822 names for mailboxes, and X.509 certificates. These names are not even vaguely similar. They're from different standards bodies. And yet the program somehow has got to bridge from one to the other. You just can't do it, other than by electronic mail pushing the problem up to the user and saying, OK I'm going to display this on your screen, it's your problem to work out whether these two different names relate to the same entity or not. And this was a cheat, because the user didn't know either.

Now I work for Microsoft and look at things like Microsoft Exchange. The latest round of this is that Exchange – in some respects – uses numeric identifiers within a domain and RFC822 mail messages outside the domain. So you've got two sorts of recipients, those that you know by number, and those that you know by RFC822 name. You also have two sorts of certificates, those certificates where the subject is a number, and those where the certificate subject is an RFC822 name. Now if you get the right sort of certificates matched up with the right sort of e-mail message, all well and good and things work swimmingly. However, there is plenty of scope for getting this drastically, horribly wrong, where the sort of certificate you've got for the thing you want to send to is not the right sort of certificate for the protocol interaction that you want to do.

It's hard to know what to do about this, other than to say that Alice/Bob discussions are in some ways deeply misleading and cause these problems. Because you have high level specification systems that talk about Alice and Bob, it smoothes over the fact that one part of the protocol stack is refining Alice as one kind of computer process-able identifier, and another part of the specification is refining Alice into a completely different human readable identifier, and you really just have got to get this right.

My final comment on naming problems is to do with the Web and the Domain Name Service (DNS), where you've got all these things happening at once. In your URL you have the DNS name. You click on security properties, see the certificate which has in it, and lo and behold, an X.500 name from something that is not only syntactically in a different form, but often is completely surprising: so you discover it was in a different country, the country codes are even different, you suddenly discover that the two different naming authorities thought the thing you were talking to was in different countries. Its name can be completely different: the name somebody is trading as, that they get as their nice friendly website address, may be very, very different from the real proper registered limited company name the certification authority gave them in the certificate.

And lastly, DNS names are a bit problematic because you can basically have any DNS name you like. You go to NSI and say I would like `flobble.com` – that's probably been taken, but you think of some implausible string that nobody else has had yet – and lo and behold you get given this implausible string. Then somebody wants to authenticate you, and even if the protocol says, I am `implausible-string`, this tells them nothing useful about who I really am, or whether they should trust whether I am the person in the real world (or the business in the real world) that they actually wanted to talk to.

It's all a horrible mess and we need to think about this very carefully when we're designing real protocols, and I think sometimes this misleading Alice/Bob discussion has got us into this problem.

Matt Blaze: OK, you've rubbed salt in a lot of wounds here. The interesting example you ended on was pointing out that the one problem that you *can* solve is binding your DNS name. From the application's point of view, that's not what you really want to know: you really want to know are you dealing with the company you wanted to. But you pointed out that we know how to solve the problem of, are you dealing with `microsoft.com`, but in fact we don't even have the infrastructure required to do that. Even though that's a fundamentally simple problem from a protocol point of view.

I think a lot of the reason that we can't do many of the things that you describe today, even though conceptually they could be simple – they're tied up in these layers of incompatible programs, incompatible certificate formats, and so on – are in fact commercial problems rather than technical problems. For example, the name `microsoft.com` or `e.com` or what have you, is issued by an NSI or by your Internet naming authority. There's no fundamental reason why at the time they agree to give you the name, they can't also bind your public key. They don't do that. Instead there is a separate business, VeriSign or whatever, that believes it can make quite a bit of money, charging far more than you paid for the name, simply for selling you a certificate that says that NSI gave you this name, even though this from a technical point of view makes no sense whatsoever. So I think it would be interesting to try to understand which problems are technical and which problems are business/commercial problems.

There's been a myth, perpetrated by those who want to sell certificates and PKI systems, that the issuance of a public certificate is a remarkably heavy weight operation. You know, you must need steam powered equipment in the basement of your facility in order to stamp out those certificates, which have to be made out of titanium or what have you. In fact we design protocols and software and systems that do the equivalent operation of issuing certificates all the time, yet for commercial reasons we've become quite commercial.

Reply: The name-binding problem is one that goes both within the technical sphere and outside into the business sphere. Purely in the domain of protocol design, we can fix the problem of different protocols using different names for the same entity. But also you get a related surrounding procedural problem, that you've got to ensure binding between the names you use within the protocols and the names that are being used in the real world which are completely outside the protocol. Even if you solve the first of those problems, you've still got to deal with the last of them.

Matt Blaze: But we haven't even solved the first one.

Reply: But we haven't even solved the first one, yes.

Ross Anderson: I'd like to add to this point saying that I don't think these problems are even in principle soluble using mechanisms which people would find acceptable, because they present real problems in the real world and you can't fix those by messing about with computers.

Users and Trust in Cyberspace

Pekka Nikander and Kristiina Karvonen

Helsinki University of Technology
{Pekka.Nikander, Kristiina.Karvonen}@hut.fi

Abstract. The underlying belief and knowledge models assumed by various kinds of authentication protocols have been studied for well over 10 years now. On the other hand, the related question of the generic trust assumptions, which underlie the settings where the protocols are run, has received less attention. Furthermore, the notion of trust, as it is typically defined, has more been based on the formal model used than the real user requirements posed by the application context and the actual people using the system.

In this paper, we approach that problem from the users' point of view. We briefly describe what are the psychological bases on which typical people build their trust assumptions on, and consider how these are reflected in a typical e-commerce setting today. Given this background, we proceed to contemplate how the systems could be made more trustworthy by explicitly representing the trust assumptions and requirements, and how these digital expressions of trust could be instrumented to and integrated with actual authentication protocols. Thus, our aim is to broaden the view from a protocol centric approach towards considering the actual users, and to provide some initial requirements for future operating systems and user interface design.

1   Introduction

The majority of computer system users are relatively ignorant about the security, or non-security, of the systems they use. In fact, if asked, they tend to claim that they do not care [1]. However, if the same people are asked to explain how they adapt their behaviour according to the situation at hand, it rapidly becomes apparent that much of their behaviour is based on the *perceived* sense of security or insecurity. [2]

Still today, most people seem to consider computer systems almost godly; the computers are considered so complex that they could be understood, and it is generally believed and explained that computers themselves are unable to err, that is, whenever a computer seems to make a mistake, the fault is presumed to lie on the user. Furthermore, the computers seem to demand ungodly amounts of sacrifice in the form of time spent in getting them to produce the output desired (and getting them work in the first place). Besides, the publicity received by the various kinds of attacks against Internet based systems, along with the general opinion starting to consider personal computers unreliable[1], is slowly deepening

---

[1] Hereby we want to thank the parent organization of the workshop organizer for educating the general public's opinion, especially in the area of reliability of personal

B. Christianson et al. (Eds.): Security Protocols, LNCS 2133, pp. 24–35, 2001.
© Springer-Verlag Berlin Heidelberg 2001

the situation. Thus, a typical unconscious attitude against a computer system may well resemble the attitude paid towards an austere god that requires blind faith and dedication.

When we consider this typical user attitude with the complexities involved in designing, implementing and verifying actual security protocols, we get an initial impression on the obstacle to be tackled. Fortunately, the work spend on analysing the underlying belief models of authentication protocols (e.g. [3], [4], [5], [6]), in modelling trust in technical sense (e.g. [7], [8], [9], [10]), and in providing infrastructures for expressing authorization and trust in open systems (e.g. [11], [12], [13], [14]), together with more user centric work (e.g. [1], [2], [15], [16]), allows us to outline a map of the problem area. Basically, we surmise that combining explicit, key oriented authorization with operating system level security and basic user interface design, could provide a sound technical basis for expressing the technical trustworthiness of a system in a way understandable to the average user. This, combined with enough of market reputation and supporting legislation, might be able to convert the Internet from its current insecure state into one where people could base their actions on reasonable security assumptions even when they do not possess deep technical knowledge about computer systems or information security.

In this paper, we attempt to give a glimpse to this possible solution approach. We start with the user centric view, considering how the aspects affecting the average user in making trust decisions, continuing to contemplate how some of these aspects could be expressed in digital form, and concluding with ideas how these digital expressions could be used in conjunction with actual security protocols.

1.1   About the Nature of Trust

The term "trust" is used in the literature to denote several different but related phenom-ena. Basically, a distinction can be made between two basic meanings. In computer se-curity literature in general, the term is used to denote that something must be trusted (e.g. Trusted Computing Base, TCB). That is, something trusted is something that the users are necessarily dependent on. If a trusted component breaks, the security of all of the system breaks. On the other hand, in this paper, as well as elsewhere in more psy-chologically oriented literature, the term is used to denote that something can be trusted. That is, something trusted is something that the users feel comfortable with to be dependent on. If a trusted component breaks, the users feel betrayed. Probably some harm is done to the security of the system, but that is less relevant to this discussion.

This distinction should be kept in mind when reading this paper. In this paper, the term trust is used to denote the psychological attitude of being willing to be dependent on something or somebody. For example, if Alice trusts Bob (in some respect), Alice is willing to delegate control to Bob (over the issues covered),

---

computer operating system and office effectiveness tools, to consider computers unreliable and untrustworthy.

thereby making herself more dependent on Bob's honesty and goodwill. Thus, whenever Alice expresses her trust, she, in fact, announces her willingness to trade a piece of her personal control for simplifying the situation. The usual reason for deciding to trust is the desire to make (future) decisions simpler. An existing trust relationship allows the user to proceed in her pursues more easily, without needing to contemplate whether the procedure is safe or not. In this respect, there is no distinction whether something is trusted because of a necessary need or due to a decision based on emotions and consideration.

The rest of this paper is organized as follows. In Section 2 we briefly describe some of the most relevant psychological aspects of trust, concentrating on how trust is created and lost in the current cyberspace. Next, in Section 3, we outline a proposal of how some of the user centric trust forming aspects could be represented in an non-forgeable digital form, while in Section 4 we consider how this information could benefit the integration of protocol level and operating system level security. Finally, Section 5 provides a brief discussion of some of the aspects involved.

2   Users and Trust

What does it mean to trust someone, or something? The concept of *trust* seems to imply lack of sufficient amount of knowledge [17], meaning that there is at least some amount of uncertainty involved [8][18][19]. On the other hand, trusting reduces the complexity of a situation. When we *decide* to trust rather than suspect — this is what it means when we talk of *a leap of trust* — the number of issues we have to consider is reduced, thereby simplifying the process of making decisions. Trusting also describes *an attitude* towards future expectations, as well as introduces the presence of implied risk in a given situation [19].

2.1   Technical vs. Psychological Trust

In the technical sense, there exists a number of reasonable well defined definitions for trust, e.g., [7], [8], [9], [10], [13], [20], and [21]. Thus, the concept of trust in a technical sense is rather well-defined, at least in comparison with the psychological definition of trust, which for the most part still remains unresolved and under discussion. In general, the technical approaches tend to consider trust as a more or less binary concept (with the exception of at least [8]); there either is trust or there is not. However, typically a distinction is made between various *types of trust*, e.g., distinguishing recommendations from "direct trust" (whatever the latter means).

A leap of trust is needed, because there is not conclusive amount of information available. This would, in fact, be the description of most real-world user situations. In this sense, Audun Jøsang's approach [8] seems to have some connections to the psychological sense of trust.

Understanding the real-world trust is crucial to understanding the actual security of any transactions on-line — maybe even more so than creating the technological solutions for these transactions. Users are often considered to be the weakest link in the security of on-line transactions, and rightly so; what else could they be, when they are not provided with sufficient amount of information and/or support on security-prone situations by the system and its user interface design? How could the users be expected to be able to make rational choices of whether an operation is secure and trustworthy or not, if they are not given the right information? This point is well expressed in the following quote by Eric Ketelaar, in his demand for trustworthy information [22].

> *"Why do we demand more of the quality of food or a car than we demand of that other essential: information? Reliability and authenticity determine the credibility and the usefulness of information. These concepts, developed in different cultures and at different times, are essential for our information society in its dependence on trust in information. In the creation and distribution of digital information, conditions should be met to ensure the reliability and authenticity of the information."*

Trust can also be viewed as a historically emergent property of human interaction that is tied to a specific form of social organization. This means that modern forms of trust are rooted in the rights, obligations, and liberties of citizenship. Throughout history, people have always tried to ensure the authenticity of a document by several means: a seal, a special mark, witnesses, placing the document in safe-keeping with a public official, etc. Modern electronic systems also have these safeguards. They use passwords, cryptography, electronic sealing, digital signature, etc. Rules are needed about form, communication, and storage of information. [23]

2.2   The Untrustworthiness of the Web

Jacob Nielsen has described the current state of the Web as one of untrustworthiness, where "customers are traded like sheep" [24]. This has also been confirmed by other user studies, e.g., [16]. In practice, this mean that e-business has not taken the customers' need for security into any consideration at all. According to Nielsen, this has to change, however, if one wants to establish any decent business on the Net. *A culture of trust* must be promoted whenever there is a need to create a functioning network in a virtual world, and that's what the electronic marketplace essentially is. Mutual trust is always needed for good-quality relationships, be they between two people, a group of people, or between a user and an on-line service.

It is interesting, however, that according to another study by Hoffman et. al. [16], it was found that the negative perceptions of security and privacy increased along with the level of on-line proficiency — the more fluent the users were with using on-line service, the more conscious they seemed to be of the lurking risks of on-line transactions. In another study [25], the likely on-line consumer was described as someone with a "wired lifestyle": having years' of experience on the Internet, receiving a lot of e-mail, and searching for product information on the

Internet, to name a few. In our studies, the behaviour of the users was exactly the opposite — the most educated and experienced users were most against and doubtful of on-line services that included transactions of money or private information [1].

2.3   Transferring Real-World Trust to On-Line Systems

Is real-world trust transferrable to the digital world? It seems that the answer is "yes". Trusting a bank stays more or less the same regardless of the media (there is, however, also some reports on studies that suggest exactly the opposite, e.g., [16]). More important than the place where the service is situated is the existing brand reputation and other users' opinions about the service provider. These elements create the *sense of place* that guides the social interactions, perception of privacy, and the nature of all transactions conducted on-line [2].

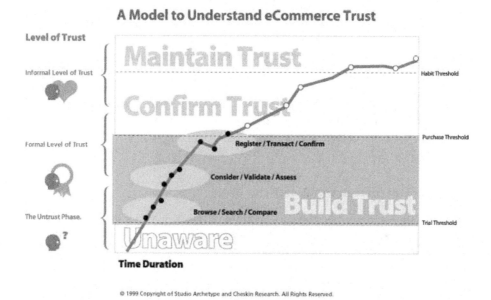

Fig. 1. An example of accumulation of trust as a function of time [15]

To start trusting is slow: trust is formed gradually, it takes quite a lot of time and repeated good experiences [15]. On-line trust can be described in terms of a human relationship. The initial stage is that of interest and suspicion; there has to be a motivation, a need, to get interested in the service, but this curiosity is stamped with distrust and suspicious cautiousness in the beginning of this flirtation with a new on-line service.

2.4 Recommendations, Rumours and Hear-Say

To become better acquainted with the object of interest, additional information is gathered of the service through various media: the mass media, but especially from other people, i.e., friends, colleagues, experts etc. We are not alone in this world but surrounded by others, some friends, and some enemies. Listening to rumours play a big role in gaining information: finding appropriate knowledge is difficult and time-consuming, and users are not really motivated to find out about the technical details of the security of the service to begin with — all they want to know is whether it is safe to use the service or not, and not why this is so [2]. Also, users may often not have any way to judge whether the information gained is trustworthy [1]. Friends are trusted, and it should not be too surprising that the information they provide often forms the basis for decision-making also when starting the use of an on-line service. Trust in people is transformed into on-line trust [1].

2.5 Imposing Laws on On-Line Behaviour

On-line trust depends on many factors, including consumer rights, freedom of expression, and social equity [26]. Trusting an on-line service provided by a well-known bank is to a great extent based on users' knowledge (or assumptions) about the laws binding all the business operations of the bank. In most studies about computer security, the users report on finding legislative intervention by the state desirable and necessary for promoting on-line trust (e.g. [27], [16]). Furthermore, behind this trust in the legality of the bank is, to put it bluntly, the sub-conscious trust in the basic structures of the society to remain stable, the trust in the status-quo instead of anarchy — in short, the trust and belief in the good-doing nature of a social contract between men, in the Rousseaun sense [28].

Another kind of "social contract" is also suggested to be executed in the cooperative relationships built on the Net: According to the study by Hoffman et. al.[16], over 72% of Web users would have been willing to provide the service provider with personal information if only the sites would provide the customers with a statement about how this information would be used. Still, it seems that users do not consider information about themselves as merchandise, to be sold to the highest-bidding offer: in the Hoffman et. al. study, most users were found not to be interested in selling their personal information.

2.6 Trusted Portals

Most user studies investigating into perceived trustworthiness of on-line services have focused on evaluating the services of single companies that offer their services directly to the customer. In our user studies, this approach formed the starting point for the inquiry. We took the study one step further, however, by introducing the users to the idea of a *trusted portal*, i.e, a third party taking care of the on-line monetary transactions, and acting as a trusted third party between the Web merchant and the on-line customer. This third party was a party that has for centuries been trusted to handle our money properly — a well-known, long-since established bank.

Third parties acting as mediators is an idea repeatedly expressed in many studies (see, for example, Hoffman et.al.), and it is also more or less the same as is behind the idea of Certification Authorities (CA) that, in form of seals of approval, or trustmarks, would guarantee the safety of the Web merchant, such as the TRUSTe [29].

In our study, the bank acted as the host of the trusted portal. Thus, in that case the real life trust placed on the back was more or less completely transferred to the trusted portal in cyberspace.

2.7   Losing Trust

While gaining the trust of on-line users may be slow and painstaking from the entrepreneur's point of view, losing trust happens quickly. A single violation of trust may destroy the achievements of trust over a period of months or even years [24], [15]. And, once broken, the recovery of lost trust is difficult, if not impossible. One cause for losing trust may be an initial misunderstanding of how the system works. To avoid these misunderstandings, the service should be meaningful to the user: The more intelligible the service and the system behind it are to the user, the less likely she is to misinterpret them and the more willing and motivated she will be to put an effort to learn to use the service in a secure and educated way, i.e., to participate [30]. Motivation can also be provided by personalised privacy tools; at present, a user with particular privacy needs and policy often lacks the means to fulfil them [31]. Users interested in their privacy often have to also conclude that the privacy information on most sites is confusing, incomplete, and inconsistent [32], even if the users would show an interest towards this kind of information. Privacy has also often be balanced against other, competing interests, both personal and others' [26].

3   Representing Trust in Digital Form

As we already mentioned in Section 2.1, a central problem lies in providing the users with information about the *real* security and trustworthiness of on-line operations so that they can make rational choices. Here, the terms *real security* and *real trustworthiness* necessarily refer to the social context of the user. That is, the user should be able to compare the security level of the system with the risks involved in the intended operation. To the average user, both the security level and the involved risks are at best vague, if comprehensible at all. Thus, the basis of the supposedly rational choices are based on the context, including individual trust decisions made by others, explicit recommendations, perceived brand reputation and other users' opinions, together with the quality of the relationships between the decision maker and the other individuals.

Today, the social context used in making decisions about the trustworthiness of services in the cyberspace cannot securely rely on the cyberspace itself [2].

That is, if I want to create an opinion of mine about the security level of a particular web server, I tend to prefer information received in real world, e.g., from my colleagues at the coffee table and through the public media.

In cyberspace, trust can be expressed. There is already a number of various techniques that attempt to express real life trust in various kinds of digital format. PGP is an example of such a system, where explicit real world trust is transferred in the digital form, and where the digital expressions of trust can be used infer the trustworthiness of previously unknown email addresses. Unfortunately, the current PGP approach is relatively rigid, and inherently bound to a single application, i.e., providing keys for securing email. [33]

Correspondingly, the PolicyMaker [11] and related approaches attempt to provide a more flexible platform for expressing authorization in a digital form. However, on that branch of security research, the focus has almost completely been on decentralizing access control systems. But, as we have argued ([11], [13]), these system can be, and should be, extended to handle also other forms of trusted information. That is, even the expressions of authorization information may be considered as a form of trust expressions, and the same kinds of certificates can be used to express many other forms of trust.

Thus, we propose that some form of authorization certificates, or rather *trust certificates*, is used for expressing *trust decisions* and *recommendations* made by the users. The same kind of certificates can also be used to represent the quality of relationships between individuals, allowing me to consider whose recommendations and opinions I trust and in which sense, and also to publish these considerations of mine. A suitable format for these kinds of trust certificates might be signed XML documents, allowing basically any XML DTD to be used to express opinions. It is noteworthy that the usage of XML might even allow to express security policies in a digital, secure format. [34]

Certificates could also be used to express attitudes about brand names, and for associating specific networked servers with specific brand names. This would require, of course, that each brand name owner would publish or certify their own public key in some secure enough way, e.g., by publishing certificate fingerprints periodically in a newspaper. Given this kind of arrangement, users could also express their opinions about specific brands by referring to the public keys of those brand names.

Already as such, these kinds of techniques could be used to create digital counterparts of our real life social networks, and to express our opinions in a digital format. However, since the certificates are in machine readable form, and since XML documents can be relatively easily parsed and handled programmatically, it would make much more sense to integrate the handling of these kinds of trust expressions directly to the future operating systems and user interfaces. That is the topic of the next section.

4 Binding Trust to Operating Systems and Protocol Runs

The purpose of the explicit utterance of trust, in the form of certificates, is to promote *a culture of trust* (which we called for in Section 2.2), and to create *a secure sense of place*, allowing the users to conduct their tasks with a feeling of security that is based on real security measures. As discussed, essential elements in these are good-quality relationships, explicit brand reputation, and other users' opinions about service provides, among other things. All of these, along with basic recommendations and expressions of trust, can be represented in the form of digitally signed documents, i.e., certificates.

In order to be real useful, the handling of these kinds of trust expressions should be integrated to the trusted computing base (TCB) of the used computing system. That is, the security mechanisms of the underlying operating system should be extended to understand where, when, and for what purpose, trust is needed when conducting transactions over the network. In practice, this means that the operating system takes responsibility for securing the network connections, and whenever running an authentication protocol in order to open a new connection, takes care of evaluating the trust requirements of the requesting application together with the credentials of the server and client programs.

To put this in slightly more concrete terms, we might consider a multi-user operating system running TCP/IP protocol stack and using the IPSEC security protocols. In such a setting, the operating system would issue a security policy on all connection requests, allowing only such connections to be opened whose trust assumptions and security credentials match. The security policy would be based on the trust expressions the user has earlier stated, augmented with on-line user interaction when needed.

On opened connections, the trust assumptions and credentials would be separately bound to each IPSEC security association (SA), allowing SA sharing whenever the needs of a new connection match with ones provided by an existing SA. [13]

As another example, we have considered how Java/Jini based ad hoc communities could be secured with SPKI certificates, and how simple application specific trust relationships could be represented in that kind of information. [35]

One area still requiring considerably more study is the relationship of these kinds of security measures, enforced by the operating system, and the user interface. It seems that something similar to the trusted path is needed.

5 Discussion

In order to be really useful, quite a lot still needs to be done. First, it is not at all clear how the various kinds of trust relationships and their expressions could be turned into certificates or other kinds of signed documents. Second, the actual user expectations and their probable reactions to various kinds of automated trust evaluation mechanisms should be evaluated. Third, even the concept of trustworthiness needs more clarification, both in the formal sense and especially in a language understandable to the average user. Furthermore, it seems inevitable that some new legislation is also needed.

For example, considering an on-line service trustworthy means, among other things, considering the information provided for the service and all the conducted transactions to remain private. This, then, means that the information will not be available to others, and will not be used out of context, for example. But defining privacy is not an easy task. Privacy is a basic human requirement we have a fundamental right to, but this does not reduce its unambiguity. What is regarded as private varies across organisations, cultures and even individuals [36].

Good example of this are the findings of a study at the AT&T Labs-Research [37] on Net users' attitudes towards privacy, where it was concluded that users could be divided into at least three groups according to their privacy assessments. These included 1) privacy marginalists, who showed little or no interest in privacy matters, 2) privacy pragmatists, who were concerned about their privacy but were ready to trust the services if there was some sign of existing privacy protection, and 3) privacy fundamentalists, who were extremely concerned about their privacy and very suspicious of the on-line services. All these different groups seem to require different user interface designs, emphasizing different aspects of the underlying systems security.

Thus, as the users' expectations vary quite a lot, the mechanisms are not quite there yet, and it is unclear how the implementation of such mechanisms would effect the design and structure of operating systems and user interfaces, this work is in the very beginning at best. However, we wish that these contemplations would lead to new ideas and points of view, preferably eventually leading to an internet that is more secure, in practice, than the current one.

References

1. Kristiina Karvonen, "Creating Trust", in Proceedings of the Fourth Nordic Workshop on Secure IT Systems (Nordsec '99), November 1-2, 1999, Kista, Sweden, pp. 21-36
2. Anne Adams and M. Angela Sasse, "Users are not the Enemy", Communications of the ACM, Vol. 42, No. 12, December 1999, pp. 41-46
3. Martin Abadi, Mark R. Tutle, "A Semantics for a logic of authentication", in Proceedings of the 10th ACM Symposium on Principles of Distributed Computing, pp. 201-216, ACM Press, Aug. 1991.
4. Michael Burrows, Martin Abadi, and Roger Needham, "A logic of authentication", ACM Transactions on Computer Systems, 8:1, pp 18-36, Feb. 1990.
5. Paul Syverson and Paul C. van Oorschot, "On unifying some cryptographic protocol logics", in Proc. 1994 IEEE Computer Society Symposium on Research in Security and Privacy, pp. 14-28, May 1994.
6. Pekka Nikander, Modelling of Cryptographic Protocols, Licenciate's Thesis, Helsinki University of Technology, December 1997.
7. Thomas Beth, Malte Borcherding, and Birgit Klein, "Valuation of trust in open networks", in Proceedings of Computer Security–ESORICS'94, Brighton, UK, 2-9 Nov. 1994.

8. A. Jøsang, Modelling Trust in Information Society, Ph.D. Thesis, Department of Telematics, Norwegian University of Science and Technology, Trondheim, Norway, 1998.
9. Raphael Yahalom, Birgit Klein, Thomas Beth, "Trust relationships in secure systems: a distributed authentication perspective", in Proc. 1993 IEEE Computer Society Symposium on Research in Security and Privacy, pp. 150-164, IEEE Computer Society Press, May 1993.
10. Raphael Yahalom, Birgit Klein, Thomas Beth, "Trust-based navigation in distributed systems", Computing Systems, 7:1, pp. 45-73, Winter 1994.
11. Matt Blaze, Joan Feigmenbaum, and Jack Lacy, "Decentralized trust management", in Proc. 1996 IEEE Computer Society Symposium on Research in Security and Privacy, Oakland, CA, May 1996.
12. Ilari Lehti, and Pekka Nikander, "Certifying trust," in Proceedings of the Practice and Theory in Public Key Cryptography (PKC) '98, Yokohama, Japan, Springer-Verlag, February 1998.
13. Pekka Nikander, An Architecture for Authorization and Delegation in Distributed Object-Oriented Agent Systems, Ph. D. Thesis, Helsinki University of Technology, March 1999.
14. G. U. Wilhelm, S. Staamann, L. Buttyán, "On the Problem of Trust in Mobile Agent Systems", in Proceedings of the 1998 Network And Distributed System Security Symposium, March 11-13, 1998, San Diego, California, Internet Society, 1998.
15. ECommerce Trust Study, Cheskin Research and Studio Arhetype/Sapient, January 1999, http://www.studioarchetype.com/cheskin/
16. Donna L. Hoffman, Thomas P. Novak, and Marcos Peralta, "Building Consumer Trust On-line", Communications of the ACM, April 1999, Vol. 42, No. 4, pp. 80-85
17. Lucas Cardholm, "Building Trust in an Electronic Environment", in Proceedings of the Fourth Nordic Workshop on Secure IT Systems (Nordsec '99), November 1-2, 1999, Kista, Sweden, pp. 5-20
18. A. Jøsang, "Trust-based decision making for electronic transactions," in L.Yngström and T.Svensson (Eds.) Proceedings of the Fourth Nordic Workshop on Secure IT Systems (NORDSEC'99), Stockholm, Sweden, Stockholm University Report 99-005, 1999.
19. M. Mühlfelder, U. Klein, S. Simon and H. Luczak, "Teams without Trust? Investigations in the Influence of Video-Mediated Communication on the Origin of Trust among Cooperating Persons", in Behaviour & Information Technology, Vol. 18, No. 5, 1999, pp. 349-360
20. Ronald Fagin and Joseph Y. Halpern, "I'm ok if you're ok: on the notion of trusting communication", Journal of Philosophical Logic, 17:4, pp. 329-354, Nov. 1988.
21. Gustavus J. Simmons and Catherine A. Meadows, "The role of trust in information integrity protocols", Journal of Computer Security, 3:2, 1994.
22. Eric Ketelaar, "Can We Trust Information?", in International Information & Library Review, Academic Press Limited, 1997, 29, pp. 333-338
23. A. B. Seligman, The Problem of Trust, Princeton University Press, New Jersey, 1997.
24. Jacob Nielsen, "Trust or Bust: Communicating Trustworthiness in Web Design", Alertbox, March 7, 1999, at http://www.useit.com /alertbox/990307.htm

25. Steven Bellman, Gerald L. Lohse, and Eric J. Johnson, "Predictors of On-line Buying Behaviour", Communications of the ACM, Vol. 42, No. 12, December 1999, pp. 32-38

26. Roger Clarke, "Internet Privacy Concerns Confirm the Case for Intervention", Communications of the ACM, Vol. 42, No. 2, February 1999, pp. 60-67

27. Kristiina Karvonen, "Enhancing Trust On-line", in Proceedings of the Second International Workshop on Philosophy of Design and Information Technology (PhDIT '99), December 15-17, 1999, St.Ferréol, Toulouse, France, pp. 57-64

28. Jean-Jacques Rousseau, Maurice Cranston (Translator), The Social Contract, Reprint edition (September 1987), Penguin Books, USA.

29. Paola Benassi, "TRUSTe: An On-line Privacy Seal Program", Communications of the ACM, Vol. 42, No. 2, February 1999, pp. 56-59

30. Elena Rocco, "Trust Breaks Down in Electronic Contexts but Can Be Repaired by Some Initial Face-to-Face Contact", in Proceedings of CHI '98, April 18-23, 1998, Los Angeles, CA.

31. Tessa Lau, Oren Etzioni, and Daniel S. Weld, "Privacy Interfaces for Information Management", Communications of the ACM, Vol. 42, No. 10, October 1999, pp. 89-94

32. Surfer Beware III: Privacy Policies without Privacy Protection, Electronic Privacy Information Center (www.epic.org), December 1999, http://www.epic.org/reports/surfer-beware3.htm

33. Alma Whitten and J.D. Tygar, "Why Johnny Can't Encrypt: A Usability Evaluation of PGP 5.0," in Proceedings of the 8th USENIX Security Symposium, August 1999.

34. Juha Pääjärvi, "XML Encoding of SPKI Certificates", work in progress, Internet draft draft-paajarvi-xml-spki-cert-00.txt, March 2000.

35. Pasi Eronen, Johannes Lehtinen, Jukka Zitting, and Pekka Nikander, "Extending Jini with Decentralized Trust Management", to appear in the Proceedings of OpenArch'2000, Tel Aviv, Israel.

36. Anne Adams and M. Angela Sasse, "Privacy Issues in Ubiquitous Multimedia Environments: Wake Sleeping Dogs, or Let Them Lie?", Proceedings of Interact '99, IFIP TC.13 International Conference on Human-Computer Interaction, 30th August - 3rd September, 1999, Edinburgh, UK, pp. 214-221

37. I. F. Cranor, J. Reagle and M. S. Ackerman, "Beyond Concern: Understanding Net Users' Attitudes about On-line Privacy", AT&T Labs-Research Technical Report TR 99.4.3, http://www.research.att.com/library/trs/TRs/99/99.4/

38. Ross J. Anderson, "Liability, trust and security standards", in Proceedings of the 1994 Cambridge Workshop on Security Protocols, University of Cambridge, UK, Springer-Verlag 1994.

39. Gustavus J. Simmons, "An introduction to the mathematics of trust in security protocols", in Proc. Computer Security Foundations Workshop IV, pp. 121-127, Franconia, N.H., 15–17 June, EEE Computer Society Press, Los Alamitos, CA, 1993.

Users and Trust in Cyberspace
(Transcript of Discussion)

Pekka Nikander

Helsinki University of Technology

I did my PhD in decentralised authorisation, but I guess now I'm jumping right through the rat hole of this conference by speaking about trust. I'm trying to look at trust from a psychological point of view, not so much from the technical point of view, and trying to point out some of the observations that have been made about how users perceive trust in cyberspace. I am presenting work that I am doing with one of my PhD students, Kristiina Karvonen. She is doing research on what trust is from the user's point of view in the Web, but I am more interested in how we could generalise these issues to uses of computer communications other than the Web, and how we could possibly make computers understand trust in some limited sense.

First I am going to speak a little bit about our motivations, then try and define what *we* mean with the word trust (and I hope it is an acceptable definition even though it's a limited one), and then I'm going to tread on thin ice and try to contemplate whether we could make computers understand trust in this limited sense.

It seems to be a fact that the Web is getting everywhere and, at least in Finland, everybody these days has to have a cellular telephone. Teenagers are the most active cell phone user group in Finland, sending short messages to each other all the time, and some schools have banned cell phones altogether. Even primary school kids have cell phones, and this has a number of privacy concerns that make me think really hard. How could I change the world so that when my daughter comes to the age that she wants to have a cell phone that the operator doesn't get all the information about her habits and friendships and so on? And in the more distant future it seems to be that these kind of devices will get integrated into our clothing and jewellery and maybe some people will turn into cyborgs! Now when we are starting to look at security concepts from that point of view, instead of an organisational point of view, so we are speaking about protecting the personal data and privacy in this kind of connected world, then we get quite a different view to what is trust, and whom should we trust, and whom have we to trust. That's what we are trying to address.

From this point of view it seems that when we are speaking about trust, it's first that trust implies lack of knowledge; so trust is a special kind of belief meaning that when we make a trust decision, when we decide to believe, it has quite a heavy emotional load from the psychological point of view. We make a commitment in trusting and we make ourselves more vulnerable when we decide to trust something or somebody. So we made ourselves *dependent* and when we are speaking about computers it seems that trust implies that we made a decision that our attitudes or perception towards the computer system is that we decide

B. Christianson et al. (Eds.): Security Protocols, LNCS 2133, pp. 36–42, 2001.

to believe that what seems to happen really happens, so that what the computer was showing us is in some way reality. That may be one of the really basic works of trust in the computer systems. When we connect into distributed systems and communication protocols we get into real trouble because in the current way things are done it is not at all clear that what we think happens is what really happens. This seems to be the case with some application programmes as well, but maybe that's not the thrust of this conference.

It also seems that trust is similar in all communications. So when you are listening to me you are making a trust decision whether you will believe in what I say, especially if you are making yourself somehow dependent on that. From the user's point of view for trust it is not at all that clear that the formal definitions that we have seen in the protocols work.

So if we look at the studies of how people consider websites as trustworthy, four factors emerge that really affect them. The first one is if it's possible to mentally transfer real world trust to on-line systems, then it makes the websites more credible and more trustworthy. Brand reputation is one issue and if we're thinking about both kind of businesses that really deal about trust in the real world like banks, which deal with monetary type of trust, then users are more willing to extend this kind of trust to the digital world as well.

Then the second issue is the social context. Many users really make their decisions based on the recommendations of other users in their local social network. So if somebody of local authority says that a particular e-commerce site is OK, it's easier for them to start to use it. One of the reasons for that is that in practice it's impossible for the end users to find out whether a website is technically secure or not. They just can't do that, they don't have enough information, and they don't have enough knowledge and understanding, and therefore they believe in recommendations, rumours and hearsay, especially if the hearsay comes from a source which is assumed to be trusted: a friend or other socially close people.

Another factor is the user experience. So if a website has been in the Web for a long time, if it's quality is high, it's contents are up-to-date, accurate, and it seems to the users that the technology has been used appropriately – all of these form also a feeling of trust to the user.

Only last comes seals of approval like TRUSTe, Better Business Bureau, *etc* and what's noteworthy is that on this list we don't see certificates or crypto or anything at all. It's hidden there in this technology, so it's only a small issue of how users perceive what is trustworthy in the Web and what is not. And we should keep this in mind when we are thinking about larger issues like making computer systems trustworthy for personal use.

There is some research which shows how trust can be created in a website. First the user is unaware that there is such a website, then we have a trust building phase where the user first starts browsing the website, then he or she considers whether the website might be trustworthy, and finally decides to make a transaction. If all of these experiences seem to be OK, at that point the user might have been about eight times to the website before making the first transaction. Then trust starts to be built and here the real trust means that the user gradually becomes dependent on, or vulnerable, because they have made a mental decision that this website is trustworthy. If after such a point it becomes evident that it is not, then there is some harm done, and in that way the user is vulnerable.

So, what do we need to trust for, why is it needed? The reason seems to be that it's easier to do things, it reduces anxiety because we start to feel safe when we have made the real leap of faith, when we have made the real trust decision. From this point of view we can say that trustful action increases vulnerability, it's directed towards parties that are not under our control, and it involves risk that might be higher than the benefit. I think this is what makes real trust different from calculated or estimated risk. If you estimate a risk and find out that the risk is less than the benefit then it's not real trust, it's just making a calculated risk.

More important is that if we think about the biological basis of trust it seems to be that inter-personal trust is continuously reinforced. So trust is very much dependent on time, it builds gradually and when it has been built to a degree it must be reinforced all the time. It's typically reinforced both by verbal communication and non-verbal communication, and when we are thinking about this type of world we lose all of the non-verbal communication these days (and even if we have video we lose most of that).

From this background I would like to find a way to make computers understand trust, because in this everyday life we are making trust decisions all the time. We're using our social context, we are using our assumptions and we are seeing how other people behave and we are basing our assumptions and our decisions on those perceptions. But in the virtual world, when everything is getting more and more digital and we are starting to use those things in our everyday life, we should have the same kind of support or possibility to make these decisions and that's not currently there. There is no reliable social context, and it's very easy to do bad behaviour and so on. I think that we need assistance so that we can make good trust decisions in cyberspace and now I am speaking from this personal point of view, I'm not referring to an organisational point of view where this probably also applies, but maybe differently.

Ross Anderson: Is this not what companies like Amazon do when they put in their reviews page large numbers of comments from named people, such as Matt Blaze from New York says that such and such a crypto book is reasonably good. If I don't hear that Matt has crashed their site out of irritation at their misquoting him, I am likely to trust the site more as a result of that.

Matt Blaze: The name I use on `amazon.com` is Ross Anderson. I don't know who this Matt Blaze is.

Reply: So one approach which tried to create this kind of reliable social context to the digital world is PGP, and it seemed to me that it might be possible to express this kind of limited sense of trust with certificates. The PGP trust root network is, I think, the kind of right approach but it doesn't go far enough. If we do this, the trust expressed needs to be expressive enough, so they really need to tell why that certificate has been written and what is the real semantic meaning of the certificate. And these kinds of certificates can be considered as recommendations and in that context it's the verifier of those recommendations who makes the real decision: whether to trust or not or whether to believe in those recommendations or not. This might form that kind of virtual social context. So we could use technologies like e-speak, PKI, PolicyMaker or KeyNote to do these types of thing as well, because it seems to me that authorisation is just a special form of trust and so delegation is just a form of recommendation and maybe we could apply the same kind of approach to trust a little bit more generally.

If we think about that and if we think also about security protocols, I came to a tentative conclusion that if we put semantics into the certificates and in the PKI then we probably should enhance our infrastructure so that even when we are running authentication protocols and when we are getting certain keys from the authentication protocols we would carry along that semantic down to the session keys used for sessions. And somehow we should bind these keys to the operating system or maybe at the application level, because in a way – from the computer system's point of view – the semantics resolve to making access control decisions for this system whether to complete an operation or to display a choice to the user between various alternative behaviours like giving full information about the identity of the user or just the peg name, depending on what is being learnt from the certificate.

Right, so the basic points that I am trying to make here are that it seems to me that computer security is becoming a more personal matter, it's not an organisational issue any more. According to the studies that we went through, actually people *do* care about security and they are actually quite security aware, but they just don't have enough information. It seems to be a tendency in corporate computer security departments that they don't give any information to the users. So the challenge is how to give the users enough information that they can fit into *their* mental model so that they can make good decisions, trust decisions and other decisions, and how the protocols can be used to create security context with semantics that are bound to the applications and where the semantics are communicated to the user.

So, I don't know what is trust. I understand maybe some misuse of trust, and not even then very well. The real question is how should we make this kind of personal trusting expressible so that we could teach our computers to understand it. We have to remember that for typical users these formalities of approval or formal authorisation don't matter, they don't understand it, and it's really the personal relationships and the total context that matter. Well, that's more or less what I was planning to say.

Tuomas Aura: There is a lot of research being done on what makes users trust websites or other electronic services, but this research is done by the marketing departments and their goal is not to increase the security or trustworthiness of the servers. Their question is how can they portray their service as trustworthy so that people will use it.

Matt Blaze: When I started using the word trust management I got a lot of flack from people who didn't understand what I was talking about because I was using the term trust the way computer security people use trust, and now that term trust has mutated into the common understanding of trust which is much harder to pin down. I've always wanted trust, as a security person, to be a very simple thing: I trust something if it's allowed to violate my security; something that's trusted is something that I don't have to worry about and if it is broken, I am broken. So I want as little trust in the system as possible, and so security people are worried about minimising trust and now suddenly we have this new set of semantics that are concerned with maximising trust, and I'm terribly confused.

Ross Anderson: Perhaps this is because the two concepts really don't have very much to do with each other. Think about non-repudiation – if you look at the terms and conditions offered by various on-line banks and credit cards, it turns out that those which make the largest, loudest noise publicly about how they are super trustworthy and the credit card on the Internet and so on, are those which have the most savage terms and conditions. It seems here that psychological trust and legal trustworthiness are at opposite ends of the spectrum.

Bruce Christianson: It's quite right that trusting something and believing in their trustworthiness are different. The point you made right at the beginning was that trust is used as a substitute for knowledge. Very often you trust something not because you believe that it is trustworthy but because you have no choice, you cannot proceed with the transaction unless you trust it. So your security policy is, you may proceed, because you want the transaction to complete.

John Ioannidis: To confuse the issue even more, when I started talking to people about trust management one of the answers I was given was that there is no trust management, there is only risk management. That seemed to be for two reasons: first the semantics of a word we use in a technical context which also has, different (similar but not identical) semantics in the social context, and second another concept that they were familiar with: the concept of risk management. There is a business world and a financial world and they said, oh this is a concept I know something about, let me see if I can map that concept that I know something about in a very precise and technical way to another concept which is given to me which seems to be similar. But the things are actually orthogonal, you could use one to manage the other, or the other to model the one. Again we have an issue of trying to define trust as we know it in our linguistic sense. I am going to bet that people from different environments from around the globe understand the meaning of the word trust differently. When I say I trust the Bank of England to give some value to a piece of fancy coloured paper, it is not the same thing as I trust my mother not to lie to me, or I trust God to save me from my sin, because you use of the same word and get three totally different contexts. So this is a well known phenomenon of linguistics. But we have a very specific problem to solve and if we try to sell a solution that we technical people know about to an audience that is not technical, but that we definitely depend on because direct or indirectly they pay our salary, then we have to make sure that we explain to them or else invent terms and then proceed to define them.

Virgil Gligor: Let me re-emphasise for a moment the traditional notion that Matt points out.

I trust the components therefore I am dependent on the components so the entity that produces that component must produce some evidence about its behaviour. So there is a liability in trust. In other words, whoever produces a component that is supposed to be trustworthy should produce the evidence. Banking people say, look I have to trust this component, I have very little evidence, therefore I'm taking a risk. So the idea of traditional security/trust/risk management is not all that different. However, what Matt pointed out that I think should be emphasised, is that the notion of trust in a commercial sense is different: there I want to maximise trust not minimise it. Security wants to minimise trust (because trust leads to liability – namely produce the evidence and so on), but here if I'm a producer of some sort of service and I have a website, my goal is to maximise trust in me without producing the evidence.

What we are told here is that there is a new kind of evidence that might be generated, such as brand recognition. This is commercial evidence.

John Ioannidis: Exactly. When I give a certificate I'm actually trying to maximise my correspondent's trust in me because what they're trying to do is minimise their trust. This is a zero sum game.

Reply: Well I'm not quite sure about maximising trust because we are not necessarily here trying to maximise the risk involved, but we are trying to maximise the dependability or the level of how automatically you can use the service without thinking. We are trying to maximise the behavioural consequences of trust so that the people will feel safe when using the service. So we are still minimising the necessary level of risk or trust in the technical, computer science sense, I guess.

Virgil Gligor: The evidence that is being produced, is not necessarily engineering or scientific evidence, it is a different form of evidence.

John Ioannidis: Often it can be scientific evidence. If you link the cryptographic parameters that you have to a legal document, then that actually makes a very ...

Virgil Gligor: But I think the discussion here is in quite a different context.

Bruce Christianson: Then you are dealing not with trust, but with knowledge. You are back to the first place where you have guaranteed inter-personal agreements and there's no need for trust.

John Ioannidis: Oh, yes, there is no use for trust in the social term of the word trust (that's like I, trust my mother).

Ross Anderson: I'm not sure if the social definition of the word is so very different. Social trust is just a statistical or thermodynamic development of the naiive computer science idea that a trusted component is one that can hose you.

John Ioannidis: Well in that case you're in a non zero sum game.

Ross Anderson: You find the same thing in Mutually Assured Destruction. Much of society is just a gentler and more diffuse version.

Reply: One of the points here is that when we are speaking about this kind of trust in the case of Web and so on, we don't necessarily have names at all and that is somehow related to the previous conversation.

Stewart Lee: Every year at this conference we manage to spend half a day on trust, we've proved very little excepting that there are 30 people in the room, there are 30 definitions of trust. I trust that we are not going to repeat this, to give another definition of trust. This is a very important issue, but we don't know how to measure these abstract notions, and until we do we should perhaps not beat our drum too strenuously.

Mike Roe: The problem is, trust means too many different things to too many different people, so if you ever use the word trust in any formal context people just misinterpret what you mean and we get into these kind of discussions. Quite frequently you can explain what you're trying to do perfectly clearly without ever mentioning the dreaded word trust.

John Ioannidis: The usual solution to that is to choose a word from a non-English language and that nobody's likely to know (for example, Greek), and use that.

Virgil Gligor: Hence the expression, it is all Greek to me.

Mike Roe: Quite frequently there is some particularly good English word for what you mean to say in the context of any particular scientific paper, rather than calling it trust

I'm particularly talking about building trust in websites. What the merchant wants is a way to protect a transaction against threat, the merchant wants the customer to pay his money rather than to go away.

Matt Blaze: I like the phrase that links Michael's talk with this one; consider the phrase, "a name you can trust", and how ambiguous that is.

John Ioannidis: There are people who have thought about the problem of anonymous reputation builders, where you don't have a name in the traditional sort of cabbalistic sense, you just have an anonymous address somewhere that does not necessarily get back to you. But by behaving consistently and by always fulfilling your promises you've got this reputation, which is another wonderfully ambiguous word, that can be used as a figure of merit for assigning risk or blame or whatever you want to call it.

Reply: If *we* can't really understand what does trust mean and what security and privacy and names mean, how can we expect the users to understand, and how can we even expect them to understand the difference between security, privacy and trust?

Ross Anderson: That's for the marketing department to explain.

Interactive Identification Protocols
(Transcript of Discussion)

Peter Landrock

Cryptomathic A/S, Denmark

I think this is one of the first times that I'll give a lecture without really getting into crypto at all; I'm really trying to broaden my personal scope when I'm talking about security protocols.

There are two extremes when you speak of protocols. One is when, as a basis, you are using very strong crypto protocols that many people like to talk about, and the other extreme is where no crypto is used at all. The latter is much more commonly used that the former, namely password in the clear, that's I guess the second most used identification protocol, the most used one being no security at all. It could be with or without tokens, for instance there are many systems – in particular implemented in banks – where you get a challenge on the screen and then you have a little device that enables you to calculate a response to that challenge and then return that. But for practical systems like home banking systems, electronic commerce and that lot, these solutions are usually considered too expensive. This may change as everybody is getting GSM because you suddenly have something that can be used as a token without paying anything for it, but I will not get into that discussion today.

So I am interested in electronic commerce, in particular I got the inspiration for this from some home banking solutions we've been building, and what the users would like to have are the following:

- They'd like to have logon for transactions from any workstation, that's what their customers are demanding – when they suddenly feel this urge to transfer some money in the middle of a night when they are sitting at some Internet cafe they should be able to do that, or when they are on their way to the USA and spending some time at the airport.
- The protocol should be protected against eavesdropping, at least from the outside and that's easy to establish using a crypto tunnel.
- They also want an authenticated transaction.

These are apparently contradicting requirements because it basically means that you're going to rely on, well I was almost going to say Java solutions, but something similar, portable code, and we know that this is prone to a number of attacks because you can't trust the workstation at all.

So this is how we got into considering possible interactive identification protocols without tokens. I should say that the first system we built (we didn't design this system but we helped build the system) was a home banking system where the bank insisted that every customer be given a little card with 25 one-time passwords and so whenever they open a session they will key in one of these

B. Christianson et al. (Eds.): Security Protocols, LNCS 2133, pp. 43–48, 2001.
© Springer-Verlag Berlin Heidelberg 2001

one-time passwords. This type of system would be prone to attacks from the workstation, but in the two years that it has been in operation no such attack has been detected. It's always interesting that we can list a number of possible attacks, but when you actually build the systems you will not see these attacks. That's one of the strange things of life, it's so very easy, I think, to kill a person with whom you have absolutely no connection and not be detected. It's much more difficult to kill somebody that you have a connection to. Yet this happens very rarely (except perhaps in the USA). [laugher]

So what are the threats here? Well, we have threats from persons with access to the workstation, so authentication is definitely being threatened and confidentiality, that's clear. But authentication *is* a problem, because the attack we're worried about is that the user will generate some transaction information that he believes is what he wants to do and then the information that's being forwarded is entirely different. That is an attack to worry about but what the banks are saying here is that yes, but whoever is launching that attack will somehow need to get hold of the money and the typical way of doing that is to have the money transferred into his bank account instead and then we know who the culprit is.

As far as threats are concerned from people without access to the workstation, the only threat is really towards confidentiality and not authentication if you are using cryptographic means on the workstation, and typically the inside attacker wants to take advantage of the authentication mechanisms. The whole point is that he wants to use the identity of the real user, he wants to pretend that he's the real user, so he needs the authentication mechanisms. So that means that an exterior enemy is a common enemy both to the attacker with access to the workstation and to the person who's entering the protocol.

What about WAP technology here? Anybody who's taking a first course in cryptography is told that it is always good to have two independent communication channels that allow you to use one for authentication. WAP technology is a possibility but in a number of transactions the monitor of your mobile telephone will not really give you many possibilities, and most of the applications I've been hearing about seems to be, well, rather advanced, and probably will not enjoy widespread use. So I think for most electronic commerce transactions you will need a proper monitor either in the form of a workstation or in a connection to a Web TV.

Now the set-up that I want to discuss is the following. Alice and the remote server share some secret information, Alice needs to prove that he knows this information. This is not a misspell, and it's neither caused by the fact that Alice went through a sex change operation, it's simply because I've learnt from these seminars that we can't really trust a name. So the point is how can we enter such a protocol where Alice just demonstrates what she knows in her mind without giving it away. To what extent is that possible? That's what the bank was asking us, and the goal here is that nobody with unlimited control over the workstation should be able to identify himself as Alice using this protocol in a new session after having monitored a number of previous sessions. The question is how many sessions can Alice enter from the same untrusted workstation without allowing anybody who is actually eavesdropping to subsequently enter another session in a successful manner.

So we'll introduce a little notation and some assumptions here: we will only consider protocols with two steps at a time, a challenge and a response, but we may do it over and over again; we will assume that the reciprocal of the probability of guessing the right answer is a constant A, which we call the threshold acceptance, so that really represents the number of possibilities for the responses being given; we will let S denote the number of potential secrets Alice and the server may share, meaning in the case of passwords the number of passwords that could be used in the system; and then we will let U denote the maximum number of protocol rounds that Alice may participate in from the same untrusted workstation before her secret is revealed in principle, if the attacker is sufficiently skilled to drag out the information that's been given to him. And this number U that really tells how secure the protocol is, we called the unicity parameter. I was inspired here by the unicity distance of a cryptographic mechanism, which is the length of the clear text that you need to encrypt before the key that you used is uniquely determined. The fact that it's uniquely determined doesn't mean that somebody can determine it – only if you have enough computational power can you take advantage of that.

So here are some examples. No passwords at all, that's $U = 0$, I can immediately impersonate anybody who doesn't use anything when he's logging on. Password in the clear is $U = 1$. A DES-based challenge response, just 64 bits challenge, 64 bits response is $U = 2$, because when you encrypted two DES blocks the DES key is uniquely determined according to some work that I think Hellman did many years ago. This would be relevant if Alice has a hand-held token that can do DES encryption, and it is an example where the fact that the key is uniquely determined doesn't mean that you can actually determine it, it depends on your computational power. I can't rely on that because I've told you that I would like to consider protocols that do *not* require a crypto engine, and the zero knowledge challenge response would have $U = \infty$ if the attacker has limited computational power and $U = 0$ if the attacker has unlimited computational power, because the zero knowledge protocols we know are based on public key cryptography and can be broken with enough computational power. The reason why I mention zero knowledge here is that that's precisely what I am after; the whole purpose of a zero knowledge identification protocol is that I as a user can enter over and over again, and the only thing that persons who are witnessing the protocol will learn from it is that I know a secret but the protocol should be built in such a way that I won't give anything away about my secret, only the fact that I know it. That's precisely what we are after.

Now can we learn anything from crypto protocols? Yes, we can actually. A typical protocol is the following: Alice and the bank share a DES key, bank sends the challenge, Alice encrypts and responds with a MAC, but often she only returns the first four bytes rather than all eight, and the advantage here is that then suddenly the number of possible keys is growing by a huge factor, in fact here the unicity parameter goes up by an expected factor of 32 due the fact that you are only giving away half of the bits and therefore there are about 2 to the 28, possible keys that could have been used in this protocol. So we *can* learn from this.

But the main problem we are finally faced with is the following: how can we build a system where a user can authenticate himself at any workstation in an inexpensive fashion yet sufficiently secure, not using hardware. So we are hoping for zero knowledge identification protocol without having computational power but with a secure fairly tamper resistant memory, namely the user's brain. I am not considering attacks where you force the user to give away his secret.

So we are in the situation as often actually arises with users where Alice's intellectual capacity becomes very important, her ability to remember, manipulate and calculate. It also has to be a user friendly system.

Audience: In your model you're allowing a shared secret.

Reply: Yes, sure.

Now here's an example, it's a very primitive example, I apologise for that, but that's because I had to make it myself. Here's a pattern that I'm just trying to make you think of constructing such protocols. I am not saying this is a good idea, what I'm proposing here is just to get you thinking the right way.

You can imagine a grid with about 400 entries and there's a pattern that helps you to recognise a field so a user may say, OK I want this one here just at the bend of the S and at the green one, in this grey pattern I want to select this always, and this, and this. Then whenever I log on I get a challenge with randomly chosen numbers all over it, in particular also randomly chosen numbers in these four fields, and then I just type in those. Clearly the U value of this, the number of safe rounds, is somewhat larger than one, because if I have 400 grids, there'll be about 40 places where any particular digit will appear, so having seen this session once you wouldn't be able to guess exactly which entries had been chosen. The shared secret is the location of the four chosen entries in the grid, and I can just suggest a number of protocols here.

The first one is that Alice just returns those numbers in the grid amongst the 400 possibilities.

Another possibility is that she has an additional secret key that she shares with a server, an audited key, say 2087, and then she adds these numbers that she selects one by one and returns 7096 as the answer. Obviously the unicity parameter goes up by adding this, but so does the demand on Alice's intellectual capacity. If Alice had a calculator we could go even further, and in fact this bank that we were discussing this with did actually contact a producer in Hong Kong and ask how much a hand-held calculator with a DES chip would cost, because they were thinking of giving that away to the user, and now we are back to the old systems with hand-held devices.

Let's look at another example, here again the key is a four digit number, say 1729, which is a very famous Cambridge number, as I'm sure you all know. For each number the user this time must remember a colour as well, say lilac, brown, green and light blue. Alice is this time given a memory template which looks like this, so here are the numbers. Again she must remember a pattern, lilac, brown, green, light blue, and this time when she gets a challenge, she must remember the chosen fields. This time it's more difficult, because it's difficult to remember whether you took the fourth down the line or the third down the line. But anyway, just to give you a feeling of what the possibilities are, her first one was lilac and she finds a 3 there and then she notices the number where her brown 7 is, let's say that's 6, so in the unsophisticated version she'd just return these numbers, 3, 6 and so on. She could manipulate and perhaps send $3 + 6$ which is 9, that's a bit more demanding, and the unicity parameter goes up.

Now if you think that I think that these systems could be adopted by users, you are absolutely wrong. I just wanted to make you start you thinking about how to build those systems, and you will very quickly get into the following considerations. Let me just remind you of what my notation was, A is the reciprocal of the probability of guessing the right answer, what I call the threshold acceptance, and S is the number of potential secrets so if it's a four digit number then it's 10,000. U is the maximum number of protocol rounds, and what we are up against is this equation here, $A^U = S$. We want to get U as large as possible. If we want to get U much larger than 1, then we have to make A very small in comparison to S. So what we have actually discovered here is that exponentially speaking most people have similar intellectual capacity.

Here we are operating in example 2 with an S value of 10^8, and in example 1, almost 20^8, which seems acceptable with an A value of 10^4 (that's the probability that somebody will just guess the right answer with the probability of guessing a PIN code), and this means that for all practical purposes $U = 4$ is about the best we can expect. So the protocol for Cambridge students we can use $U = 4$, for Cambridge dons $U = 3$ and for the rest of us, $U = 2$.

I don't usually reveal the fact that I can be very naive, but I must confess when I first started thinking about this I thought that I could reach a much larger U value. But I really can't and so I was about to give it up, as this basically means that if we built a protocol that a Cambridge student could handle mentally or intellectually then after 4 identification protocols he would have given his secret away. I am sure we will have a few students that can manage 5, but we are building systems for the masses because we want to make money on this. But at least it's nice that U is larger than 1. So, is this useful? Yes, it's very useful combined with other means of verifying the transaction. For instance, what we've discovered is that Alice can log on at least once from the most insecure workstation in the whole world, without having her ID stolen if we are using such a protocol. Even with $U = 2$ that will be all right. And we could always build into the system that if she has this urge to log on from the same insecure workstation every now and then she must go home and alter her key first.

Matt Blaze: As a designer of world's most insecure workstations, here is the way I would design such a thing. It rejects your first transaction, "sorry the transaction didn't go through, you must have typed it in wrong, try again", until I reach your U value.

Reply: Yes, so we'll have to tell her not to fall for that trick. But even so we have to worry about the subsequent transaction. A phenomenon that we call wysiswys, what you see is what you sign, and that's an independent question because we can easily build systems where what is being transmitted is not what was authorised by the user. But here we can make use of the WAP technology and we can authenticate that by other means. I don't want to get into that, that's actually a system we are building right now.

So, I think it is useful because it doesn't cost anything and it was certainly useful to go through that consideration.

The question still is, when she goes to this place with that insecure workstation, is the person with control over that workstation able to take advantage of the fact that she's there, that's not so clear.

John Ioannidis: My fundamental objection to tokens and other such handheld devices is that when they fail I have no recourse; if my hand-held authenticator fails while I'm at a conference I have to resort to much more primitive means of communication which involves calling the person in charge of that and yelling at them. By knowing the kind of insults that we utter, they will figure out it was me and not Matt and authenticate it that way. Also one thing I found useful is to have a throw away password, so normally I will have my hand-held authenticator but if I lost them or if they got compromised or they broke, I have a hard-wired password which could be used once to send an emergency message somewhere.

Virgil Gligor: Is there a requirement here that Alice knows she is talking to the bank? Say for example an intruder fakes the bank caller, finds out what Alice responds to that, so next time he'll know where Alice ...

Reply: It's very easy to break this protocol but that's not the issue; the issue is an examination of how many times you can expect to run the protocol before the secret is given away, and even though you can easily imagine man in the middle attacks, banks are not really concerned about that because they think it's so unlikely that they will happen that they don't worry about it.

The money they have lost is not significant enough to move to chip card solutions, for instance.

Vilgil Gligor: What about insiders putting out fake responses and attacking the user?

Reply: Oh yes, you can list lots of possibilities where it wouldn't work, I agree, but at the end of the day the bank has to take decisions on what sort of risk it wants to run.

They like this for the purpose that they are using it for, because it's very low cost. Even the system where the users are using a one time password (and they get this list of 25 one time passwords), the bank is very happy with because so far the two years they've used this there's been absolutely no mis-use.

Open Questions
(Transcript of Discussion)

Peter Ryan

I wasn't too sure what to give as my title because it's a fairly open ended thing, I'm just trying to raise some issues and questions which have come to my attention recently, so I just called it "Open Questions". My talk will be quite quick (I think) as long as it doesn't turn out to be too controversial.

Matt Blaze: Don't use the word trust!

Ross Anderson: Or the word security!

One issue that's been on my mind for some months now is that there are two entirely different styles, schools if you like, in doing analysis of cryptographic security protocols. There's the cryptanalytic way of doing it: trying to do reduction proofs showing if you could crack the protocol it would be equivalent to breaking RSA or that sort of thing. Then of course there's the formal types of analysis: BAN, all of the CSP model checking type stuff that I've been involved in, and so on. Hitherto as far as I am aware, those two communities have been completely separate, haven't really talked to each other, and nobody really understands how these two forms of analysis might gel together. In some sense they're kind of complimentary, they're analysing different aspects of the problem, but neither of them clearly analyses the whole thing, so in principle you could conceive of protocols which might survive both types of analysis and yet because of some subtle interaction between the protocol and the cypto-algorithm might still fall over.

So, it would be interesting to try and bring these styles of analysis together in some way. The only really serious attack on this that I'm aware of is the work by Lincoln *et. al.*[1], where they set up really quite a complex framework, a sort of probabilistic process algebra framework, and try and address this problem. But very quickly you get into a great deal of complexity.

Some of the things that I'm coming on to touch on some of the things we raised this morning. Another way of viewing this that it's kind of another symptom of the well known refinement problem for security, which is certainly something which is very well recognised in the computer security community and people have known for a long time, since say John McClean, that security does seem to be a particularly tricky problem and trying to develop step wise refinement ways of dealing with it seems to be particularly difficult, and so that impinges on our discussion this morning about whether a layered approach to this works which is essentially you're trying to do a sort of incremental refinement approach to your design.

There's a whole bunch of ways you can look at this. Another way is: it would be great if you could capture all the underlying assumptions. Say in the case of a

---

[1] A Meta-Notation for Protocol Analysis by I. Cervesato, N.A. Durgin, P.D. Lincoln, J.C. Mitchell and A. Scedrov

B. Christianson et al. (Eds.): Security Protocols, LNCS 2133, pp. 49–53, 2001.

crypto protocol if you could capture all properties that the crypto algorithm had to satisfy in order for a particular protocol design to be valid. It is actually quite difficult to identify and capture and formalise all the relevant properties and be sure that you caught them all, so you quite easily fall into the trap that Larry mentioned where you've got a very nice protocol which has been analysed to a high level of abstraction, been shown to be OK, then someone goes ahead and implements the cryptographic primitives in some way which causes the whole thing to collapse.

So these are, I think, all inter-related problems, if you like different ways of looking at it and yet another way of looking at it is this issue of re-use of proofs. If you've done an analysis such as Larry has done and then decided to use different primitives to implement it, it would be nice not to have re-do the entire analysis from scratch, but be able to build on your proof and just show that the new primitive didn't introduce some new factor which caused your proof to fall over.

Apart from just this issue of doing an analysis of the abstract protocol and then worrying about the different implementations, another aspect of this re-use of proof which occurred to me recently is that we have a whole a bunch of cryptographic primitives which are used in a variety of ways, so there's obviously encryption: for integrity, for binding, and so forth, and sometimes people use similar primitives to achieve different ends, I mean sometimes to achieve secrecy, sometimes to do binding,

Recently I was looking at a particular protocol which is rather analogous to the STS[2] protocol but instead of using encryption to do the binding of terms it uses signing. So the question that comes to mind is, can you map the proofs say done on STS into this alternative protocol by mapping between the primitives and mapping in some sense between the purpose of the rôles they're playing? It struck me that if you knew how to do that, as a natural spin off you'd actually understand, perhaps much better, the rôles of the primitives.

Another thought which, particularly listening to this morning's discussions, occurred to me, when we were talking about the distinction between communication and computer security and cryptography and other system security approaches is, as far as I know nobody has really asked this question, let alone answer it, but if somebody is aware of this in this room please tell me, it occurred to me a little while ago that, and we already know that quite a lot of security requirements can be fulfilled using cryptography. Confidentiality, access control, delegation, and so forth can be done cryptographically, and this does seem to pose the obvious question, is there any kind of computer security requirement which couldn't be done cryptographically if you felt like it, which might be quite a useful thing to do because in some sense cryptography strikes me as a better understood mechanism for providing these than quite a lot of the system security solutions that people suggest.

---

[2] W. Diffie, P.C. Van Oorschot, and M.J. Wiener, "Authentication and Authenticated Key Exchanges," in Designs, Codes and Cryptography, Kluwer Academic Publishers, 1992, pp. 107

I was chatting to Dieter last week about this and he points out there's one obvious limit here, presumably ultimately you'll have to protect your keys in some non cryptographic way. I assume that to be accepted wisdom, I'm not sure if it's a theorem.

Virgil Gligor: Why don't they encrypt them?

Just to return to this question of how might you bring these two styles of analysis together, recently I was listening to Birgit Pfitzman give a presentation introducing the way crypt-analysts define the notion of when an encryption scheme is secure or indeed when a protocol is secure. In essence what she does is to allow a spy to produce two chosen messages to present to the system, the system then does an encryption, does a manipulation, and then in arbitrary order spits out two results. The criterion is that if the spy can't distinguish with better than evens chance between these two then you deem the system to be secure. And that set me thinking, because one of the things that I and others have been quite interested in the computer security context, is notions of things like non interference, when you're trying to say that information doesn't flow across a particular interface, and one of the ways you can do that is to cast the whole thing in a process algebraic context and reduce the whole thing to indistinguishability between two systems in a process algebraic sense.

So if a high level user indulges in two different activities or, if you like, you put two high level users interacting with the system, and then you think about the observations the low level guy can make of that system through his interface, if he can't distinguish those two then you deem a system to be non interfering and secure. So, in that context too, you're thinking in terms of testing equivalence which would be quite analogous to the way the cryptographic people are thinking about the problem. So that does suggest there might be a way of linking these two styles of analysis. This is highly speculative at the moment, I still haven't pushed it through very far. One thing, for example, you'd need to do (and it's not entirely obvious how to do it in a tractable way), is to introduce these notions of probability which the cryptographers would think about, into process algebra. Probabilistic process algebra is notoriously difficult. In fact most of the conventional non-interference definitions talk about things in a possibilistic rather than probabilistic sense, so that's one hurdle you'd have to get over.

All this seems to be related to how you encode the notion of encryption in a non-interference style. If you have high level data sent out over an encrypted channel, that doesn't really fit in the usual non-interference, at least naively, because you clearly are having some influence flowing from high to low; but nonetheless if the encryption algorithm is good you would think it's secure.

Ross Anderson: Curiously enough, at tea-time, George and I have been talking about the possibility of doing this with non-deducability security, because there you have the much simpler requirement. You assume that your encryption is indistinguishable from one time unconditionally secure authentication. Now I don't know how strongly that can be taken, but I'm not a process algebraist.

Reply: That is one possible angle. Another way of looking at it perhaps is to think in terms of ensembles of tests in systems, experiments if you like, which are I think boils down to the same thing.

Virgil Gligor: You accept that the adversary has some probability of advantage, but somehow you have to quantize that advantage. The crypto people have formalised this.

Reply: Yes, that's right. The Lincoln *et. al.* work I think makes a step towards that because they have a metric on your notion of equivalence, so, as you still push up the parameter like the length of the key you say that this parameter has to fall off towards zero.

Virgil Gligor: The advantage is not based on the length of the key at all, there is a notion of advantage which presumably is independent of the length of the key.

Reply: Thank you, well let's talk more off-line, I've already going for longer than I expected. I think I've pretty much finished. In a recent paper Steve Schneider and I[3] suggest one way of doing this in a process algebraic framework where the trick basically was (it's a bit of a cheat really, but in a sense it's no more of a cheat than is done in the spy calculus), to project down the bits, the ones and zeros of the encrypted channel, and just project them down to a single event. Then you can show that it gives you kind of what you'd expect in the sense that the spy can tell the length of the message that's been sent but can't distinguish which one it is. But that's obviously not very satisfactory because it completely misses the fact that, if you've got two crypto streams which are the same, the spy can at least detect that which set me wondering whether this is a little bit like some of the stuff people do in data independence where you've got just equality checks, where the absolute value of various parameters is not significant but you do assume that equality of value is significant, and this is all trickery that people used in model checking to try and reduce the models and claim that if you've got a data type you can actually just do model checking on perhaps two or three elements and it effectively exhausts them all. That has the same feel as the problem here, and it also seems to have analogies with anonymity, but I don't think we have time to go into that.

Ross Anderson: Perhaps the thing to do is to look at a paper by Rushby and Randell[4] (about 20 years ago) on doing non-deducability security on a network on Unix workstations, some of which were unclassified. They encrypted the data, made packet lengths the same, and generated padding traffic there was nothing going on. If you have non-deducability security in this sense, then you have got anonymity of transactions. It all seems to hang together in a non-deducability context.

---

[3] Process Algebra and Non-interference by P Y A Ryan (Defence Evaluation and Research Agency) and S A Schneider (University of London)

[4] A Distributed Secure System by John Rushby and Brian Randell, IEEE Computer, Vol. 16 no. 7, Jul 1983, pp. 55-67

Roger Needham: Also some 20 years ago[5], David Gifford tried to use cryptographic methods for access control. He managed to do it, but it was not a thing of beauty.

Reply: So you're suggesting the answer to that earlier question is maybe you can push it quite far, but it's a dog's breakfast. The motivation for wondering whether it's possible is that maybe you can get a higher degree of assurance easily if you're using cryptographic mechanisms. So, more speculation than anything...

---

[5] Communications of the ACM, Volume 25, Number 4, April 1982 Selected Papers from the Eigth Symposium on Operating Systems Principles

David K. Gifford: Cryptographic Sealing for Information Secrecy and Authentication. 274-286

Looking on the Bright Side
of Black-Box Cryptography
(Transcript of Discussion)

Matt Blaze

AT&T Laboratories Research

I'm going to talk about something a little different from trust management, which is what I usually talk about here. What I'm going to present is joint work with Matt Franklin, now at Xerox PARC. Moti Yung and Adam Young had a paper at Crypto '96 called The Dark Side of Black-Box Cryptography[1], quite a nice important paper that shows essentially that if you have a crypto-protocol that's being implemented by hardware that you don't trust – or hardware that you do trust but you shouldn't – then in most cases that hardware is in a position to leak messages if it is so inclined.

I'm going to look at the bright side of black-box cryptography, *i.e.* could we eliminate the possibility, for specific protocols, of a black box implemented crypto-system compromising our secrets?

Black-box cryptography essentially involves the use of a secure hardware cryptographic co-processor, and the idea of these hardware cryptographic co-processors has been around for a while. Operating systems that run on general purpose computers are hopelessly insecure and we'll never be able to secure them, so let's build small special purpose hardware that never reveals long term secrets, in particular that never will reveal a key simply by speaking to it through its normal interface. Hardware cryptography at worst should reveal keys only with the use of electron microscopes.

You need some kind of forward secrecy built into the device. By forward secrecy, I mean that if you break into the system in which the box is installed you can't learn about past or future traffic. OK, that's not the definition you were expecting, let's not worry about words. In particular, such a hardware crypto-system needs access to a good reliable source of "randomness", which is a requirement for forward secrecy[2].

A black-box crypto-system should represent its owner's interest rather than the manufacturer's interest. Our general purpose here is that we want to limit the damage if the system, or the black-box itself, is stolen or its environment has been compromised in a way that allows one to see what traffic is going in and out of the black-box. Now the down-side to this is that you have to actually have a

---

[1] Adam Young, Moti Yung: The Dark Side of "Black-Box" Cryptography, or: Should We Trust Capstone? CRYPTO 1996: 89-103

[2] The requirement not to be able to see into the future requires unpredictability. The requirement not to be able to infer the past requires un-retrodictability. Cryptographically strong pseudo-randomness is good enough for both, provided the seed is kept secret. This can be done by the black-box, or by some external mechanism.

B. Christianson et al. (Eds.): Security Protocols, LNCS 2133, pp. 54–61, 2001.

specific black-box, so there's some additional cost involved. But aside from that additional cost problem, at the moment you also have to trust the manufacturer of this black-box.

A system that uses a black-box for its cryptography is hard to audit, you can't be sure that the box is doing exactly what you think it's doing, particularly if it's generating and then holding on to your secrets for you. There might be subliminal channels leaking secrets, there might be trapdoors, there might be simple bugs, its (pseudo-)random number generator might not actually be working properly, and it might not actually be implementing anything even remotely close to the crypto-system that you think it is. In particular, if these black-boxes are sold in pairs where one encrypts and the other decrypts, then you have no way of knowing whether or not it's in fact using any kind of secure cipher.

Let's call this the NSA model of a black-box: you put clear text into it, something happens inside, and you get cipher text out, and with an analogous black-box you take cipher text and put it in, and get the clear text back out. Now we can verify that the cipher text doesn't look like the clear text externally, and we can verify that if you take a pair of these boxes and put them back to back you get the same clear text out the far end as you put in in the near end, and we can probably count the number of cipher text bits that come out, but aside from that we can't really do much to assure ourselves that this black-box is in fact representing our interests.

So the problem essentially is: does this thing that I can't actually look at, always act in my best interests, even when I'm not looking, and even though I don't actually know necessarily what it's supposed to be doing. This is the model which we're encouraged to believe is more secure than doing cryptography in software – we'd rather rely on the hardware vendors to make our mistakes for us than the writers of software.

It is certainly possible to set up a system of audits for the manufacturer's chip, but that still doesn't help in answering the question whether or not the protocol that it should be running is correct, or whether or not the particular chip you have is actually implementing that protocol.

So what I want to propose is a better version of black-box cryptography, or a slightly more nuanced version of the black-box, in which the black-box has a trusted and an untrusted side. I should preface this by saying, I'm not interested in solving the general problem of replacing all applications of all kinds of black-boxes, but I'd like to look at the problem of certain specific protocols that are characterized by certain specific things.

In particular, in the cases that I am going to be describing, we assume that the black-box should protect the interests of the owner of the black-box, who in normal operation is actually controlling it. So this does not handle the case, for example, of the chip-card in your set-top box, in which the person who is controlling the interface has interests that are different from the person controlling the internals of the black-box[3].

---

[3] Analogous, but subtly different, arguments can be made in the case where the black-box is an embassy for a foreign domain. In this case protocols may require the host to

So I'm looking at the case of a crypto co-processor in a general purpose computer, used for straightforward crypto-protocols such as message encryption and message decryption for electronic mail, for example, rather than the general case of all types of black-box crypto protocol. In particular, we assume that inside this black-box are algorithms and protocols that are publicly known, where the algorithms and the protocols are understood and trusted by the users of the black-boxes as being the algorithms and protocols that they want. Whether or not these algorithms and protocols are correct is a separate question. Also inside is a good source of on-line randomness[4], and a key store that's capable of storing state over long periods of time and not revealing the contents of the keys stored in this state.

Now we'd like the algorithms to be publicly known, and we'd like the random store to have a forward secrecy property, in the sense that it shouldn't be possible to derive its past or future behaviour from any current information about the interface[5]. Ideally it should be impossible, even under hardware reverse-engineering, to learn the random bits, but that's not really that strong a requirement here, and it's fine if you relax it. Keys need to remain secret under whatever kinds of threats you're concerned with.

Mark Lomas: Putting the source of randomness inside the same box as the secret key store is potentially dangerous.

Reply: I'd like a random source both inside and outside the box. It's not clear you actually need a random source inside the box at all if you have a good random source outside the box, but the problem is that getting a good random source outside the box is a hard problem.

Here's the easier problem you get if you have one of these boxes: are the public protocols being followed? You know what the protocol is, you just want to know if the black-box is actually implementing it. Are "good" choices being made when the random numbers are being used, where "good" is deliberately in quotes, and is the box leaking secrets? This is an easier problem than the general problem: is whatever this thing is doing the whatever it is that I actually want it to be doing. We'd rather have these more specific requirements.

Here are some simplifying assumptions that I'll impose. The current user – whoever has physical possession – is trusted to know anything that's sent to and from the black-box in the current session. So the user is trusted to know what the input and the output to the black-box is while he or she is using it. We don't want the user to be able to learn anything from following its interface about past and future traffic going through it. So if you're physically holding the box, then

---

have the ability to monitor and audit what the set-top box is doing before deciding whether to allow a transaction to proceed.

[4] This may be deterministic cryptographically strong pseudo-randomness, provided that the initial key (or seed) really is a strong secret with sufficient diversity, chosen in such a way that the box cannot influence the probability distribution of the outcome. Matt discusses later how to achieve this.

[5] For example, it suffices to derive the random stream (r_k) from the initial seed s_0 using a cryptographically strong hashing function and setting $r_k := h(0|s_{k-1}); s_k := h(1|s_{k-1})$.

you can know what is going in and out of it now, but not in the future or in the past.

Long-term secrets in the key-store are RSA keys, because of what I am going to say a couple of slides from now. We can modify some protocols to allow user audit. We don't need to be able – and I'm not trying – to solve the problem of putting this black-box transparently inside an arbitrary cryptographic protocol. What I'd like to be able to do is to use this black-box to build new protocols that solve specific problems. And we'd like to be able to rely on the black-box as a randomness source and as a key store, in particular.

The first thing to do when you buy one of these black-boxes is this. The initial user, the user who will have the ability to audit the box – I should say that the first user is the user who will have the ability from now and in the future to audit the black-box – does a shared RSA key generation such as Boneh and Franklin's protocol[6]. Briefly, the interface to this protocol is that two users can get together and generate a shared RSA key that has the property that the two users end up knowing shares of this RSA key, but neither user as part of this creation protocol can sabotage the RSA key, as long as one of the users follows the protocol well. As long as one of the users provides sufficient random bits, we know that the output of this will be a robust RSA key.

So, the user and the black-box get together and do this protocol. At this point the user has to supply some randomness as part of the initialization protocol, but that only has to be done once when the black-box is bought. It can literally be done by flipping 128 coins, or one coin 128 times, you don't actually need 128 different coins. The box uses whatever its random hardware source is[7] and the user generates random bits however they wish. At the end of the protocol the user does something not anticipated by the Boneh-Franklin protocol: the user reveals their share to the box.

Now what do we have? Well both the user and the box learn the public key associated with this shared RSA key generation. The box now has enough information to determine the corresponding private key. The user has a public key that she knows she contributed to, but only the box can decrypt or sign using the corresponding RSA private key.

How do we do audit-able sessions? At session start, the box (2) picks a random number from the internal source, (2) increments a counter value, and (3) receives an input from the user[8]. The user input is a user-chosen random value for the session. The box then computes the RSA signature, using the private half of the shared RSA key, of its own random number, the user's random number and this incremented counter. The box uses this signature value – or more accurately a

---

[6] Dan Boneh, Matthew K. Franklin: Efficient Generation of Shared RSA Keys. CRYPTO 1997: 425-439

[7] There may be actual non-determinism inside the box, or the box can use a stored secret key initialized by some previous leak-proof physical interaction with a forward-secret random source.

[8] The order is important, as Mark Lomas points out later: the box must commit to the values (1) and (2), without revealing them to the user, before it learns the value (3). The box can do this by, for example, revealing $h((1)|(2))$.

digest with fewer than half the number of bits of the signature so that it gets good randomness – to seed a deterministic cryptographically-secure pseudo-random number generator that's used to provide all bits for the encryption of the session in order. So now all bits of the session are determined by the random numbers, the counter value, and the unshared secret RSA private key for which the user knows the public key.

Mark Lomas: Is the counter in the box?

Reply: The counter is in the box, the counter is part of the box's state that it can write and rewrite. It's incremented, and it's a permanent value.

How does the user then audit the session? Remember that the user knows the public key. The box sends the random value (1), the incremented counter value (2), and this signature value that's being used as the seed for the random number generator, back to the user over the trusted channel. The user has to verify two things, first that the counter value has in fact monotonically increased since the last time this was invoked – this is necessary to prevent leakage of past bits across sessions – and second that the signature value verifies, using the box's random number (1), the counter (2) and the user's random number (3), together with that shared public key that was generated at initialization time.

So the user is now in a position to simulate the box's function, and compare what the box produces with what the box should produce, for most kinds of straightforward crypto protocols. For example, message encryption works quite straightforwardly here.

The parameters obviously have to be large enough to prevent things like birthday attacks by the box and so forth, but those are just issues of tweaking the sizes of the parameters. The algorithms here, in particular the hash function that is used to hash the signature value, and the pseudo-random number generator that is being used to actually generate the session of secure bits, also have to be secure, but, those are obvious crypto details.

What this suggests is that for some kinds of protocols it may actually be possible to have black-box crypto-systems whose behaviour is audit-able, on a session by session basis, by the owner of the black-box. Now does this work for the kinds of protocols we actually care about? The obvious one is message encryption, also possibly hybrid public-key/secret-key message encryption. Diffie-Hellman key exchange is another example where this would work.

There's an interesting point with the protocol here of whether or not it's vulnerable to subliminal channels, whether it can leak information through its choice of parameters. Essentially there is a trade-off: if the user can supply session randomness, it makes it harder for the box to leak secrets[9], but providing session randomness is one the things you want the box to do for you.

---

[9] Unless the user supplies input which the box cannot predict, then the box can choose the value of the low order bit of the hashed signature value, by repeatedly examining and discarding successive random numbers until the chosen value of the hashed signature bit appears. This is the low bandwidth covert channel for leaking secrets: the sequence of bit values chosen by the black-box may actually be the master secret, encoded under a DES key known to the manufacturer. The owner of the box has no way of assuring themselves that this is not happening. If the box is to

Formally, what are the requirements for the key generation protocol and the pseudo-random number generator? We think we've nailed that down pretty well, but in any case I think this is an interesting area for further work: designing protocols that can be implemented by secure hardware in a way that can be audited by the party whose interests are supposed to be maintained here.

Mark Lomas: If the box supplies its own randomness the auditor must be sure that that box's randomness (1) is not chosen after it has seen the user's randomness (3), for example using hash values. Unless you're very careful the box can still choose whether a bit is a one.

Reply: Yes, that's right, there's the low bandwidth channel there, yes. So the question where the session randomness comes from is a difficult problem. At a first approximation, if the box itself supplies the session randomness, you have to be very careful to avoid the low bandwidth key leakage: if the box doesn't supply randomness then the user can supply it, but if you have to supply session randomness yourself this limits the usefulness of the black-box approach. What you do is design protocols in which we assume the box is being malicious in its own choices, so that we're still robust against that.

Mark Lomas: Can't we turn it to the user randomness, can't the auditor just set the random number before the input is given?

Reply: Yes, that's certainly an approach you could do if you hold the box to the value it committed to, but again you have to be a little bit careful. There are some attacks here where you still get the low bandwidth covert channel.

Frank Stajano: The obvious thing is to have the randomness provided by someone else.

Reply: Yes, that certainly ameliorates the problem greatly in practice. But what I want is something which really allows me to say at the beginning, I don't have to trust these hardware vendors.

Mark Lomas: Why not physically divide the box?

Reply: That's precisely the way you can avoid this problem. You can actually solve this problem by having two separate boxes, the protocol becomes a bit hairy which is why I didn't describe it here[10]. But you still have to trust the

---

be prevented from leaking a stored key, then a covert channel bandwidth of even a fraction of a bit per session is disastrous. By examining an average of $p = 1+\epsilon$ choices per session, the box can communicate about $\log_2 p \approx (10/7)\epsilon$ bits per session. Raw random numbers produced by the box are even more dangerous, since they provide a high bandwidth channel for leaking secrets. The "random" values (1), which are chosen by the box in a way which the user cannot predict, must be kept in quarantine and never revealed even after auditing is completed.

[10] The half of the box which is the key-store must be sure that it is receiving exactly the bit-stream which is being generated by the other half of the box which is the randomness generator. But the random half of the box must not have access to any output from the key-store half if the two halves are to be prevented from colluding to leak keys.

component that's generating the random numbers, if that's your sole source of session randomness[11].

John Ioannidis: I also like the idea of marketing randomness – we're more random than those other models. "Randomness you can trust." What's the target market for these things?

Reply: Researchers. (laughter.) Seriously though, the same people who demand open source for security reasons in software. Some users would very much like to have such a box. It's not clear that the average PC user who uses a very well known operating system would care about such a thing, but banks do. The people who want this mustn't be wanting secure hardware for performance reasons, because you don't gain any performance[12]. If you want to audit it, you have to simulate its performance in software anyway.

Of course, you needn't audit it every time. But if you want to be sure, you can audit it every time and still gain the secure key store. The problem is that in practice, right now secure hardware is being bought by two kinds of people, people who want to put their secure hardware in your computer, and this doesn't help you there with the set-top box example, and people who want the performance increased, for example, so they can do better, faster SSL on their web server, and this doesn't help them either because to audit it they have to simulate it.

But there's also this other class of people, who simply want the architectural benefits of having their crypto encapsulated in a hardware device that isn't under the control of their operating system, and that would include people like me and probably the people in this room.

Ross Anderson: There's a very general attack on hardware which I'm not sure you've addressed, which is that the hardware is programmed to look for the string "beeblebrox", whereupon it spits out of the serial port all its long term secrets. I don't think there's a defence against that.

On the other hand, in banking you have security modules with no covert state in them, except for the master key. All the transactions that are done on the system are all well understood, they are all documented, and you can check statistically that the thing is doing what is in the specification. So there's a bit of difference between what can be done easily and what probably cannot be done at all.

Reply: Yes, I certainly agree with your first point. This does not address the problem of essentially having a secret interface to the box that allows you to do the equivalent of hardware analysis of it[13].

---

[11] If several sources of "randomness" are deterministically combined, then it suffices for each interested party to trust at least one source. But again, the process which validates that the deterministic combination has been correctly done must be incapable of leaking any of the input streams to the outside world.

[12] Unless the security context is such that the user is willing to do auditing in arrears.

[13] Or to gain access to the quarantine area, which is just as bad.

Ross Anderson: Suppose that I have bought this box and put it in my PC to do secure banking and now there's a completely secure environment, and something goes wrong with my credit card transaction. It's now my fault.

Reply: Well it's already your fault as far as the banks in the UK are concerned.

The box still wouldn't be able to be used as an oracle, because of the monotonically increasing counter. If the box is behaving faithfully then the monotonically increasing counter prevents that, if the box isn't behaving faithfully you'll detect that because you'll see it's not increased.

Markus Kuhn: The crypto-box primarily protects the key, so it's only useful on occasions where the key is significantly more valuable than the plain text. For example, credit cards are one of the main ...

Reply: Right, because none of us would ever have designed the credit card system as a transaction model in the first place, because there's a fixed key. I think for e-mail messages, as an example, this probably has some benefit.

Michael Roe: How can I verify that the box is doing the decryption properly and giving me back the right clear text, if there's random padding[14] and stuff in there?

Reply: If the text being encrypted is just a session key, then you could just re-encrypt it. Otherwise you get technical details[15]. The long term key in the box is the one you generated using the shares, so you can be sure that the public key is the one that you contributed the initial randomness to.

---

[14] Which, incidentally, the corresponding box at the other end had better not have chosen!

[15] The box needs to reveal the padding, or the padding can be a hash of the encrypted text.

Government Access to Keys – Panel Discussion

Michael Roe (chair), Ross Anderson, Bill Harbison, and Mark Lomas

Michael Roe: I will start this with a disclaimer that nothing I say is Microsoft's official opinion. Microsoft may have an official opinion on some of these issues, but I am not allowed to make up what that opinion is. So all this is just opinion on my part.

Matt Blaze: You found it necessary to say that now, but not during your talk before!

Michael Roe: (pause). Yes. (laughter).

People from the US may be surprised that we're talking about Government access to keys. You're going to say, Clipper, all this kind of stuff, dead and buried long ago, it's all gone away. Unfortunately here in Europe, just like we get movies six months later than you, we also get policy a couple of years later than you. Currently going through the UK Parliament is a bill called the Regulation of Investigatory Powers (RIP) Bill, which gives various kinds of powers to the police, intelligence agencies, customs and excise, and a long laundry list of government agencies that you didn't know existed. Part of the RIP Bill concerns cryptography.

The reasonable compromise with key escrow that was proposed a few years ago was to have some measure where, if law enforcement officials demand you hand over a cryptographic key, you have to give it to them. This effectively is in the legislation, but with a nasty twist: it's *have or have had* a cryptographic key and failing to provide it, that is the criminal offence. So there is a worry now: what happens if I no longer have that session key? If you read the Bill carefully[1], you have to prove on the basis of *balance of probability* that you no longer have the key. Otherwise you are committing a criminal offence which renders you liable to imprisonment.

Proving that you no longer have a copy of a session key is a somewhat tricky problem. So this has led to both vigorous political campaigning to try to get it out of the Bill, and protocol-theory to try to think up some silly protocol that actually gives us this guarantee.

That's a bit of the UK political background, and now without further ado, here's Ross Anderson.

Ross Anderson: I suppose I've been involved to some extent in the campaigning. I'm against it, yes.

The idea of government access to keys, rather than government powers to have you decrypt, initially came from somebody in Anne Campbell's private office – she is the MP for Cambridge – and she took the heat when people started complaining about Labour's proposals for crypto-controls while they were still in opposition. We have set up an organization called the Foundation for

---

[1] The text refers to the draft of the RIP Bill as it was at the time of the Workshop. Some of the more objectionable features have subsequently been removed, but a great deal of "interest" remains.

B. Christianson et al. (Eds.): Security Protocols, LNCS 2133, pp. 62–73, 2001.
© Springer-Verlag Berlin Heidelberg 2001

Information Policy Research (FIPR[2]) – with generous support from Microsoft – and the function of this organization is to have somebody full-time to run around educating lawmakers, journalists, and people like that. The Advisory Council that directs FIPR (on which I sit) contains many of the principal players in the UK, and is an interesting mix of lawyers and computer scientists. We're starting to get lawyers and computer scientists to actually talk to each other for a change, rather than past each other.

What can one do about proving that one doesn't have a key? Government would like us to believe that you say "honestly, I don't have this key anymore", and if the judge believes you then you get off, and if the judge doesn't believe you then you don't. As Mike pointed out, this is a little bit contrary to the usual standards of proof at criminal trials. So what can one do?

We are rapidly coming to the conclusion that the only way you can satisfy – or if you like, defeat – the RIP Bill in a way that is compatible with current products, is by using tamper-resistant hardware. If you are allowed a free hand designing everything from scratch – you can redesign the Internet, and you can redesign PGP, and compatibility of people in foreign countries doesn't matter – then there are probably things that you can do at the protocol level. You can build in anonymity and deniability and all sorts of stuff like that. But if you are faced with the problem, how do you show you no longer have access to a key which is useful for decrypting PGP messages, for example, then about the only way you can do that is by having an auditable black box that you control.

If I've got an auditable black box, and I get somebody to spend a few months programming PGP into it, and I have somebody else verify correctness, and I'm happy with this, then I can put in an extra twist. I can instruct the box never to decrypt anything twice. This isn't quite obvious, because you've got to worry about blinding attacks, and you've got to keep some kind of hash table with the clear text keys that have been decrypted, you've got to check the format of packets, and there is a laundry list of developments for other things you want to do, but these are all doable.

So you end up being more or less compelled by UK legislation to construct equipment with all these things. I think that this isn't quite reasonable, but though we've tried to explain this to the authorities once or twice, they either don't get the message or they are determined to get the Bill through Parliament and then worry about it later.

It will be interesting to see whether this assessment is right, that we must have tamper resistant hardware and this can then trivially defeat the legislation. Would this mean that in the next round of regulations we will be told our hardware must be audited by GCHQ because of the ease with which tamper resistant hardware can be turned into an instrument of larceny? And from the scientific point of view, with regard to the question is there anything we can't do in cryptography, I think the answer is "yes" because with cryptography you can't forget keys. This is only one of the ways in which mathematics isn't expressive

---

[2] www.fipr.org

enough for the purposes that are now enforced upon us by statute, and we have to move away from mathematics towards metal.

William Harbison: I got involved in this in a slightly different way. Perhaps I could give a bit of broader background to the RIP Bill to show some of the arcane complexities which may be going on. This Bill is being brought in in order to comply with the European Convention on Human Rights, which is becoming established into UK law later this year (2000 AD). There are current statutory instruments, most noticeably one called IoCA, which is the Interception of Communications Act – for our North American cousins this is the equivalent to CALEA[3] – and IOCA actually breaches many of the terms and conditions of the European Convention of Human Rights. The RIP Bill is in part allegedly trying to fix these issues, and it also covers and legislates about all sorts of activities which before were not particularly legislated either for or against. It covers things like private investigators, which weren't discussed before, it supersedes IoCA, but it does nothing with other laws which deal with either interception of communications or their subsequent understanding. For example the Wireless Telegraphy Act 1968 still has extremely broad powers, and I'm surprised no-one has mentioned it yet, because it isn't touched by the RIP Bill. And of course we have various security bills which enable the security forces to do whatever is in the best interests of the country.

The part of the RIP Bill about key escrow came through another route. That legislation was originally in the Electronic Commerce Bill, which Ross and many others fought successfully to get it excluded from. It was that part of the Electronic Commerce Bill that got moved into this Bill, and so the RIP Bill deals with everything from what is called lawful – or in North American terms, legal – interception, through to the regulation of private investigators, through to the handing over of messages in the clear. The RIP Bill is very specific about how it deals with this. The bill enables orders to be placed on any communication service provider – and that, from what I can see, covers almost everybody in the world including individuals – to hand over the clear text, the plain text, of any message.

Michael Roe: Or the key, at their discretion. You don't get to choose, the law enforcement officer gets to choose what he's going to ask you to provide, and he can ask for both.

William Harbison: I am not a lawyer and I haven't actually been through the depths of this Bill, but Mike has talked about establishing things on the burden of probabilities. If I recall English law correctly, that's the civil burden of proof, criminal law is beyond all reasonable doubt.

Michael Roe: Except for this clause. There are other exceptions in criminal law, but they're fairly rare and it's usually fairly obvious what you have to do to avoid getting yourself in the situation where you have to prove your innocence.

William Harbison: Now, the sting in the tail is this. Setting aside the whole set of social issues about the rights of the individual versus the rights of the state and all of those discussions which are going on, the fact of the matter

---

[3] Communications Assistance for Law Enforcement Act 1994.

is that it is not clear, at this point in time, that technical solutions currently exist to meet some of the provisions of the Bill.

Since we don't have the detailed requirements, it is a bit difficult to know whether we have the solutions. But in the legalistic sense it is possible that we will get into our statute books a law which makes it a criminal offence to do something which nobody knows how not to do. So that in itself is a difficult problem.

The RIP Bill is enabling legislation which basically just provides just a framework within which the actual details (called "orders in council") operate separately and don't have to come through the same legislative programme. The government has a statutory obligation to consult on these, but at the meeting a couple of weeks ago, basically what I heard the minister say was, yes, we heard what you say and we're not going to change our minds about it. So we have now been consulted.

The sting in the tail, I was going to say, is that there are many organizations which undertake activities which involve encrypted data, on behalf of others. And they are governed in those interactions by separate laws and sometimes by separate jurisdictions. So it seems that there is a strong possibility that we will have an act on our statute books where if you don't do something you are breaking the law and if you do do something you are breaking another law, which is not a particularly comfortable position to be in.

Mark Lomas: I'm currently responsible for information security at Goldman-Sachs. It's probably best to explain what Bill was alluding to there about cross jurisdictional problems, by means of a particular example. One of the members of Goldman-Sachs Group is Goldman-Sachs and Company Bank in Zurich, which is a Swiss bank regulated under Swiss law, and I am responsible for the security of that bank, as well as various other organizations. One of the things that I was advised when I took on this responsibility was that under Swiss law, client confidentiality is utmost. It actually takes precedence over various criminal laws in Switzerland. So a law enforcement officer must not breach the confidentiality of the client other than under very specific exemptions to do with drug trafficking, money laundering, etc.

If I were to reveal information about those clients I would be committing a criminal offence under Swiss law. Also, the directors of the bank would also be committing a criminal offence, even though they were not able to prevent me from revealing the information. Under the proposed British regulations I commit a criminal offence if I refuse to reveal something subject to a British intercept warrant. Also the directors of the company for which I work are separately subject to this criminal act, they have committed a criminal offence even though they had no good way of preventing the information from being revealed. So, I'm stuck in this position where I'm damned if I don't, and damned if I do.

One of the ways we might avoid that, which people have mentioned before, is the use of tamper proof equipment. It would be my recommendation that we put tamper proof equipment in wherever we've got opportunity, just as Ross suggested, so that I have the defence: I have no access to those keys, I never have had, there is no practical way of me getting them. Unfortunately that is a bit inconvenient for business practice in organizations, particularly if they want to audit things themselves. It means they are actually suggesting that I ought to reduce the audit capabilities of my bank in order to comply with this regulation, because that's the natural result of what they're planning to legislate.

There are various other problems associated with complying with an intercept warrant. I might be presented with the result of an intercept – let's imagine there is a perfectly legal intercept warrant, they've tapped one of our links and they get a recording of several days of cipher text, and they come to me and they say, here is a warrant, would you please tell us what is in there. Now in theory I might have access to the keys, but all I know is I've got a piece of cipher text. I have no way of identifying which key it is. I might have to search all over my bank in order to work out who it was that actually generated this thing, and I've got no reasonable way of doing that, short of adding an awful lot of additional infrastructure that I don't need, just in order to be able to comply with these sorts of warrant.

There are similar problems for an ISP that was served with an intercept warrant, please hand over all of the data that Mark Lomas sends across your link. If they happen to be trying to tap our link between London and New York, for instance, we have about 2000 people in London sending data to New York, and we multiplex all of their data together. How is the ISP going to find my traffic in the middle of that? I don't know. But fortunately that is their problem not mine.

There is supposedly an exception: under certain circumstances, you can actually refuse to hand over the key. One of those circumstances was supposed to be if the use of that key is only for signatures. There is a slight problem with that as well. A signature key is part of a key pair, so imagine a public/private key pair. I've got my private signature key and I've only ever used it for signatures, but a police officer decides he'd really like my private key. Now the problem with the legislation as drafted is, the police officer can take my public key, encrypt something, and then say, this key is no longer only a signature key. It's the key that is necessary to decrypt the message that was just sent. I have no sensible defence against that. The policeman isn't doing anything illegal, he doesn't accuse me of doing anything, he just says, I've discovered this message, which when decrypted happens to say "meet you at the Eagle at five o'clock." He's not committing a criminal offence, he's just sending me a confidential message.

Michael Roe: He sends you the message, and then serves a warrant on you, which he's perfectly entitled to do, and then you are committing a criminal offence by not complying with the warrant. It wasn't as bad as some of the previously suggested ways the legislation could have been worded, where the police office could invent some random bits, hand them to you, demand that you decrypt them, and you are committing a criminal offence if you don't. At least that has been fixed: now the prosecution has to show, beyond reasonable doubt, that you have or have had the key. So in a case where the message has nothing to do with you, your defence is: nothing to do with me, never had the key.

William Harbison: In the UK, there are currently over 200 licensed telecommunications operators. The number of ISPs is probably around 500 or so. Now I think we all know that not all of those people have their own dedicated lines or use dedicated facilities. In fact you clearly get people who are hosting services using other people's equipment who may themselves be using other people's equipment. So there is this whole issue about to whom this notice is served and their ability to comply with it.

Apart from the European convention on human rights the other big initial driving force for all of this was: oh my goodness, people are not using their telephones as much as they used to, they're using e-mail. We used to be able to tap the telephones, so we need to be able to tap the e-mail. There's not that problem in North America of course, because there's a distinction between voice and data in North America. This distinction is not made in Europe, I might say, let alone just the UK.

Matt Blaze: It seems to me that one could straightforwardly get around this with properly designed protocols, if the courts are rational. In that case simply designing software protocols so that the encryption keys for messages are never kept around in the long term would solve the problem. If the courts are rational they will accept the explanation: look, here is the software that I have, see, it throws the keys out, what more can I say. On the other hand if the courts are not rational then nothing you can do will influence things.

So I'm not sure how much of this is a technical question, how much is a question of the wording of the law, and how much of this is simply an issue of trust (I hate using that word trust). How much do you trust the process to respond to this in a rational way.

Ross Anderson: In practice the courts are somewhere in-between being rational and being irrational. The one thing you can't do in court, here in Europe or in America, is to be too clever for the judge. If you turn up and produce a mathematical proof in court then you'll get thrown in jail.

I have some experience of giving expert testimony about crypto-matters, and believe me it is a jolly hard thing to do. It's even harder if you've been arrested at three o'clock in the morning and told, you can either hand over the key or you can spend the weekend in jail and we'll let you talk to your lawyer on Monday morning when you'll be charged with an offence that gets you three years in jail. Even if you believe that your rights are completely solid under European law, it takes an awful lot of courage and an awful lot of money to be determined to fight the writ for the twelve years or so it takes, especially if you're the first case that comes up.

William Harbison: There are also issues of where the servers are actually kept. I believe that the Home Office were asking for volunteer ISPs to work with, to help look at some of the solutions that might be involved. And AOL said, yes please come and have a look, we've got all these long lines and all of our servers are over in North America.

Ross Anderson: Using an ISP which is located in the Isle of Man costs absolutely no more than using an ISP that's located in the mainland UK, but it falls under a different jurisdiction. Now, need anything more be said.

William Harbison: We're providing a market for Matt's box here, if we could logically prove that we can't access the keys.

John Ioannidis: What happened to "innocent until proven guilty"?

Ross Anderson: All these things have been undermined again and again: with terrorism legislation, with seizure of drug assets, with losing your right of silence in front of a Department of Trade and Industry Company Inspector. There are articles in the press from time to time that give a list of all the rights we had in the 19th century, and the particular laws that took them away. The process continues, nobody seems to care, it's as if human laws like everything else accumulate barnacles over time, and every two centuries somebody has to press Ctrl-Alt-Del.

John Ioannidis: But if nobody cares about fundamental and phenomenally easily understood things like drug seizures, what will they care about a bunch of geeks and their obscure mathematics?

Ross Anderson: Exactly. It's very hard to get this issue into the mainstream press at all, they prefer to put it into their computer comics. Computer Security is an issue that does not run.

William Harbison: The RIP Bill does in fact distinguish between two classes of data, which are *seized data* – stuff they can normally get hold of *i.e.* stored on your local machines, on a disc, or on the ISP system – and *intercepted data*, *i.e.* that which is flying along in real time along the communications links. Clearly there are different technical problems and technical solutions to do with these different problem domains.

John Ioannidis: Any technical solution that you come up with for today's laws can easily be rendered illegal in next year's laws. Outlawing encryption would solve this problem entirely. If they catch you with encrypted data, you're dead.

Ross Anderson: That was in fact the position of the French government till a year and a half ago. I was fascinated to read about the history of telex in Tom Standage's book, The Victorian Internet. Exactly the same situation arose with the telegraph in the 1850's, and different countries took their own separate routes. In France, for example, the use of any kind of code whatsoever was just about a guillotining offence, and other countries like America were much more liberal. And in the end this didn't work, because telegraph messages flowed from one jurisdiction to another to a third.

Eventually in 1865 they had to get together a conference – the International Telecommunications Union – which finally set down some laws to the effect that, yes you can use codes if you want and the government through whose jurisdiction some bits go has got absolutely no business whatsoever to interfere with them. The curious thing was that this was motivated by the French, who suffered more than anybody else from their original maximalist position.

So perhaps what we're going to need some time in the next ten years or so is a remake of the International Telecommunications Union, and that is something that people working for a large international company, like Microsoft or AT&T, should be motivated to push for through the various available channels.

Michael Roe: This being a protocols workshop, I think maybe the task for us as protocol designers – rather than as general political activists – is to assess what impact on protocols these kinds of legislation will have. If it really is absolutely impossible to comply with these things even under the kind of benign interpretation that a court might put upon the law, then we just say, it can't be done. On the other hand, maybe some of these things can be done: they might be imposing a duty of care on everybody in the UK, that you have got to construct and use protocols in a particular way that will allow you to comply.

Matt Blaze: Can I clarify what the law says here? My understanding of what you said earlier is, that this law does not impose any new, explicit obligations for a key, only to reveal keys that you have had in the past. But does it require explicitly that you save any key that you've used?

Michael Roe: No, but it does require you to be able to prove that you lost it. Effectively it requires that you either provide the key or a proof that you no longer have it. So getting stuck in the middle like we do at the moment, where we just kind of let keys fade away, is not acceptable. I remember some of the people from the Home Office saying, well surely you have proper procedures in place for key destruction, and we go, umm, well actually we don't. (laughter). This is really a fault in the protocol and I think we should be able to prove when and where a session key was destroyed.

It's for the courts to decide, but my personal opinion is that registered key death would be probably be enough.

Mark Lomas: We've had legal advice that that's what we ought to do. However, that would prevent certain types of audit practice, where I actually wish to retain some of my keys. Not because I particularly want to comply with the warrant, but because I would like to audit certain transactions in my system without making it obvious to the people by whom this transaction has been done.

Markus Kuhn: Is it the crypto-text or the plain-text that you audit?

Mark Lomas: Potentially both.

Ross Anderson: There is an alternative approach to this, which also involves trusted hardware. Instead of being sure that you destroy a key, or being sure the keys expire after a certain amount of time, you ensure that the keys can only be used in a controlled way. The obvious way to do this is through biometrics. IBM used to sell a signature tablet as an accessory to the 4753, and it would be trivial to program it so that it would only decrypt a message when it witnessed your actual signature.

Now much of what the security and intelligence services appear to want to achieve, is to have covert access to past traffic and to future traffic, without you knowing what traffic they have selected. If you bind the authorized user into a decryption loop, then this might provide a somewhat less confrontational way of persuading the government that's its maximum wishes are in fact counterproductive. If Mark at Goldman-Sachs has to physically sit there and draw a squiggle every time a message is to be undone, then normal reasonable law enforcement needs can be met, as can all audit needs, but the unreasonable felt-needs of the intelligence services can't be, so they will probably go away.

John Ioannidis: Let me throw another monkey wrench in here. There's some industries where, at least in the US, you're not only allowed but you are obliged to keep traces of everything in the transaction, for audit purposes. Very frequently you need to be able actually to do what creative government agents want to do: an audit which will try to trace and find something, and in fact the company secrets are being insider-traded. You really do want to do the audit without that person's co-operation. Not because you are not going to get their cooperation, but because you don't want to tip them off that you are investigating them. So there is actually legitimate use for this kind of ability.

Ross Anderson: But that's always false within my model, which requires the knowledge and co-operation of one of a small number of named known individuals in the company.

John Ioannidis: But the issue is that the originator of the traffic sometimes should not have to be consulted. On some occasions.

Ross Anderson: Oh sure. If you do have a corporate wide escrow key which will act as a universal unlock code, then there should be strict controls on its use. What I'm saying is that you should engineer your system such that it is not at all possible for the company to give the cleartext value of that universal unlock code to any person, including the cops. Especially including the cops, because there's so many stories of bent cops.

Mark Lomas: The problem is, we do have audit procedures in place. If they were to say, I want to see Mark Lomas's bank account records we can bring them out, but that's fair enough and we don't mind that. What I *do* mind is the point which Ross has mentioned about the corporate-wide escrow key, which we have mainly for internal purposes. I would mind very much if we were served a warrant for that particular key, because I have no idea which information they're actually trying to use it to get at. They might claim that they're trying to do it in order to convince themselves that they've got the correct account records which reference Mark Lomas, when in fact what they're doing is looking at our trading strategy.

Bruce Christianson: I think there is an issue here about the difference between the requirements of an internal auditor and those of an external agency. Superficially they're all very much the same in the kind of looking around that they want to do, but they quite possibly have very different agendas. How do you separate them?

Michael Roe: In particular, any internal auditor is going to be careful not to do things that will badly hurt your business. A law enforcement officer is under no such obligation. He's trying to solve some crime, and that's all he's interested in and quite properly so. He will serve that warrant on you whether or not it might be inconvenient or expensive for you. Or even put you out of business.

Mark Lomas: He might not even realize the value of a piece of data. Suppose they decide to investigate somebody who happens to be involved in a very large deal. Let's say it has not yet become public that a particular company is going to be floated, and we are advising on that. That information is, we would argue, highly confidential. And let's imagine an intercept warrant were to be served upon one of the advisors to this deal, and so some arbitrary police officer ends up with something that he has no idea of the sensitivity of. If that information got out, it could cost people millions.

Ross Anderson: Here's perhaps a better model than biometrics. Suppose that in your company you keep a log of all the messages that have ever come in or out, which in many banking applications is the case. Suppose that you were using something like PGP for example. Then you just require that all messages are carbon-copied to the escrow department.

Suppose that the escrow department then deciphers the session keys, re-enciphers them and holds them in a database, along with the messages. You've got a perfectly explicit database that says, this is the escrow key to unlock message 12345. Then the policeman comes along with his warrant and you say, which messages to you want to decrypt. All of them? I'm sorry, you may not have all of them, legal privilege etc. And if he says, well he actually wants all the stuff in 1996 relevant to transactions with bank X in New York you can say, that's fine. Here you are, a total of 347 keys, here's a floppy disk, have a nice life.

Now that completely complies with what appears to be the spirit of the law, but it's going to make the intelligence agencies very sore indeed if that's what everybody does. Perhaps this highlights the tension better than talking about biometrics.

Stewart Lee: It seems that there has been some concentration upon the immediate burning of keys at the end of a session. There are various ways that the data can remain encrypted and decryptable, by re-encrypting it with some other key.

But this doesn't fulfill the primary reasons for keeping keys around. There are at least two reasons for keeping keys around. One of them Mark has just illuminated: auditors will probably not be happy with data that has been re-encrypted with some other key by some process that may or may not be trustworthy, in some box that may or may not be trustworthy, under the control of some guy who probably isn't trustworthy, and so on.

The second reason for doing this is non-repudiation. Non-repudiation needs the keys that were originally used.

Ross Anderson: And many dumb banking systems encrypt and then sign!

Michael Roe: I personally think it's quite reasonable if I'm served with a warrant to decrypt particular messages with a key that I still have, I'm quite happy to do that. Decrypting messages with a key that I don't have any more is a bit of a problem for me, *because* I don't have it any more.

William Harbison: But the Home Office have said that they will only charge you if you are guilty.

Ross Anderson: There is another interesting aspect to this. I am sorting through applications from people who want to come and do a PhD here at Cambridge and I reckon over half of them want to do work on things like anonymity, steganography, plausible deniability, and so on. It's hard to believe that this would be the case had the government not introduced this legislation.

I believe after Clipper some NSA people expressed bitter regret at ever having raised the subject. I believe they said in essence, well we should just have let AT&T sell that stupid phone, they would have sold fifty and then dropped the product, and that would have been the end of it.

Now I think that in ten years' time it is quite predictable that spooks and law enforcement people alike will come to bitterly regret the stupidity of all the influential people who got together and pushed this Bill through, because they have really shot their successors in the foot. In fact they have shot their successors' feet off.

Michael Roe: By having alerted people to the fact that interception is taking place. If they'd just kept quiet probably everything would have been in the clear, and they'd have been quite happy, but all this fuss has publicised cryptography no end.

Ross Anderson: But publicising anonymity and steganography is far worse, because mostly what the police get from communications intelligence is not the content, but who called whom.

And if we start seeing widely deployed stuff like zero-knowledge, and anonymous re-mailers integrated with a stable file system, which is what one or two people want to do ...

Matt Blaze: Here is a technical solution that, if I were a judge I'd throw you in jail for implementing, but which I think probably meets the technical requirement, since we're technical people.

I proposed the scheme at Eurocrypt with Martin Strauss[4]. The idea it uses is an atomic proxy property. Two parties get together and create a a public function that allows them to atomically decrypt and re-encrypt into a new key.

The significant point is that although the function is public, it doesn't reveal the intermediate plaintext. So one way of strictly meeting the requirement would be to publish your public key, create a proxy key to a second key, and immediately burn the first secret key.

Every time you receive a message, you go through a two-step process, apply the proxy function and then the secondary secret key. You can honestly say the key that this message was encrypted with no longer exists, and you've met the letter of the law.

Now if I were a judge and I actually understood what you did I'd be very angry, but strictly you have met your requirement.

Ross Anderson: I think that the central problem here is who controls traffic selection. If we remember that report from 95 or whatever, even the NSA admit

---

[4] Matt Blaze and Martin Strauss, Atomic Proxy Cryptography, Eurocrypt 1998.

that traffic selection is the biggest headache, it's where most of the resources go. What the government is trying to achieve with the current legislation is to have control over traffic selection. If you're an ISP and they want you to do the traffic selection, because it's a headache to pull traffic out of a enormously heavily multiplex multi-gigabit link, they can tell you to do it.

If on the other hand they want to do the traffic selection because they don't want you to know which of your employees they're snooping on, because they're snooping on the managing director or the security manager, then they can say look give us the master keys and trust us. Now the corporate response to this should probably be, *we* will control the traffic selection, or at the very worst, the traffic selection will be under the control of the judge, and it will be an accountable, auditable process and costs will be paid. Now without this intellectual parity what's going to happen is that everybody will just redesign their systems so that, using biometrics or secure hardware or whatever, the company controls the traffic selection and there's no play in the situation.

William Harbison: I'm surprised nobody mentioned the multi-part key with one part held offshore. I suppose this is similar in some ways to proxies, but it would certainly provide a lot of people with a headache.

Making Sense of Specifications: The Formalization of SET

(Extended Abstract)

Giampaolo Bella[1], Fabio Massacci[2,3],
Lawrence C. Paulson[1], and Piero Tramontano[3]

[1] Computer Laboratory, University of Cambridge
Pembroke Street, Cambridge CB2 3QG, England
{gb221,lcp}@cl.cam.ac.uk
[2] Dip. di Ingegneria dell'Informazione, Universià di Siena
via Roma 56, 53100 Siena, Italy
massacci@dii.unisi.it
[3] Dip. di Informatica e Sistemistica, Università di Roma I "La Sapienza"
via Salaria 113, 00198 Roma, Italy
{massacci,tramonta}@dis.uniroma1.it

1 Introduction

The last ten years, since the seminal work on the BAN logic [6], have seen the rapid development of formal methods for the analysis of security protocols. But security protocols have also developed rapidly, becoming more and more complex. Protocols for electronic commerce are the *béte noir*: six pages were enough to describe the Needham-Schroeder protocol in 1978 [15], six hundred pages were not enough to describe the SET protocol of VISA and Mastercard [11,12,13] twenty years later.

This increase in complexity is a challenge to both protocol designers and protocol verifiers. The sheer size of the documentation makes it likely to contain bugs and inconsistencies. The same size makes it difficult to analyze of protocol formally. Model-checking approaches are likely to founder in the enormous state space, while inductive proof may become unfeasible in the presence of so many subgoals to consider.

After Kailar's [8] analysis of simple electronic commerce protocols, there have been attempts to model more realistic protocols such as Kerberos [2], TSL/SSL [18], Cybercash coin-exchange [4,5], and C-SET (a version of SET reduced for smart cards) [3]. However, to the best of our knowledge, no attempt has been made to formally analyze the SET protocol. This paper describes the work we have done in this direction.

2 The SET Protocol

The SET protocol [11] has been proposed by VISA as a standard protocol for securing electronic transactions on the Web. It has been standardized by

B. Christianson et al. (Eds.): Security Protocols, LNCS 2133, pp. 74–81, 2001.

a large consortium including the major credit card companies (VISA, Mastercard, American Express) and software corporations (Microsoft, Netscape etc.). SET aims to protect sensitive card-holder information but does not support non-repudiation.

The overall architecture of SET is based on a rooted hierarchy of *Certification Authorities* (CA). The top level is a trusted root followed by centralized certification authorities corresponding to credit card brands. Two levels down are certification authorities (corresponding to banks) that deal with customers. The task of these CAs is to provide customers with public keys and digital signature certificates for signature and encryption. It is worth noting that CAs do not need to have access to the private keys of customers, who must generate and safeguard their own keys.

Customers of this systems can be grouped in two major classes: *Card-holders* (C) and *Merchants* (M). Besides them, it is foreseen to have *Payment Gateways* (PG) to play the role of clearing-houses [16]: their task is to settle the payment requests made by Merchants and Cardholders when buying goods. The protocol descriptions are complex [11,12,13] and make heavy references to the PKCS standards by RSA Security [19,20].

The cryptography algorithms used in SET are of three main types:

1. public key cryptography for encryption
2. public key cryptography for signature
3. symmetric key encryption (typically for session keys and digital envelopes)
4. hashing and message digests

The first two kinds of keys are deemed to be different, despite being based on the same algorithm. These basic types are composed in various forms: for instance one may use a strong signature that signs a whole document or a weak one that signs only a digest. Or one may prepare a digital envelope by encrypting (with a public key) a symmetric key and the hash of a message plus nonces and then concatenate this message with proper envelope which is the actual message plus the hash of symmetric keys, etc.

The SET protocol consists of five phases. The first two phases are used by the agents participating in the protocol to register their keys and getting the appropriate certificates. The remaining three phases constitute the electronic transaction itself.

Card-holder Registration. This is the initial step of the protocol for card-holders. The agent C sends to a certification authority CA the information on the credit card he wants to use, the CA replies with a registration form, which is compiled by C and sent back together with the signing key that C wants to register. Then the CA checks that the credit card is valid (this step is outside the protocol) and releases the certificate for C who stores it for future use. All this information (such as credit card information) must be protected and this makes the protocol steps complicated. A couple of things are worth noticing:

- a user may register as many public keys as he wants to;

 – the user identity is not stored in the certificate but just an indirect information on its primary account number (PAN): that is, its credit card number.

Merchant Registration. This phase is analogous for the Merchant M. In contrast
with the card-holder registration phase, M can register a public key for encryption and a public key for signature. The process is shorter because there is no
confidential information to be protected.

Purchase Request. We reach this phase if the card-holder has decided to buy
something. C sends to M the order and the instruction for payment. M process
the orders and forwards some of the payment instruction to the PG. This last step
is needed because SET aims to keep some card-holder information confidential.
The PG, in cooperation with credit card issuers, banks and other institutions,
checks that everything is all right (this step is outside SET). Then we are ready
for the next stage.

Payment Authorization. The PG sends the payment authorization to M and M
sends to C the confirmation and possibly the purchased goods. C acknowledges
the result and M passes to the next stage.

Payment Capture. In this last phase, M sends to the PG one or more authorizations and the corresponding card-holder authorizations. The PG checks that
everything is satisfactory and replies back to M. The actual funds transfer from
C to M is done outside the protocol by the credit card company.

3   General Principles behind the Formalization

The formal analysis of a complex protocol like SET requires two steps. The first
step tries to obtain a high level description of the protocol, eliminating some
of the technology dependent features. It should clearly describe the operating
environment and the semantics of the messages.

Once a protocol reaches the stage of an RFC (Request for Comments), it is
often specified in an elaborate but unsatisfactory manner. The meanings of the
fields of a message are only given informally. Often it is hard to know precisely
what the recipient of a message will do with it or when a particular message will
be sent. It is often unclear what counts as a successful outcome. Such ambiguities
can be resolved by discussion and reflection, but there is no guarantee that other
readers of the specification will interpret it in the same way.

When it comes to syntax, we have the opposite problem: too much detail.
The fields of each message are specified down to the last bit. Contemporary
theorem-proving technology is not up to the job of reasoning about real-world
cryptographic algorithms. For an abstract understanding of protocol correctness,
it does not matter whether hashing is done using MD4 or SHA-1; we merely
expect hashing to be collision-free and non-invertible. Similarly, the RFC will
name specific cryptographic algorithms, when for abstract purposes it only matters that encryption guarantees confidentiality and (perhaps) integrity. We have

to assume perfect encryption, even though this may hide some protocol flaws. Having abstracted away the particular algorithms, we can also simplify those parts of a protocol concerned with choosing the algorithm, though we need to ensure that such pragmatic fields are received intact.

We make the further assumption that there is no type confusion. For instance, if two certificates have the same form except that one has a key where another has a nonce, then they can never coincide in our model. This aspect agrees with the real world, since typically the two certificates differ in other details, such as the length of the key/nonce field. However, for each protocol that we model, we have to check that the certificate formats indeed satisfy this assumption. Since data sent in clear can never give security guarantees, type confusion is relevant only for integrity-protected data.

As usual in protocol verification, we assume a worst-case environment. An active attacker controls the network and also possesses a long-term key and other credentials. We can model weaker assumptions, such as a passive eavesdropper, if the protocol is intended to work in that type of environment.

4   On Modelling with Inconsistencies

The second step in the formalization process involves a deeper understanding of the specifications and, possibly, a further simplification of the protocol to obtain a manageable analysis. We eliminate protocol steps or messages that are not relevant to a particular claim. For instance, recall that we assume that no message can be decrypted without the key. Then, if the specification says that the only purpose of a nonce in a message is to avoid a dictionary based attack and that it will not be checked by the recipient then we can dispense with this nonce. So the obvious way to analyze of SET is as follows:

– eliminate all optional parts (which should always give a SET compliant protocol)
– eliminate all parts which are introduced because of non-perfect cryptography (which are inessential for the formal analysis)

As one would expect, it is difficult to understand the specification of a complex protocol such as SET. Moreover, the SET designers also made clear that "if a discrepancy is found between the Formal Protocol Definition and the other books, the Formal Protocol Definition should be followed."

We found that this does *not* work. The first major problem is that the Formal Specification [13] is not sufficient to clarify key issues: it does not specify what agents has to do with messages (do they have to check nonces?) or how certificates are handled. One must look elsewhere, such as in the Programmer's Guide [12] or in the Business Description [11].

Unfortunately, this is not a safe procedure. The Business description [11], and in particular its figures, are most misleading. For instance, the description of the Payment Authorization phase suggests that each merchant will receive the primary account number of the customer, whereas this is not the case. So we were forced to use the Programmer's Guide [12] as the ultimate reference.

The second, more serious, problem is that many "options" are not really optional. So one cannot omit the options and obtain a working protocol. For example, the specification of the Card-holder registration phase specifies that if the software of the card-holder can use symmetric encryption then it should encrypt a certain message using a symmetric key and send the key in another message. The field where the key is stored is tagged as optional. Even though everything seems to imply that it can be left out, it cannot be. Elsewhere it is said that if the key field is missing then the Certification Authority reports an error. To solve the inconsistency the only way is to fall back on the Programmer Guide [12] where, however, things are only informally explained.

Another example is the optional use of certificates. For instance, the card-holder registration phase is structured in such a way that it can be interrupted and resumed much later. (We do not know whether this is intended.) Thus, the Certification Authority always sends the certificates (or better its thumb-prints) for the signing keys. The rationale that we figured out is that the CA may want to offer the card-holder the possibility of always getting the most recent key there is. However, certificates for encryption are always optional and sometimes even missing. Yet, the card-holder can receive a message encrypted with a public key for which he may never have seen a certificate if we leave options out.

Other inconsistencies can be found in the use of nonces, which are sometimes sent, sometimes are optional and, worse still, even when they are sent they may not be checked in subsequent messages (so one may wonder what they are for).

These inconsistencies could be solved easily if there were a precise specification of what each step of the protocol should accomplish. Unfortunately, there is no equivalent of the specifications as set forth by Abadi and Needham [1], Gollman [7] and Lowe [9] for authentication protocols.

The broad goals are clear: at the end of the Card-holder registration phase, the Card-holder C should have registered his public key his chosen Certification Authority. They are also spelled out in the Business Description [11, p. 4]. However, many questions remain unanswered:

1. How many keys can a card-holder register with a certification authority?
2. Can two different users register the same key with the same certification authority?
3. Should confidentiality of primary account numbers be protected?
4. Can be the registration phase be interrupted and resumed at any later stage?
5. Should each message be linked to a previous message to identify the protocol run?

Even such reasonably high level goals are not specified in the Protocol Description and, as we have already noticed, the Business Description can be misleading.

For instance, we would expect that Question 2 deserves a straightforward answer: No. Yet in the Business Description [11, pp. 25, 44] and in the Programmer's Guide [12, pp. 146-161], no such requirement is mentioned. So, it seems that SET lets two users have the same private key.

Question 3 is more intriguing. It is explained at great length in the Programmer's Guide description of the Card-holder Registration phase that the card-holder account will not be visible in the certificate. So, when modelling the protocol, this seems a crucial requirement. However, when looking at the Business description of another protocol step, when the Payment Gateway transmits the card-holder data to the Merchant for the payment authorization, the information about the Card-holder are transmitted in clear. In this case, we have decided to be on the safe side and stick to the Programmer's guide.

We can only prove properties of a protocol after we have arrived at a formal model of it. As we have indicated, we had only general indications from the SET book, so we had to rely on common sense.

5   The Isabelle Formalization

Notwithstanding the obstacles mentioned above, we have formally specified the SET Cardholder Registration phase (SET-CR in the sequel) using the inductive method [17,18]. Compared with other protocols that have been analyzed formally, SET has some unusual features. These include (1) several certification authorities may participate in the protocol and (2) the cardholders are entitled to issue and submit their own keys for certification. The inductive method may be easily extended to account for these features.

The datatype for agents must allow for a single root certification authority and an unbounded number of certification authorities

```
datatype agent = RCA | CA nat | Friend nat | Spy
```

which requires minor updates to a few of the existing lemmas.

The protocols analyzed so far by practically any formal method [9,10,14,17,18], [21,22] presuppose that every agent possesses long-term key. By contrast, SET-CR aims at establishing such association for card-holders. Some certification authority creates the association at the end of the protocol by means of a certificate. Therefore, we only define a pair of signature keys (one public, one private) for the root certification authority; each certification authority has two pairs, for signature and encryption. For the sake of convenience, we refer to these as *crucial keys*.

Existing models of key-distribution protocols issue session keys that are fresh. Our SET-CR model does not require freshness of the key pairs that a card-holder wants certified. He can submit any pairs that differ from the crucial keys, perhaps to different authorities in separate protocol runs.

6   Conclusions

The official descriptions of SET [11,12,13] describe the composition of messages in minute detail, while failing to provide a satisfactory semantics for those messages. A formal specification by the inductive method does provide an operational semantics for the protocol and identifies several ambiguities in the documentation.

Our work has focussed on the cardholder registration phase. We have unveiled some potentially dangerous omissions. Different agents may collude and register the same key with different authorities. The protocol will not prevent them from obtaining the requested certifications. We have not yet investigated the consequences of this scenario.

Our future work will cover the remaining phases of the protocol. Having formalized the specification, the greatest task is behind us. We expect to be able to derive further properties of SET with an acceptable amount of effort.

References

1. M. Abadi and R. M. Needham. Prudent engineering practice for cryptographic protocols. *IEEE Transactions on Software Engineering*, 22(1):6–15, January 1996.
2. G. Bella and L. C. Paulson. Kerberos version IV: Inductive analysis of the secrecy goals. In *Proceedings of the 5th European Symposium on Research in Computer Security*, volume 1485 of Lecture Notes in Computer Science, pages 361–375. Springer-Verlag, 1998.
3. D. Bolignano. An approach to the formal verification of cryptographic protocols. In *Proceedings of the 3th ACM Conference on Communications and Computer Security* (CCS-96), pages 106–118, 1996.
4. S. Brackin. Automatic formal analyses of two large commercial protocols. In *Proceedings of the DIMACS Workshop on Design and Formal Verification of Security Protocols*, page 14pp, September 1997.
5. S. Brackin. Automatically detecting authentication limitations in commercial security protocols. In *Proceedings of the 22nd National Conference on Information Systems Security*, page 18pp, October 1999.
6. M. Burrows, M. Abadi, and R. Needham. A logic for authentication. *ACM Transactions on Computer Systems*, 8(1):18–36, 1990.
7. D. Gollmann. What do we mean by entity authentication? In *Proceedings of the 15th IEEE Symposium on Security and Privacy*, pages 46–54. IEEE Computer Society Press, 1996.
8. R. Kailar. Reasoning about accountability in protocols for electronic commerce. In *Proceedings of the 14th IEEE Symposium on Security and Privacy*, pages 236–250. IEEE Computer Society Press, 1995.
9. G. Lowe. A hierarchy of authentication specifications. In *Proceedings of the 11th IEEE Computer Security Foundations Workshop*, pages 31–43. IEEE Computer Society Press, 1997.
10. G. Lowe. Casper: A compiler for the analysis of security protocols. *Journal of Computer Security*, 6(18-30):53–84, 1998.
11. Mastercard & VISA. *SET Secure Electronic Transaction Specification: Business Description*, May 1997. Available electronically at `http://www.setco.org/set_specifications.html`.
12. Mastercard & VISA. *SET Secure Electronic Transaction Specification: Programmer's Guide*, May 1997. Available electronically at `http://www.setco.org/set_specifications.html`.
13. Mastercard & VISA. *SET Secure Electronic Transaction Specification: Protocol Definition*, May 1997. Available electronically at `http://www.setco.org/set_specifications.html`.

14. C. A. Meadows. Formal verification of cryptographic protocols: A survey. In *Advances in Cryptology - Asiacrypt 94*, volume 917 of Lecture Notes in Computer Science, pages 133–150. Springer-Verlag, 1995.
15. R. M. Needham and M. Schroeder. Using encryption for authentication in large networks of computers. *Communications of the ACM*, 21(12):993–999, 1978.
16. D. O'Mahony, M. Peirce, and H. Tewari. *Electronic payment systems*. The Artech House computer science library. Artech House, 1997.
17. L. C. Paulson. The inductive approach to verifying cryptographic protocols. *Journal of Computer Security*, 6:85–128, 1998.
18. L. C. Paulson. Inductive analysis of the internet protocol TLS. ACM *Transactions on Information and System Security*, 2(3):332–351, 1999.
19. RSA Laboratories, RSA Security - Available electronically at `http://www.rsasecurity.com/rsalabs/pkcs`. 19: Extended-Certificate Syntax Standard, 1993.
20. RSA Laboratories, RSA Security - Available electronically at `http://www.rsasecurity.com/rsalabs/pkcs`. 20: Cryptographic Message Syntax Standard, 1993.
21. P. Syverson and C. Meadows. A formal language for cryptographic protocol requirement. *Designs, Codes and Cryptography*, 7(xxx):27–59, 1996.
22. P. F. Syverson and P. C. van Oorschot. On unifying some cryptographic protocols logics. In *Proceedings of the 13th IEEE Symposium on Security and Privacy*. IEEE Computer Society Press, 1994.

Making Sense of Specifications: The Formalization of SET (Transcript of Discussion)

Lawrence C. Paulson

University of Cambridge

How do we pay for things on the Internet? The way it is done now is using SSL. SSL is a fairly straightforward protocol, at least it's straightforward enough to have already been analysed using methods that I like, but it isn't really a satisfactory way. Now the SET protocol is a very complicated thing, its take-up has been very low at present, and it may be that it is not the protocol which will eventually solve this problem. What is certain is that some better protocol than SSL will appear. I think that ordinary customers are going to demand it, and even small vendors as well, because just sending your credit card number isn't really a very happy solution.

Now the idea of SET is that you have trusted intermediaries whose job it is to pay the vendor. You trust the intermediaries, banks or whatever, because you think that they are not going to hoover your account of all its money. They then pay the money to this strange vendor who is based in Luton; the strange vendor is not meant to get hold of your credit card number. SET is very complicated compared with SSL, which is a relatively straightforward protocol which has nine messages if I recall properly and is just *one* protocol. Whereas SET consists of five sub-protocols, each of which is quite complicated in its own right.

To give you some idea of what is involved here – you have these certification authorities which are arranged in a hierarchy which is about five levels deep. There is a "super" one at the top and then as you go down there are ones corresponding to countries and ones corresponding to banks *etc.* and eventually you get right down to the people who actually pay the vendors. Naturally you have the people with credit cards who want to buy goods and you have the merchants. You also have the payment gateways which, I believe, are the agents which actually hand out the funds while keeping the credit card numbers secret. There are five phases to this protocol, of which we have only looked at the first one: card holder registration. A quick overview of the way you use the entire protocol; first you have to register your credit card with SET and choose a private key that you are going to use. The merchant, this obscure vendor in Luton, also has to sign up with the protocol. Then you have to order your widget from the vendor and then I believe, although I don't really know how it works at this point, it is the vendor's job to go to the payment gateway to say what you have ordered and to ask for the money. If that is all right, then the final phase is for the money to be delivered.

Card holder registration is a whole sub-protocol and I have no idea what is really in there; all I can say for certain is that, even though this one is only five

B. Christianson et al. (Eds.): Security Protocols, LNCS 2133, pp. 82–86, 2001.

messages, there is a lot going on. There is a great deal of private, public and symmetric key-bashing just for what looks like a trivial task of the card holder saying "I want to use this private key for my transactions".

Here is an overview of the card holder registration. First the card holder asks to register and the certification authority agrees and gives the card holder the CA public key certificate. The card holder asks for a form to fill in with his mother's maiden name *etc.* and he chooses a random symmetric key which he sends encrypted with the public key of the CA. (Notice that this is the kind of thing that the BAN logic could not deal with because you just create a key and send it along and use it at the same time, which is not something the BAN logic was meant to deal with.) The card holder also chooses a private key, so it is the card holder's responsibility to choose his own keys and to safeguard them. I don't quite know how this would work in practice. The process would be computerised of course; the average man on the street does not know how to choose keys so it would all have to be done by the software and you would hope it would be done reliably. The CA sends back the necessary form which the card holder fills in with their home address, mother's maiden name *etc.* and the CA takes this to VISA to ascertain that the details are correct. If they are, then finally the card holder gets some kind of digital credentials which he can use to buy things. Remember that this is not all of SET, this is just card holder registration.

The people who did this had a rather daunting task. I complained yesterday about SSL being described by 150 pages of plain ASCII, well this is a lot worse. It is at least in PDF but there are 600 pages spread over three documents which do not agree with each other. There is apparently a statement in the Formal Protocol Definition saying that it is the absolute one and that the others are merely explanations, but my impression is that only the Programmer's Guide really gives you the nuts and bolts. All the documents disagree with each other and it is not a lot of fun reading 600 pages of extremely boring material. What we are really trying to do is what the protocol designers should have done in the first place, which is to give a very brief, two-page description of what the protocol is trying to accomplish. I just cannot understand why the designers are not capable of doing this. We all know that when you have English language documents, they are going to be full of vagueness and inconsistencies. Even if we do not prove a single theorem, but merely reduce the whole thing to formal specification then at least we will have something to take as a starting point for analysis. And if we get it wrong, then the programmers are going to get it wrong as well, because the documentation is full of holes and the people who are coding it in C have got an even harder job than we have. We just have to render it in logic, which is a good deal easier than coding it in C so that it will actually work with all the performance demands *etc.* So somebody has to go through the documentation and find out what it really means.

One of the more amusing statements in the documentation is "optional is not the same as not required". So you find Piero trying to minimise his work by leaving out all the optional parts of the protocol, only to discover that they are absolutely necessary in another phase. This meant that there was nothing for it but to read and digest all 600 pages and try to work out which parts were *really* optional and which weren't. Although the documentation said that some optional things were still required, it did not really give any advice as to how to determine which was which. There are a great many things which are left unclear. For example, are you allowed to have more than one private key? Can two people have the same private key – clearly they should not because that would result in their identities being merged, but there is nothing in the protocol which stops two people from registering the same key. I think that what Giampaolo did in the end was to decide that with a particular certification authority the protocol will insist that a given private key is associated with only one person, but even with that you cannot stop different people registering the same key with *different* certification authorities. It is not clear what happens then, presumably one of these people can masquerade as the other.

Now of course there is a very basic question on the credit card number confidentiality. I think that the whole point of SET was to keep card numbers confidential, but apparently a lot of the big vendors would rather like to have them, and so a loophole was put into SET which seems to say that some people are allowed to get them and other people aren't. Now this of course is not so much a design flaw, it's more a political problem that some people want to be able to grab your credit card number, but it certainly raises conflicts when you're trying to formalise SET and what its goals are. As I recall it wasn't entirely clear which people were allowed to grab these credit card numbers and which weren't but it's meant to be in the protocol itself somewhere.

Ross Anderson: What happened was that all the big players in the USA said that they were not using SET unless they got the credit card numbers because they used them to index their data bases. The banks said that the credit card holder agreements forbade them from doing that, but the big players said that they did it anyway and so they needed to be given the credit card numbers. The decision is basically up to the bank that acquires the merchant's transactions whether or not it supplies the merchant with the credit card numbers.

Reply: But it wasn't very clear in the documentation – I think the documentation actually claims that they're kept confidential, which of course is not the case. It's again for political reasons that the documents want to say certain things to some people, and other things to other people, but how you're meant to implement such a situation I do not know.

Markus Kuhn: Is the card holder notified that the merchant is going to get the credit card number?

Reply: I've got no idea, but I expect some hacker will publish them on his Web page.

Anyway, just to show you that we have been doing things on a computer, we have here a formalisation of something which we put into the design to say that a certification authority will only allow a public key to be associated with one person.

Briefly to conclude – we can say that the existing state of formal methods is sufficient to look at protocols like SET. There are as usual details that we have left out, and we've only looked at one phase of it, but nonetheless it is feasible. The main difficulty is not to do with logic at all, it's simply to do with digesting all the documentation. It really is a political problem, or a standards problem, of getting these documents written to a higher standard so that people can make sense of them. As you can see, we've only just started.

Ross Anderson: I suppose the big problem of designing SET was that you had a very large cacophony of voices making input into it, but the guy from VISA who was driving the whole process wanted to get this to a conclusion by March 1996 (I think it was). So he had to say "yes we'll do this, no we won't do that, we'll accept this but we'll cut that" and so you ended up with a very bloated protocol with a very unclear description. From the point of view of this community, the interesting question is whether by adopting some formal discipline (whether it's logic or whether it's just curly bracket notation) you can actually make a useful contribution to the process. If you insist that all protocol modifications are written out in curly brackets, or in some logical formalism, then can you prevent people hustling in inconsistencies in order to advance their own political agenda? And if you prevent these political trade-offs happening, can you actually end up with a protocol that's always as it was intended to be?

Reply: I think a strictly formal notation, completely formal, would be a mistake. If you look at how programming languages are specified, we can specify the syntax of programming languages, but for the semantics one uses a lot of English, at least in the beginning. We don't know enough about protocol semantics to impose a formalism on people at this stage, but we can still demand a lot more than we get. The key thing I think one needs is a brief listing of the protocol messages without details of the crypto algorithms, or at least without unnecessary details like bit lengths and field lengths and all that sort of thing, in which you just say abstractly what is going on. This should not merely be a pretty picture, but should be part of the official definition. Then when you say it's 128 bits and is computed using this algorithm and that algorithm, one should argue that this is actually a refinement of the original abstract specification that you gave. So the people like us who want to look at the abstract properties can read a ten page document instead of a 600 page document, and any ambiguities can be resolved by looking at the ten page document. The rest of the 600 pages is needed to tell you about how you get the exact values and the bits that are needed using particular algorithms, but the exact choice of algorithms usually isn't relevant for the properties most of us are worried about.

Audience: Should some statement of the goals be included in the definition?

Reply: Yes, you can't analyse a protocol if you don't know what it's for.

Mike Roe: I was about to add that one of the main problems that you see is that the goals are not clearly stated. There's a conflict there as to whether the protocol lets you give an identifier for the customer to the merchants, to let them link the transaction to the customer, or whether it doesn't. That's why that option about giving the credit card number is there or isn't depending on what kind of merchants they are. Some of the need is for unique identifiers that are needed for database indexing but there are other people inputting things into the specification about anonymous protocols and clearly the merchants should not be able to find this out.

Reply: Yes of course, and there is a difference between anonymity and just giving them an identifier on the one hand, and on the other choosing the particular identifier that lets you loot them of thousands of pounds.

Ross Anderson: I don't think this was a concern back in 1995/96, because at that time people had not yet really become aware of the idea that you could do mail order shopping without giving your name and address. That you could for example buy an upgraded Microsoft Word or whatever over the net giving an anonymous credit card number, and letting Microsoft merely know that someone who knows the private key corresponding to the following public key is now an authorised user of Word. That really didn't enter into the equation at that time.

Mike Roe: There is a little bit about anonymity in SET. They had a go at providing the kind of anonymity you're talking about, and I think it probably turned out that this was a mistake.

Reply: I suspect that most people actually don't want anonymity and most of your ordinary shoppers aren't bothered about anonymity. They're not buying sex toys, they're buying books and CDs.

Mike Roe: Anonymity is a very strong requirement that gets you into all kinds of problems. One thing we need to be clear about in the specification is whether it is supposed to keep the user anonymous or not because this has very, very serious consequences.

Reply: Yes, as I said I don't know that we'll ever see SET deployed, but I suspect there will be protocols that let you buy things that will be better than SSL, and they will be a lot more like SET than they'll be like SSL. I think that something that will let people buy things without giving up their credit card numbers will actually be necessary, if people are going to start buying things from as many different vendors as people would like to see out there.

Ross Anderson: But if you're going to transfer liability from the bank to the customer, then that's highly undesirable.

Reply: Well, I don't want to get into that, I think it's time for another speaker!

Lack of Explicitness Strikes Back

Giampaolo Bella

Computer Laboratory — University of Cambridge
New Museums Site, Pembroke Street
Cambridge CB2 3QG (UK)

Giampaolo.Bella@cl.cam.ac.uk

Abstract. Provable security [4] is a study of confidentiality within a complexity-theoretic framework. We argue that its findings are highly abstract. Our argument is supported by the mechanised inductive analysis of a protocol based on smart cards that was shown to enjoy provable security and then implemented. It appears that the protocol grants no reasonable guarantees of session key confidentiality to its peers in the realistic setting where an intruder can exploit other agents' cards. Indeed, the formal argument on confidentiality requires assumptions that no peer can verify in practice. We discover and prove that the lack of explicitness of two protocol messages is the sole cause of the protocol weaknesses. Our argument requires significant extensions to the Inductive Approach [9] in order to allow for smart cards.

1 Overview

Lack of explicitness is the main reason for misunderstandings. When misunderstandings occur between the agents running a security protocol, they may result in severe and unwanted tampering by an intruder. Sensed by Abadi and Needham in 1994 [1], the problem was demonstrated by Lowe in 1995 [8] on the public-key Needham-Schroeder protocol and came to public knowledge.

Meanwhile, smart card technology has become inexpensive. Despite their small dimensions, smart cards may store crucial data such as long-term cryptographic keys and offer sufficient computational power to perform cryptographic operations. Their use in security protocols aims at overcoming an intrinsic weakness of the field: agents' knowledge may become compromised to an intruder. For example, no secure protocol may prevent an agent from revealing his password either by accident or corruption. Smart cards are supposedly more reliable than agents, in the sense that it should be very difficult to discover the secrets they contain. Significant research effort is being devoted to make the cards more and more robust to external attacks (e.g. [6]).

Developed in 1996, the Shoup-Rubin protocol [10] aims at distributing session keys to a pair of peers and presupposes that every agent is endowed with a smart card. It was shown to enjoy provable security: an intruder cannot discover the session key if a PRF (pseudo-random function) generator exists. A PRF

B. Christianson et al. (Eds.): Security Protocols, LNCS 2133, pp. 87–93, 2001.

generator can be approximated by suitable hash functions that are implemented on commonly available smart cards, so the protocol was implemented in 1998 [5].

However, selling smart cards and related protocols to a careful company requires convincing answers to questions of the following sort. Are your smart cards tamper-proof? Does your protocol achieve strong goals if the smart cards it relies on are tamper-proof? Can the agents running the protocol practically take advantage of such goals? While other research addresses the first question (e.g. [6]), we show that an affirmative answer to the second question does not logically imply an affirmative answer to the third. Shoup-Rubin offers a counterexample with its confidentiality goals because it lacks crucial explicitness. We have discovered that the protocol does enforce strong session key confidentiality if the intruder is prevented from using those smart cards that belong to the key's peers. However, such guarantees of confidentiality cannot be applied by the peers, who are not able to verify their assumptions, but can be applied by their smart cards. Adding little explicitness to two of the protocol messages is sufficient to make the guarantees also useful to the peers.

The Inductive Approach [9] can support the mentioned experiments. A new free type for smart cards, card , must be introduced, while the association between agents and smart cards can be formalised by an injective function, Card . An intruder, Spy , has corrupted all cards' data buses in such a way that cards may process their inputs in a random order, process some inputs more than once, or ignore others. Therefore, an output cannot be associated to a specific input. The spy has got hold of an unspecified set of cards, stolen , which she may query conforming to their functional interface, and has cloned another set of cards, cloned , learning the long-term keys they contain. New events intuitively formalise the interaction between agents and smart cards. In particular, Inputs $A\,C\,X$ and Outputs $C\,A\,X$ may occur for an agent A, a card C, a message X. The definition of agents' knowledge based on message reception [2, §3] is adopted and extended to account for the new events. An exhaustive treatment can be found elsewhere [3].

2   Modelling Shoup-Rubin

The details of Shoup-Rubin are intricate and difficult to grasp from the designers' treatment [10], as observed by the implementors [5]. The smart cards are not pin-operated. The protocol assumes the means between agents and smart cards to be secure.

No agent knows any long-term secrets, but the cards belonging respectively to protocol initiator and responder agree on a long-term secret with the help of a trusted server using a technique due to Leighton and Micali [7]. The initial phases of the protocol are omitted from figure 1 because they do not influence the confidentiality goals directly. The initiator A obtains some credentials from the trusted server, along with a nonce Na and its certificate from her smart card.

$$\text{IV}: \quad 6. \quad B \quad \rightarrow C_b : A, Na$$
$$7. \quad Cb \rightarrow B \ : Nb, Kab, Cert(Na, Nb), Cert(Nb)$$

$$\text{V}: \quad 8. \quad B \ \rightarrow A \ : Nb, Cert(Na, Nb)$$

$$\text{VI}: \quad 9. \quad A \ \rightarrow Ca : B, Na, Nb, Cert(Na, Nb), Cert(Na)$$
$$10. \ Ca \rightarrow A \ : Kab, Cert(Nb)$$

Fig. 1. Three phases of the Shoup-Rubin protocol.

Phase IV sees the responder B forward A's identity and nonce (received from the network) to his card. The card issues a new nonce Nb for B and uses it to compute the new session key for A and B. These components are output along with two certificates, one associating the two nonces together, the other verifying Nb.[1] The certificates are encrypted with long-term keys, so they are not intelligible to agents. Conversely, the cards may inspect them and verify their contents.

In phase V, B forwards his nonce and one of the certificates to A. In phase VI, A uses these components along with her own nonce, its certificate and B's identity to query her card. The card computes the copy of the session key for A and outputs it along with the certificate for Nb. Note that this session key is not new because it was previously output by B's card.

All phases of the protocol can be modelled inductively, yielding a protocol model that is a set of traces (i.e. lists of events) [3]. Each trace records a specific network history that is admissible by the protocol. Investigating the confidentiality goals from the viewpoint of agents does not require a formal specification of the structure of the certificates, though this becomes necessary when reasoning from the viewpoint of smart cards, which can decrypt the certificates and inspect their structure.

3   Detecting the Lack of Explicitness

Session key confidentiality is one of the primary goals of key-distribution protocols. Paulson's strategy for proving the corresponding guarantees on traditional protocols [9, §4.6] scales up to protocols that are based on smart cards. The strategy aims at deriving that the session key remains unavailable to the spy on any trace on which it is issued. While investigating the goal on Shoup-Rubin from B's viewpoint, the relevant event is the one formalising message 7 of the protocol, where B's card issues the session key

$$\textsf{Outputs} \, (\textsf{Card} \, B) \, B \, \{\!| \textsf{Nonce} \, Nb, \textsf{Key} \, Kab, \, \textit{Cert1}, \, \textit{Cert2} \,|\!\}$$

---

[1] Both the recipient of such verification and how the verification is performed are strictly related to the key used to encrypt the certificate. The matter is irrelevant to the purposes of this paper.

We stress that both *Cert1* and *Cert2* are free variables because agent B cannot verify that they yield the expected certificate.

We must also assume all conditions aimed at preventing the spy from learning the session key. Obviously, B must not be the spy. Since the protocol model allows accidental session key leaks, it must be assumed that no leaks have occurred to Kab. Besides, both peers' cards output the key, so the spy must not be able to use them. However, no assumption is in fact required on B's card because it always issues new session keys, so Kab is not at risk even if that card could be exploited by the spy.[2]

We realise that no assumptions can be stated on B's peer's card because that agent does not appear in the statement of the theorem being designed. Attempting to prove that Kab is confidential on the current assumptions leaves two subgoals unsolved, both arising from the formalisation of message 10 of the protocol. One highlights that B's peer might be the spy. The other shows that B's peer's card could be stolen or cloned, so the spy could use it to compute Kab. To do this, she only needs to forge a suitable instance of message 9: Nb and the certificate for Na and Nb can be intercepted from the network; Na and its certificate can be obtained by illegally using the card to run the initial phases of the protocol.

Specifying the structure of the certificates formally makes B's peer explicit. We have tested that the theorem can be proved in this model under the assumption that the spy cannot exploit B's peer's card. However, this guarantee is only applicable by B's card.

Verifying the same goal from A's viewpoint must be done on the event that formalises message 10 of the protocol

$$\text{Outputs}\,(\text{Card}\,A)\;A\;\{\!|\text{Key}\,Kab,\,Cert|\!\}$$

Obviously, A must not be the spy. Since A's card computes Kab (rather than issuing a new one as B's did), it must be neither stolen nor cloned so that the spy cannot exploit it to obtain the key Kab. However, A's peer previously issued that key, so the current assumptions do not suffice to enforce confidentiality. As a matter of fact, two subgoals, arising from the formalisation of message 7 of the protocol, remain unsolved from the proof attempt. They highlight that A's peer could be the spy and that A's peer's card could be stolen or cloned.

As with the preceding theorem, specifying the certificates clarifies the identity of A's peer. Assuming A's peer's card not to be usable by the spy lets us terminate the proof, though the resulting guarantee is only applicable by A's card.

4 Fixing the Lack of Explicitness

The failed proof attempts emphasise that, upon reception of an instance of message 7, B does not know who the session key is meant to be used with. Neither does A know this information upon reception of message 10.

---

[2] The model cards always issue new session keys when replying to a query of the form of the sixth message. Even if the spy tampers with the cards' internal algorithms, the probability of generating a specific, old key is negligible.

Even if B recalls the sessions he is participating in, he has no criteria with which to choose the session for which the key just obtained is meant. Message 7 clearly lacks explicitness, thus violating a well-known principle [1, Principle 3] that insists on quoting agent names if they are essential to the meaning of a message. In this case, if the key contained in message 7 is meant to be used with A, then the message should say so. Similarly, message 10 should be explicit about the peer of the session key it contains. We suggest to upgrade the protocol according to these considerations, as underlined in figure 2.

$$7. \quad C_b \rightarrow B : Nb, \underline{A}, Kab, Cert(Na, Nb), Cert(Nb)$$

$$10. \ C_a \rightarrow A : \underline{Nb, B}, Kab, Cert(Nb)$$

Fig. 2. Fixing the lack of explicitness in the Shoup-Rubin protocol.

Adding the nonce Nb to message 10 may appeal to some sort of aesthetic symmetry but, in fact, has deeper importance. Since our model allows the leak of a session key along with the nonce used to create it, such extra explicitness becomes useful to weaken the assumptions of the confidentiality guarantee for A (see below).

A significant guarantee can be proved on the upgraded protocol model. Theorem 1 expresses session key confidentiality on assumptions that B can verify in practice. However, following the considerations of the previous section, it is necessary to assume that the card belonging to A (B's peer) is neither stolen nor cloned, and that no oops event occurs on the session key. Hence, they constitute the *minimal level of trust* within which B has to interpret the theorem.

Theorem 1. *If neither A nor B is the spy, A's card is neither stolen nor cloned, and evs contains*

Outputs (Card B) B {|Nonce Nb, Agent A, Key Sk, Cert1, Cert2|}

but does not contain the oops event

Notes Spy {|Key Sk, Nonce Nb, Agent A, Agent B|}

then

Key $Sk \notin$ analz (knows Spy evs)

Assuming that neither A nor B is the spy, and that neither of their smart cards is stolen or cloned allows us to obtain the same conclusion as that of the preceding theorem, provided that evs contains

Outputs (Card A) A {|Nonce Nb, Agent B, Key Sk, Cert|}

but does not contain the oops event. If message 10 quoted no nonce, then the nonce of the oops event would not be bound. A stronger assumption would be necessary, requiring that no oops event occurred for any nonce. The theorem expresses a guarantee of confidentiality from A's viewpoint because A can check its assumptions within the minimal level of trust on B and his card, and on the oops event.

5   Conclusion

Provable security [4] is a fascinating field of research. The security of a protocol is reduced to the existence of PRF generators, which appears to be the very limitation of modern security. However, subtle but crucial features of the protocols may be missed.

When an agent running the Shoup-Rubin protocol [10] receives a session key, he gets no information on the identity of the peer with whom the key is shared. The session keys are computed by the smart cards, and the spy is granted the ability to exploit certain cards. In this setting, the agent cannot derive the confidentiality of the key because the card belonging to his peer, who is unknown, should be assumed to be safe from the spy. This is a minimal assumption. Adding little explicitness to two messages pinpoints the peers of the session key and makes it possible to terminate the confidentiality argument from the viewpoint of both peers within a minimal level of trust.

The Inductive Approach [9] tailored to the analysis of protocols based on smart cards [3] confirms to offer valuable insights into protocols even when other protocol guarantees are available.

Acknowledgement

David Richerby and David von Oheimb made several comments on this paper.

References

1. M. Abadi and R. M. Needham. Prudent engineering practice for cryptographic protocols. Research Report 67, Digital - Systems Research Center, 1990.
2. G. Bella. Modelling agents' knowledge inductively. In *International Workshop on Security Protocols*, volume 1796 of *Lecture Notes in Computer Science*. Springer-Verlag, 1999. In press.
3. G. Bella. Inductive verification of smart card protocols. Submitted to *Journal of Computer Security*, 2000.
4. M. Bellare and P. Rogaway. Provably secure session key distribution — the three party case. In *Proceedings of the 27th ACM SIGACT Symposium on Theory of Computing (STOC'95)*, pages 57–66. ACM Press, 1995.
5. R. Jerdonek, P. Honeyman, K. Coffman, J. Rees, and K. Wheeler. Implementation of a provably secure, smartcard-based key distribution protocol. In J.-J. Quisquater and B. Schneier, editors, *Smart Card Research and Advanced Application Conference (CARDIS'98)*, 1998.
6. O. Kömmerling and M. G. Kuhn. Design principles for tamper-resistant smartcard processors. In *Proceedings of USENIX Workshop on Smartcard Technology*, 1999.
7. T. Leighton and S. Micali. Secret-key agreement without public-key cryptogrphy. In D. R. Stinson, editor, *Proceedings of Advances in Cryptography — CRYPTO'93*, volume 773 of *Lecture Notes in Computer Science*, pages 456–479. Springer-Verlag, 1993.
8. G. Lowe. An attack on the Needham-Schroeder public-key authentication protocol. *Information Processing Letters*, 56(3):131–133, 1995.

9. L. C. Paulson. The inductive approach to verifying cryptographic protocols. *Journal of Computer Security*, 6:85–128, 1998.
10. V. Shoup and A. Rubin. Session key distribution using smart cards. In U. Maurer, editor, *Advances in Cryptology — Eurocrypt'96*, volume 1070 of *Lecture Notes in Computer Science*, pages 321–331. Springer-Verlag, 1996.

Lack of Explicitness Strikes Back
(Transcript of Discussion)

Giampaolo Bella

University of Cambridge

I guess we are all familiar with the principle of explicitness in the context of security protocols and know what the disastrous consequences could be when explicitness is lacked. But I'm going to show you another example of a protocol that actually does lack explicitness despite the fact that it's been analysed formally by some kind of approach.

Before I show you the protocol, I'll go through the main steps of its history. In 1996 the protocol was defined by Shoup-Rubin, it was presented at Eurocrypt 96 and it was analysed by using the provable security approach developed by Bellare and Rogaway. Shoup-Rubin just updated the formal approach to deal with smartcards, and developed this protocol that actually makes use of smartcards.

They proved two properties. One is key distribution, one is confidentiality. Actually there's no formal account for the proof of key distribution, they just say it's pretty obvious looking at the protocol, that the session keys are distributed correctly. But there is a proof of confidentiality developed by pen and paper; it is a complexity theoretic proof. They show that an intruder has a limited advantage on discovery of the session key, and that's their idea of confidentiality. Then three years later the protocol is implemented at the Centre for Information Technology Integration of the University of Michigan, and the implementers are actually pretty happy with it. They say – we have some kind of formal statement about the protocol, we have this implementation that works perfectly on commonly available smartcards, inexpensive cards, so we are pretty happy with it; this protocol should be secure enough.

That's interesting, but let's see if we can get a deeper insight into the protocol. Here is an abstract view of a few steps of the protocol. I should say that you don't have 600 pages explaining what this protocol is for, but when you read a paper based on provable security, there's a lot of mathematics so the gist of the protocol isn't that easy to grasp, let alone the details. So I should say it took me some time to get to this abstract view of the protocol. Clearly we would want to know where all these items come from and what they are meant to achieve. I'm not showing the exact form of these certificates, I'm not showing what they're meant to do because this is irrelevant to my discussion here, but they are there to achieve specific goals of authentication.

So, looking at the protocol, A and B are just the peers Alice and Bob, CA is the smartcard that belongs to A and CB is the smartcard that belongs to B. So in step 6 we see that B inputs A's identity in the nonce N_A received from the previous steps of the protocol to his card, and the smartcard in step 7 computes for B a fresh nonce N_B, a session key K_B that's actually computed out of the nonce N_B and two certificates. Then B forwards these components to A, and A

B. Christianson et al. (Eds.): Security Protocols, LNCS 2133, pp. 94–99, 2001.
© Springer-Verlag Berlin Heidelberg 2001

inputs her card with B's identity, her nonce N_A, the nonce just received, and two other certificates. After that the smartcard computes the session key out of the nonce N_B for A, and another certificate. The reason why I'm not showing the form of the certificate is that, from the view point of the agents, they are just un-intelligible ciphers because they are encrypted using long term keys that the agents don't know. Incidentally in this protocol no agent knows any long term keys, which should somehow increase its robustness (but that's not a formal statement). So, again, the certificates are un-intelligible, all the agents see from participating in the protocol are these components shown here – so these are just ciphers.

As I said, my idea was to try to make sense of this protocol, analysing it in inductively, and I needed some extensions. First of all I had to allow for this new object, for the smartcards, but that was pretty easy, they're just a new type in the language. Then you define some set of events that are possible, formalising the interaction between agents and cards, so you have input events for agents and the inputs to the cards and vice versa, you have output events. Then you have to allow the spy somehow to exploit certain cards if you want your analysis to be realistic. So here I have two levels of exploitation: there's a set of lost cards – lost or stolen if you want – that the spy has got hold of but she hasn't tampered with; and there's another set of cards, clone cards, that she manages to tamper with, to reverse engineer, to discover the secrets of and ultimately to build clones of. I won't be more precise about this.

The definition of agents' knowledge must be refined to account for the new events. Don't worry about the word knowledge here, it just means what the agents can handle from participating in the protocol. So agents know the messages they can send, or the messages they can receive, or those that they input to the cards or those that they receive from the cards. Then we have to account for the assumption of what secure means, so in this protocol the session keys are actually sent in clear from the smartcard to the agents using step 7 and 10. In fact the protocol assumes that the spy cannot listen in between me and my smartcard but, as Marcus pointed out once, it's just this protocol that makes this assumption. So if you want a general approach you should somehow allow, in certain circumstances, with certain protocols, for the spy to sneak in.

So I guess I've reached some kind of general approach for the analysis of protocols based on smartcards, and at this stage I could formalise the entire protocol, all its eleven steps. The obvious goal to try to prove was confidentiality. So obviously Shoup-Rubin is still a session key distribution protocol, all it is trying to do is distribute the key K to both A and B.

So my first attempt was trying to prove that the session key K is confidential on the basis of this assumption here, which formalises the seventh step of the protocol where the card belonging to B outputs the session key and the nonce and the certificate to its owner B. The interesting thing at this point was that you do the proof, you apply the usual kind of strategy (you have to account for this new event, but that's fairly reasonable), but at some point you realise that the proof doesn't terminate; you're left with two sub-goals that can be falsified because they either depict a realistic situation in which B is actually talking to the spy, or a situation in which the card that belongs to B's peer is cloned, and is somehow available to the spy.

Now this is fairly obvious. Clearly if I'm talking to the spy my session key won't be confidential in the sense that it will be known to the spy if the protocol distributes it correctly. But the second scenario is more interesting, it's something that I didn't realise before I actually got to that stage of the proof. What happens if I'm talking to Larry and he's not the spy but his card is actually cloned, it's compromised to the spy. What happens is that the spy could intercept the entire communication between me and Larry and exploit Larry's card of which she has a clone, and basically impersonate Larry with me. So he wouldn't realise anything of the protocol and I would have the feeling of talking to Larry when in fact I'm talking to the spy. Again in this case, this would clearly be a failure of authentication, but here we're just talking about confidentiality, certainly I wouldn't manage to prove that the session key isn't known to the spy.

The same problem arises when the session key K is delivered to the smartcard that belongs to A, the initiator of the protocol. I have again the same problem. What if A's peer is in fact the spy, what if the card that belongs to A's peer is cloned – the session key would not be confidential. Then, OK, when you realise that the proof doesn't terminate you try to add assumptions, you try to refine it somehow. So I said I'd like to assume that everything is OK with B's peer here, so that he's not the spy probably and that his card is OK and is safe from the spy. But when I try to add this assumption I realise that here basically A's peer is not visible at all.

So at this stage it looks pretty straightforward; clearly B receives the session key K, but the message fails to state the peer with whom session key is meant to be shared. At this stage we all know about explicitness. So when you think that the protocol was designed after explicitness was widely known, and then the protocol was analysed for provable security, I found it quite surprising that this point had not been noticed. And the same problem here, A receives the session key K but still A's peer identity, say B, is not mentioned.

What happens in fact is that these certificates *do* contain the identities I'm talking about, but because they are unintelligible to the peers, the peers will never realise it. So my idea was that at some stage here these messages should mention explicitly the identity of the intended peers. So by doing this, we have a fairly straightforward upgrade to the protocol, I'm just mentioning A's identity here and B's identity here. I'm also adding the nonce N_B out of which the session key is created, but in fact this is not strictly necessary, it's just a matter of completeness.

Also you should note that if you look at the entire protocol, there's no message at all stating explicitly this association between a session key and both its peers, there's no message that says that. So these upgrades are actually relevant.

On this protocol, upon refining the previous proof, indeed it was possible to prove, out of this assumption here, that the session key is confidential, provided merely that A is not the spy and that A's card is not cloned, it's safe from the spy. And note that these assumptions here are minimal in the sense that looking at the previous proofs we realise that if we don't use them, then we are going to have scenarios in which the spy can actually violate the goal that we're talking about – in this case confidentiality. So in this sense they are minimal, and I can still prove the session key K's confidentiality, reasoning from the viewpoint of A. So out of the events that A sees from participating in the protocol, the session key K is confidential.

Using a similar strategy and similar assumptions, I can also prove the goal of key distribution in a strong form. Basically if I run the protocol with Larry, I would have evidence at some point that Larry indeed knows the key, and similarly he would have evidence that I know the key.

To conclude, I think that Shoup-Rubin lacks explicitness, despite the fact that we had formal guarantees available about it. I think that the proof of security is a highly abstract property, although I still consider that it is a wonderful piece of complexity theoretic research. It seems that the inductive approach based on theorem proving does scale up to the analysis of these complex protocols. Shoup-Rubin is 11 messages long, I think it's probably the longest that's been analysed so far. An interesting thing, I believe, is that even if I didn't know anything about principles of prudent protocol design, at some stage the proof would have shown me that there was something wrong; the proof would have depicted some situation that indeed violated my goal. So this is how we learn from theorem proving, the theorem proving gives reasons why things work or why things don't work. So I could have reinvented the principle of lack of explicitness, of explicitness in general.

Geraint Price: You say that the proof of security is a highly abstract property – what exactly do you mean?

Reply: I mean that it can't cope with these details that I mentioned. Basically you can prove confidentiality from the viewpoint of the server that distributes the keys, but if you were running the protocol you would have no evidence – you wouldn't see any events, any messages, any items – from which you could infer that the session key is confidential, or from which you could infer that the goal of key distribution is indeed met. So, abstract in the sense that it can't reason from the viewpoint of the peers participating in the protocol.

Larry Paulson: One of your points that I would like to discuss is the guarantees that you put there because the name of B isn't mentioned, so A doesn't know what assumptions it has to make. The cards know what the assumptions are, but obviously cards don't think. In this case it's pretty obvious what certain of your assumptions should be, so I just wondered whether in a more complex protocol, there might be other assumptions that were less obvious.

Reply: Yes I see your point, but the claim here is more basic. I'm saying that there's no message of the protocol that says who the person I'm talking to is, in the sense that I don't know which agent this key I see is associated with. Clearly even if the cards do know this, there's no message of the protocol where the cards actually tell me, so if I am the process that's going to run the communication, I don't have this sensitive information, and so I run the risk of talking to the spy.

Virgil Gligor: I read the paper, of about 1994, about entity authentication written by Bellare and Rogaway in which they claimed that most of the logic-based analysis methods were at that stage insufficient to analyse the authentication protocol. They claimed that in fact the only thing that you can do is to find errors but not demonstrate correctness. I'm not sure how that matter was resolved.

Reply: Yes, I agree with you that the property isn't well defined. I'm actually discussing this with the implementers of the protocol, because I suspect that the explicitness I'm talking about is crucial and that they had to have it. But it's not stated either in the designers' paper or in the implementers' paper.

Virgil Gligor: The other question which I wanted to pick up on is – in what sense are they talking about provable security in peers? In their follow-on work there is a technically strange notion of what provable security meant.

Reply: Yes, it means that an adversary cannot discover this key bit with probability more than a half or something like that.

Virgil Gligor: That means that the adversary's advantage is negligible.

Reply: Yes. So encryption is a pseudo-random function generator. It's an entirely complexity theoretic approach and is a wonderful piece of research, but it fails to deal with detailed features like what components you have in the messages and what you actually can infer from them.

Virgil Gligor: One of the things that I discussed last year was about their provable security approach. They proved the security of counter-based encryption, and it turns out that while they could carry out this proof, you can produce a protocol which is utterly insecure under such an assumption. For example, if a counter for the encryption is not initialised with a random value, you can break the security of the key. What I found out later is that people now understand that some of that provable security approach refers to only certain kinds of attack, but not to security in general. So this is why it makes sense to be very explicit about what provable security means and also for what property you have provable security – you may produce an encryption scheme which is really secure, subject to all sorts of attacks, but it is provable security only in a particular sense.

Larry Paulson: This is inherent in any use of use of logic or mathematics. No-one claims they have a monopoly on how to prove something correct, because one always makes an abstract model that looks at some things and ignores other things. Its the things that one's ignoring that lay one open to attack.

Ross Anderson: You need different people, using different methods.

Virgil Gligor: Or they should admit what the limits of the particular assumptions are.

Reply: Yes, I think that one limit is reasoning from the viewpoint of the single peer running the protocol.

Larry Paulson: The problem with their approach is that so few people can understand what they're doing, that it's difficult for people to take a critical view of it.

Reply: I don't think it's so straightforward to get the details of what the protocol actually achieves out of their notation. But I understand that this view could be entirely subjective.

Review and Revocation of Access Privileges Distributed with PKI Certificates

Himanshu Khurana and Virgil D. Gligor

Electrical and Computer Engineering Department, University of Maryland,
College Park, Maryland 20742
{hkhurana, gligor}@eng.umd.edu

Abstract. Public-key infrastructures (PKIs) that support both identity certificates and access control (e.g., attribute, delegation) certificates are increasingly common. We argue that these PKIs must a lso support revocation and review policies that are typical of more traditional access control systems; e.g., selective and transitive certificate revocation, and per-object access review. Further, we show that PKIs that eliminate identity certificates, such as the SPKI, resolve only selective revo cation problems and, at the same time, make access review more complex.

1 Introduction

The distribution and revocation of identity certificates in Public Key Infrastructures (PKIs) have been extensively addressed in the literature [7, 8, 12]. Various PKIs, such as X.509 [6, 10], SPKI [2], SDSI [11], and PKI applications [1,8], also include access control (i.e., attribute, delegation) certificates, which are commonly used for the distribution and revocation of access privileges. These certificates incorporate group membership or access privileges that are distributed selectively and, sometimes transitively, to principals.

Certificate revocation policies are supported by the certificate authorities that issue the certificates, and are typically implemented by mechanisms based on off-line Certificate Revocation Lists (CRLs), on-line revocation authorities, or a combination of both. However, these policies are somewhat limited in scope; e.g., they primarily address the notions of frequency and timeliness of CRL updates [9], frequency of on-line certificate validation.

In this paper, we argue that the benefits of using of both identity and access control certificates in PKIs have an unanticipated consequence in practice, namely, that of having to support selective and transitive certificate-revocation and access review. These policies are common in access control systems, such as capability-based systems [3]. The requirement for such policy support is the result of having to enforce typical dependencies that appear between access control and authentication properties, and among access control properties themselves [4, 5], in much the same way they are enforced in traditional access control policies. An additional consequence of introducing attribute (i.e., group membership) certificates in PKIs is that caching such certificates makes it difficult to provide guarantees for revocation immediacy.

B. Christianson et al. (Eds.): Security Protocols, LNCS 2133, pp. 100–112, 2001.

The rest of this paper is organized as follows. In section 2, we review a typical access authorization and a privilege distribution method based on PKI. In section 3, we provide examples of typical dependencies between access control and identity certificates, and explain the need for selective and transitive revocation in PKIs. In section 4, we show that one of the best-known PKIs, namely SPKI [2], eliminates the need for selective revocation, but offers no support for transitive certificate revocation despite allowing transitive certificate delegation. We also point out that SPKI introduces substantial difficulty for access review. Section 5 concludes this paper.

2   Access Authorization and Privilege Distribution with PKI Certificates

In Figure 1, we illustrate an access request whose authorization uses PKI certificates. Access authorization requires client *Bob* to present a *Request* signed with *Bob*'s private key $K_{Bob}{}^{-1}$ to server P for access to object O owned by the server P. Furthermore, client *Bob* must present (or specify where server P can find) a signed *Identity Certificate* and a signed *Attribute Certificate*. Access to object O is controlled by an Access Control List (ACL) maintained by server P. As usual, the identity certificate associates the client's name (*Bob*) with a public key K_{Bob} that matches th e private key that signed the request. The attribute certificate defines the group membership for the client and associates the client's name with a group ($G1$), which, in this figure, can be found of the server's access control list (ACL). The identity certificate is issued by a certificate authority $CA1$ and the attribute certificate by authority $CA1'$.

Figure 2 shows that client *Bob* obtains the necessary certificates for accessing object O of server P from $CA1$ and $CA1'$. It is assumed that server P trusts certificate authority $CA1$ for issuing an Identity Certificate for client *Bob*, and $CA1'$ for administrating group definitions and issuing attribute certificates for groups found on the server's ACL for object O. Since an attribute certificate associates a client's identity with a group, certificate authority $CA1'$ verifies the validity of client *Bob*'s registrat ion and identity by checking *Bob*'s identity certificate before issuing the attribute (i.e., group membership) certificate. The only valid proof of identity available for the d ynamic addition of a user to a group is the identity certificate issued by $CA1$. Hence, there is a d ependency between the attribute certificate issued to *Bob* by $CA1'$ and the identity certificate issued to him by $CA1$. (In section 3, we argue that this dependency must be enforced whenever client *Bob*'s identity certificate is revoked.)

Upon receiving the access request, server P authorizes it as follows. First, P verifies the validity of the identity certificate using public key K_{CA1}; i.e., it checks the issuing certification authority's ($CA1$) signature on the identity certificate ($CA1$ is trusted by server P to issue identity certificates.) Second, P checks the authenticity of the *Request* by verifying the request signature against the client's public key, K_{Bob}, obtained from the identity certificate. Third, P verifies the validity of the attribute (group membership) certificate using public key

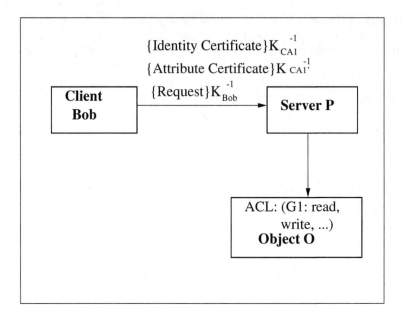

Fig. 1. Access Request with PKI (X.509 v.3) Certificates

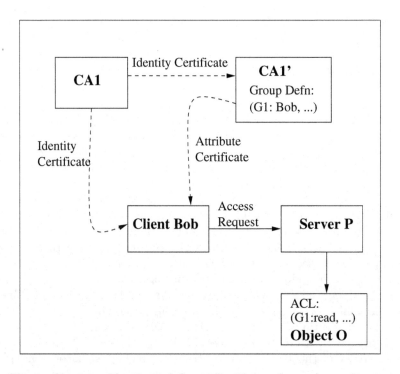

Fig. 2. Obtaining Identity and Group Certificates for an Access Request

K_{CA1}; i.e., it checks the issuing certification authority's $(CA1')$ signature on the attribute certificate ($CA1'$ is trusted by server P to maintain group membership and issue attribute certificates.). Fourth, P retrieves the group identifier ($G1$) from the attribute certificate and verifies that the ACL of object O identified by the client's *Request* associates that group ($G1$) with the access privilege(s) requested by the client. If all verifications pass, server P performs client *Bob*'s request to object O. Otherwise, P denies the request.

If access privileges are distributed (possibly transitively) via delegation certificates, then these certificates must be provided by the client and verified by the server to ensure that the client's name can be securely associated with a group name that may be found on the server's ACL.

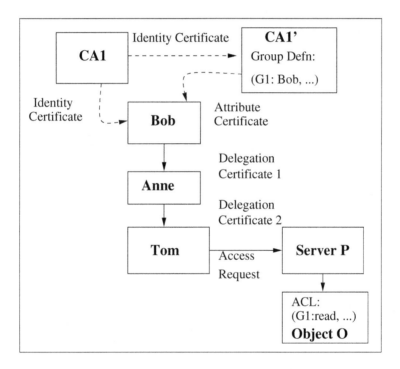

Fig. 3. Obtaining Delegation Certificates for an Access Reques

In Figure 3 above, we illustrate access authorization with delegation certificates. In this e xample, we allow transitive delegation of attribute (group membership) certificates by *principals* (clients/servers registered with $CA1'$) and such delegations can form delegation chains (i.e., transitive distribution of group membership privileges). Only a principal that has an attribute certificate can issue the first delegation certificate in such a chain. The delegation certificate defines transitive access to a group member's access permissions via a mapping of the subject's name to the issuing principal's name. Since a delegation chain originates at an attribute certificate, all principals in the chain obtain transitive access to the group's access permissions defined by the attribute certificate. Specifically, in Figure 3, *Bob* issues *Anne* a delegation certificates based upon the identity certificate obtained from $CA1$ and the attribute certificate obtained from $CA1'$. *Anne* further issues a delegation certificate to *Tom*, who can obtain access to object O by sending an access request. The access request must, however, include the entire delegation chain such that the verifying principal can associate the requesting principal's name with the name present on the accompanying attribute certificate. Since delegation certificate(s) are issued upon verification of the attribute certificate, there is a dependency among these access control certificates. (In section 3, we also argue that this dependency must be enforced in certificate revocation.)

3   Certificate Revocation Policies

The use of multiple types of certificates in a PKI, namely, identity, attribute, and delegation certificates makes it necessary to analyze potential dependencies between different uses of such certificates. These dependencies are intrinsic to access control and authentication policies of any system, and cannot be attributed to implementation detail. In this section, we consider two types of dependencies and illustrate how their enforcement leads to selective and transitive certificate-revocation policies. We also show that certificate caching - a mechanism used to bypass the expensive certificate validation mechanism - makes revocation immediacy difficult to obtain in practice.

The first dependency considered is that of authorization and management of user accesses upon user registration, unique identification, and authentication. In PKIs the issuance of a signed group-membership certificate to user, which is needed in access authorization, requires that the user be registered and identified, as evidenced by a signed certificate bearing the identity of the user.

The second dependency is that among access management properties. For example, (1) privilege revocation depends on privilege distribution, since transitive (e.g., delegated) distribution requires transitive revocation of privileges; and (2) access review depends on distribution/revocation of privileges, since the distribution/revocation of privileges must allow per-object and per-subject review of access privileges. In PKIs, support for transitive delegation of access control certificates from one user to another also requires the transitive revocation of certificates. Furthermore, whether per-object review of privileges (i.e., obtaining the answer to the question: "who has access to object O?"), is possible depends on whether an identity-based PKI and access control (e.g., X.509 based) or a capability-like PKIs (e.g., SPKI) is used. In the former, per-object access review is possible, and indeed simple, whereas in the latter it is complex, if at all possible, in practice.

3.1   Selective Revocation

The dependency between the use of these attribute (group) certificates and the identity certificate must be enforced during certificate revocation because, otherwise, a principal may be able to retain access in an unauthorized manner and later repudiate it. This is particularly relevant in applications where principals are registered in different infrastructure domains serving different user coalitions, or $ad - hoc$ networks, with overlapping and dynamically varying membership.

Consider the example illustrated in Figure 4. Client Bob is a member of two user coalitions, or $ad - hoc$ networks, having two separate infrastructure domains. When member Bob registered in Coalition 1, certificate authority $CA1$ issued him an identity certificate (corresponding to key K_{Bob}) and, based on this, certificate authority $CA1'$ issued him an attribute (i.e., group membership) certificate for access to object O (controlled by server P). Thus Bob is a valid member of group $G1$ maintained by $CA1'$. Bob is also registered in Coalition 2, where certificate authority $CA2$ issued him an identity certificate (corresponding to key K'_{Bob}). Membership in Coalition 2 does not entitle Bob access to object O. This means that server P trusts $CA1$ and $CA2$ for issuing identity certificates and trusts $CA1'$ for issuing attribute certificate to members registered with $CA1$ in Coalition 1.

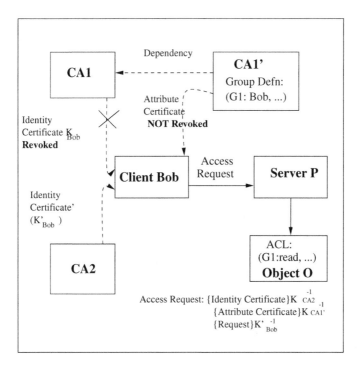

Fig. 4. Unauthorized Retention of Access Privilege

Suppose that *Bob*'s identity certificate has been revoked by $CA1$ upon *Bob*'s departure from Coalition 1. Also suppose that *Bob*'s membership privileges to group $G1$ are not (selectively) revoked upon $CA1$'s revocation of *Bob*'s identity certificate, since it is assumed that *Bob* cannot sign access requests after his identity certificate is revoked. In the absence of selective revocation, *Bob*'s attribute certificate will still be valid, and *Bob* can now use his alternate identity certificate issued by $CA2$ (corresponding to key K'_{Bob}) and the still-valid attribute certificate to obtain unauthorized access to object O. *Bob*'s access will be allowed by server P because the attribute (group) certificate is issued to the identity "Bob" and, upon verification of the access request, P will find a valid identity ("Bob") and a valid identity certificate (issued by $CA2$ to *Bob*) for that identity. Though allowed, this access illustrates an unauthorized retention of access privileges by *Bob* after his departure from Coalition 1, despite the intention of $CA1$ to ensure that *Bob* can no longer sign access requests to Coalition 1 objects (such as O). Furthermore, in the absence of access logging, *Bob* can later repudiate his unauthorized access to object O.

This problem is compounded further if delegation certificates are used in access requests to objects. We illustrate this with the following example, which extends the previous one to include delegation certificates.

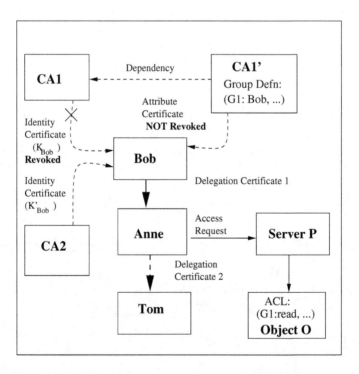

Fig. 5. Unauthorized Retention of Access Privilege with Delegation Certificates

Suppose that *Anne* and *Tom* are members of Coalition 1 registered with $CA1$, but do not have access to object O of server P. Also suppose that $CA1$ has just revoked the identity certificate issued to *Bob* (K_{Bob}). If *Bob*'s attribute (group) certificate is not revoked, then he can issue an unauthorized delegation certificate to *Anne* for access to group $G1$, using an alternate identity certificate (K'_{Bob}) and the still-valid attribute (group) certificate. This delegation, and any subsequent access requests by *Anne* to object O are considered to be valid by server P because *Bob* has a valid identity and a valid attribute certificate for that identity. If *Anne* and *Bob* are acting in collusion, then they can circumvent the intent of the access control policy of Coalition 1 because via this unauthorized delegation *Anne* receives access privileges delegated by a user (*Bob*) that was revoked from Coalition 1. Again, *Bob*'s attribute (group) certificate must be selectively revoked upon revocation of the identity certificate that was used to obtain the access control certificate.

The main cause for the problem of unauthorized retention of access illustrated above is actually that the (group membership) privilege distributed to the user is valid is all domains, not just that of Coalition 1. Hence, revocation of the privilege distribution must match the selectivity of privilege distribution; i.e., revocation must be effective in all domains, not just that of Coalition 1. Further, finer degrees of selective distribution privileges (such as, distribution to a key as in SPKI [2], or to a user in a specific domain) must be matched by corresponding selective revocation.

Could the above problem of unauthorized retention of access be avoided without support of selective revocation in practice? The answer to this question appears to be negative. Consider some possible alternatives, which prove to be inadequate. One way to avoid unauthorized is by brute force; i.e., revoke *all* identity certificates of a principal upon revocation of *any* single identity certificate. This would require a global authority across multiple dynamic coalitions, which cannot be easily supported for both practical and political reasons. Another way would be to assign different identities for a particular principal in different CA domains (e.g., qualified by CA identities). This would require a global name and authority hierarchy, which may not be practical in all applications since it practically rules out the use of non- hierarchical forms of trust. Yet another way might be to "link" the attribute and identity certificates cryptographically when the attribute certificate is issued, and require verifying servers P to check that both certificates are linked by certification authorities of the same coalition, domain. However, this could limit the sharing of objects amongst multiple coalitions. Lastly, we note in section 4 below that SPKI, which distributes access privileges to individual public keys - not to identities - eliminates the selective revocation problem, but at the same time, introduces an access review problem.

Selective revocation requires that the attribute certificate of a principal whose identity certificate has been revoked (and was used to obtain the attribute certificate) be selectively revoked as well. In coalition or $ad - hoc$ network applications where group-communication mechanisms are usually available, selective revocation could be supported by sending revocation messages between CAs that distribute and revoke dependant certificates.

Supporting selective revocation can also simplify the solution to a common caching problem that is not unique to PKIs but, nonetheless, can cause problems as explained below. For rapid dissemination of revocation information throughout a distributed system where real-time operations between entities are necessary, cached credentials (keys, privileges or certificates) pose the problem of unintended delays in the dissemination of revocation information. Upon verification of a principal's credentials for access control, the verifying principal typically caches (for a limited duration) the identity certificate (for authentication purposes) of the sender. This reduces the cost of verifying the identity certificate of the sender on every access request. However, if the identity certificate is revoked but the cached credentials (identity certificates) are still valid, an intruder may be able to obtain unauthorized access to objects until caches are flushed and access validation takes place anew (which may take a substantial amount of time).

In Figure 6, assume that server P has cached Bob's identity certificate (corresponding to Bob's public-key K_{Bob}) and this cached credential is valid for a certain period of time after Bob's identity certificate has been revoked by $CA1$. Suppose that Bob's identity certificate was revoked because an intruder X compromised his secret key, $K_{Bob}{}^{-1}$. X can now sign access requests using $K_{Bob}{}^{-1}$ to obtain unauthorized access to object O until server P flushes its cache and re-verifies certificates. The access request is accepted by P because the signing key $K_{Bob}{}^{-1}$ will not be verified, as P has already cached Bob's identity certificate. Furthermore, if the attribute certificate is also cached, the registered user himself might be able to obtain access to objects based on cached credentials of the attribute certificate that may have been revoked. Thus, there is an effective delay between the revocation of Bob's identity certificate and access revocation.

Could the above problem of revocation immediacy be avoided in practice? In preliminary analysis, the answer to this question appears to be negative. One alternate way would be to verify all concerned identity/delegation certificates at every access request, which would be prohibitively expensive. The second option would be to invalidate all cache locations upon revocation of the root key. This is difficult to implement because the cache location that needs to be revoked is not known centrally, and global cache invalidation is both impractical and expensive.

Selective revocation can simplify the cache invalidation approach to resolving the revocation immediacy problem. With selective revocation, only the attribute certificate needs to be verified on every access request, while the identity certificate may be cached. This is because if the identity certificate were revoked, the attribute certificate would also have been selectively revoked. Further, by doing this we enforce verification of a certificate (attribute) that will be revoked more often (than the identity certificate).

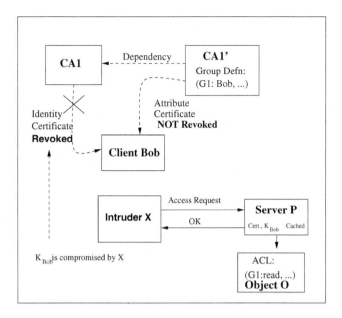

Fig. 6. A Problem of Revocation Immediacy

3.2   Transitive Revocation

Delegation certificates obtained through attribute certificates provide transitive access to a group member's privileges. Hence, distribution of delegation certificates entails transitive distribution of access privileges. If the access management policies support *transitive distribution*, then they must also support *transitive revocation* of these access privileges. That is, if an attribute certificate is revoked, then all delegation certificates issued in a chain originating at that attribute certificate must be revoked as well. Or, if any delegation certificate in a chain is revoked, then all delegation certificates further down the hierarchy in the chain must be transitively revoked. This can be more intuitively understood if we observe that delegation certificates are issued after verification of identity and attribute certificates and, if relevant, verification of delegation certificates higher up the delegation chain. That is, the validity of any delegation certificate is implicitly embedded in the validity of all certificates that its distribution depends upon. Hence there is a dependency between these access control certificates that must be enforced during certificate revocation.

Furthermore, if delegation chains become long it will be expensive to verify the entire chain, including the attribute certificate, on every access request. Hence, verifying principals typically cache these chains to hasten the verification of access requests. Usually, on an access request only the signing key and the delegation certificate owned by the requesting principal are verified. The cached delegated credentials, in effect, cause an unintended delay in dissemination of revocation information in a manner similar to that discussed in section 3.1 for identity certificates (revocation immediacy). Supporting transitive revocation will also resolve this problem as the requesting principal's delegation certificate would have been transitively revoked.

Cached certificates can cause more complex security problems if the entire delegation chain is not re-validated whenever a new delegation certificate is issued. In that case, a principal whose attribute certificate has been revoked can get back his access privileges by simply issuing a delegation certificate to a cohort assuming that the verifying server would retain his revoked certificate as a valid cached credential. If the entire chain were re-validated upon distribution of a new delegation certificate, this problem would not occur. Alternatively, if transitive revocation were supported then this problem would be eliminated as well, because the principal wishing to issue such an unauthorized delegation certificate would be unable to do so, as his delegation certificate would have been transitively revoked.

4   Access Review

The notion of access review includes per-object review and per-subject review of privileges. With per-object review, one is typically interested who has access to a particular object, whereas in with per-subject review one is interested in discovering all access privileges a subject or a principal has. In this paper, we refer only to the per-object review capabilities supported by PKIs that support access control certificates.

In traditional PKIs with identity and attribute (group membership) certificates, per-object review is achieved easily as the names of all group members are present in the group definition (maintained in the group owner's database; e.g., a CA) and the access privileges assigned to that group are available on the ACL of the object. In contrast, SPKI [2] supports the notion of *authorization certificates*, where access is directly granted to a public-key (or hash thereof) bypassing the need for an identity certificate. Therefore, SPKI does not support identity certificates and does not rely on access control lists associated with objects. As a consequence, access privileges are not assigned to principals and groups either in a central database or on an object basis. Since access privileges are explicitly present on authorization certificates, determining the access privileges amounts to solving the per-object review problem for capability-based systems - a rather problematic task [3].

By eliminating the identity certificate from the access control verification process, SPKI appears to offer a solution to the selective revocation problem. If access is granted to a public-key either directly by the object owner or delegated via a chain, a principal can neither have multiple signing keys that correspond to the same identity nor does he have a cacheable identity certificate. However, in their effort to motivate a transition process to SPKI certificates, Ellison *et al.* [2] re-introduce identity certificates, called name certificates, along with access control policies of the form that map *authorization* → *name* → *key*. One can define groups by issuing multi ple (name, key) certificates with the same name

- one for each group member. Authorization certificates can then be issued to names present on a name certificate that behaves like a group membership certificate. Thus, we have an access control scenario that is identical to one discussed in Figures 3-5 and are faced with the same problems of selective revocation of attribute certificates as discussed in Section 3.1.

Though SPKI offers a partial solution to the *selective revocation* problems, it does not resolve the *transitive revocation* problems discussed in section 3.2, as it supports *transitive distribution* of access privileges via delegation certificates but does not support *transitive revocation* of these delegated access privileges.

5   Conclusions

We have shown that revocation policies of access privileges distributed and revoked with PKI certificates need to support both selective and transitive revocation. Our analysis is motivated by (1) the fact that access management policies that support selective (or transitive) distribution of access privileges must also support selective (or transitive) revocation, and (2) the ability of registered users to circumvent the intent of revocation in the absence of selective and transitive revocation. We also point out the requirements for supporting access review functions in PKI systems.

In order to support selective and transitive revocation, the dependant certificates, as defined in section 3, must be revoked upon revocation of the certificate that is depended upon. Such an implementation would require maintenance of dynamic links between servers of dependant certificates. These links would then be used to send appropriate revocation messages across the distributed system to enforce selective and transitive revocation. Furthermore, maintaining and utilizing these links should put minimum communication and storage requirements on the servers, and avoid introducing any centralized components in the distributed system. An additional requirement of the solution is the ability to provide access review functions. The solution to these problems must be verifiable to ensure that the security exposures mentioned in this paper are eliminated.

Acknowledgments

This works was supported in part by the National Security Agency LUCITE program under contract No. MDA904-98-C-A081 at the University of Maryland, and by the Defense Advanced Research Projects Agency and managed by the U.S. Air Force Research Laboratory under contract F30602-00-2-0510. The views and conclusions contained in this document are those of the authors and should not be interpreted as representing the official policies, either expressed or implied, of the National Security Agency, Defense Advanced Research Projects Agency, U.S. Air Force Research Laboratory, or the United States Government.

References

1. 1. M. Abadi, M. Burrows, B. Lampson, and G. D. Plotkin, A Calculus for Access Control in Distributed Systems, ACM Transactions on Programming Languages and Systems, Vol. 15, No. 4, September 1993, pp. 706-734
2. C. M. Ellison. SPKI Certificate documentation, http://www.clark.net/pub/cme/html/spki.html, 1998.
3. V. D. Gligor, Review and Revocation of Access Privileges Distributed Through Capabilities, IEEE Transactions on Software Engineering, Vol. 5, No. 6, November 1979, pp. 575-586.
4. V. D. Gligor and S. I. Gavrila, Application-Oriented Security Policies and their Composition, in Proceedings of Security Protocols 6th International Workshop. Cambridge, UK, April 1998.
5. V. D. Gligor, S. I. Gavrila, and D. Ferraiolo, On the Formal Definition of Separation-of-Duty Policies and their Composition, Proceedings of the 1998 IEEE Symposium on Security and Privacy, Oakland, California, May 1998.
6. R. Housley, W. Ford, W. Polk, D. Solo. Internet X.509 Public Key Infrastructure: Certificate and CRL Profile (draft-ietf-pkix-ipki-part1-08.txt). PKIX Working Group. Internet Draft. June 16,1998.
7. S. Kent. Privacy Enhancement for Internet Electronic Mail: Part II: Certificate-Based Key Management, RFC 1422, IAB IRTF PSRG, IETF PEM WG, Feb 1993.
8. B. Lampson, M. Abadi, M. Burrows and E. Wobber, Authentication in distributed systems: Theory and Practice. ACM Transactions on Computer Systems 10(4): 265-310, November 1992.
9. S. Micali. Efficient Certificate Revocation. Technical Memo MIT/LCS/TM-542b, Massachusetts Institute of Technology, Laboratory for Computer Science, Mar. 1996.
10. M. Myers, R. Ankney, A. Malpani, S. Galperin, C. Adams. X.509 Internet Public Key Infrastructure: Online Certificate Status Protocol - OCSP (draft-ietf-pkix- ocsp-03.txt). PKIX Working Group. Internet Draft. March 1998.
11. R. L. Rivest and B. Lampson. SDSI - a simple distributed security infrastructure. (See SDSI web page at http://theory.lcs.mit.edu/cis/sdsi.html.)
12. S. Stubblebine and R. Wright. An Authentication Logic Supporting Synchronization, Revocation, and Recency, Third ACM Conference on Computer and Communications Security, New Delhi, India, March, 1996, pp. 95-105.

Review and Revocation of Access Privileges Distributed with PKI Certificates (Transcript of Discussion)

Virgil D. Gligor

University of Maryland

What I'd like to do today is to speak about review and revocation of access privileges distributed with public key certificates. The subject is actually similar to that in a paper that I published in 1979[1], so this is a recycled talk in a new context.

The idea is to ask whether the review and revocation policies that were defined for capability systems apply to public key certificates also. The reason why there is some speculation in this talk that they might apply, is because recently (meaning in the last three years) people have started introducing attribute certificates or authorisation certificates into public key infrastructures. So the thesis here is that once you do that, you have brought on yourself the liability of having to support a number of the policies of revocation that we dealt with in the capability days. Whether this is a justifiable argument remains to be seen. All I am trying to do here is to provide some examples of why it might be a justified conclusion that you have to recycle the old policies.

What kind of policies do we have? That is, what do we mean by this policy of review revocation. Generally, when you do access review you ask, possibly in disguise, two different questions. One is – who has access to a particular object, and this is called per object review. The second one is – what are all accesses of a particular subject, and this is called per subject review. You need, for example, per subject review if you want to determine whether the rôles or duties in a particular system are separated properly. So you pick these two principals that are supposed to have separate duties and you ask the question – what are all the accesses. You then find out whether they have access to the same kind of objects or to the same kind of operations and then make a decision as to whether their duties are separated properly.

In revocation, we have a number of policies. In selective revocation, you revoke a user's access to the objects accessible from a particular group. So you revoke the user membership to a group or you revoke a particular user privilege, but you do not revoke all the privileges that a user might have to an object. For example, you might revoke their write privilege to a particular object but the user might still have read-execute privileges to the object. So selectivity here means that you actually delete a particular privilege but not all privileges.

Transitivity means essentially that you have transitive distribution, that is if a user grants a particular privilege to another user, then you have the possibility

---

[1] Review and Revocation of Access Privileges Distributed through Capabilities, IEEE Transactions in Software Engineering, November 1979.

B. Christianson et al. (Eds.): Security Protocols, LNCS 2133, pp. 113–124, 2001.
© Springer-Verlag Berlin Heidelberg 2001

that the latter user can pass the privilege on further. What you would like to do in this circumstance is to also implement transitive revocation. In other words, if I delete the privilege or if I revoke the privilege of a user to whom I pass the privilege, then anybody else who received that privilege from the user to whom I distributed it, should lose it as well. If you recall, this is one of the basic policies that database standards have. For example, the SQL standard has transitive revocation built into it, because it also has transitive distribution. It turns out that if you have transitive distribution of rights, you have to have transitive revocation. Otherwise the revocation makes no sense. The reason being that if I receive a privilege from a source, and I distribute it further, then if I lose that privilege, then the target of my distribution could be one of my cohorts who is going to redistribute it right back to me. So the fact that I was revoked of that privilege would have no effect. Once again, the conclusion is that, if you have transitive distribution of privileges, you must have transitive revocation. In other words, you cannot simply have one level of revocation, if you have transitive distribution.

Revocation also has to be independent and that is again one of the aspects of the SQL standard which was also captured, before the SQL standard, in capability systems. That means that if a particular principal receives the same privilege for the same object via two different routes, the principal could lose the privilege via one route but not necessarily via the second route – so the revocation is independent.

Now the revocation has occasionally to be immediate. This is a very controversial kind of policy because we are unable, very often, to define just how immediate revocation could be. The notion of immediacy appeared very distinctly in early operating systems in which protection played a major rôle, such as in Multics. In Multics, revocation could be really and truly immediate in the sense that if you revoked a privilege and it disappeared from an ACL, it turned out that it would also disappear from the set of descriptors that the process would have. This happened because there was a list of back pointers from the ACL to the descriptor table of that particular process. In Unix the revocation is not particularly immediate, in the sense that you could lose the privilege from the protection bits of Unix but the process running on behalf of the user who received that privilege can run for a long time and still maintain that privilege because you have it via your descriptor tables in hardware and file handles and so on. So the immediacy in the Unix sense, is that at the end of the life of the process that received this privilege, revocation takes effect.

It is not clear that immediacy is always a good property to have. For example, it might be illegal to have immediate revocation in some cases. If you have a contract between two users and one party does not satisfy the contract and you revoke its privilege, there is always a grace period which is sometimes regulated by law. For example, if you don't pay your rent you cannot be evicted from your apartment immediately or in the middle of the night. So it is unclear how immediacy should be defined, what the policy for immediacy should be, and what immediacy means.

These are some of the policies that you have in access control systems. Let's now see how these policies may or may not apply to public key infrastructures once you add the authorisation or attribute certificate.

Firstly, we want to agree, if we can, on how public key certificates are used in access requests. These are traditional public key infrastructures and public key certificates in the sense that we have the notion of identity certificates. In SPKI[2] we don't, at least not at the basis for SPKI, but in most of the traditional PKIs we do. So this identity certificate, as usual, associates an identifier, or a name, with a public key and its also signed by some certification authority. You also have an attribute certificate which typically means that you have a user belonging to a group, and that membership is actually determined by some other certification authority. Finally, you have a request, maybe "read from this file" or "read from this object", which is signed. Now the key with which it was signed was the key associated with the ID by the identity certificate. These certificates, the identity and the attribute certificates, can actually be pushed on to a server or a principal can pull them from a convenient place. So in that case, the client only has to send in the signed request.

So what does the server do to authenticate the request? First the server determines whether or not he accepts the signature on the certificate from a particular certification authority. If he does, then he uses the public key from the identity certificate to determine that this is a reasonable signature. So at the end of the authentication, the server knows that this request comes from this ID. Furthermore, what the server wants to do is to determine whether this ID has access to a particular object. The way the server does that is he determines whether or not he accepts that certification authority's signature on this attribute certificate, which says that the ID belongs to the group which authorises access. This attribute certificate is usually a group membership certificate. After these two actions – determining whether or not this request comes from a particular ID and determining whether or not this ID belongs to a particular group – the server determines whether the particular client has access to the object. This is pretty much standard. Whether these certificates are cached or whether or not they are pushed on the server or pulled is not important at this point.

Now let us look at how these certificates got there and what they mean. Obviously we have a certification authority that produces in a traditional PKI an identity certificate which our client Bob has. We may have another certification authority, CA2, which maintains the group membership and determines who belongs to various groups or who has particular privileges. The membership of a particular identity to a group is based on the certification for this particular ID, by CA1 in this case. In other words, as CA2, I am not willing to attach a particular member to a group, unless the particular member has a public key certificate and an identity certificate in this sense. So the user has been registered and has been given a public key certificate before I am going to allow the member to belong to this group, and sign that membership.

---

[2] RFC2693

So once these things are done, our client Bob can actually make a request to server P. In this case, server P accepts CA1's signature for the identity certificate, namely for the public key, and it accepts CA2's signature on the attribute certificate. Accept here means trust. In other words, it trusts that these two parties have properly registered and signed this certificate and that the CA2 has the authority to manage those groups.

With delegation, this process can be extended a little bit but it is essentially the same, namely that Bob receives the attribute certificate from CA2 and Bob can delegate this certificate further without CA2's involvement. As with transitively distributed privilege and access control systems, it is possible here to construct a delegation certificate which accompanies Bob's certificates to Anne and Anne can further use Bob's certificate and the delegation certificate to delegate further to Tom. The request from Tom to the server would have a slightly different format because now Tom has to push on to the server not only his ID certificate and his request signed with the private key corresponding to the public key of the ID certificate, but Tom would also have to push the attribute certificate coming from Bob, transitively to Anne, plus the delegation certificate guaranteeing that Tom was delegated access. So now there is the server who checks the request by using the public key from the ID certificate, we check the delegation certificate saying that in fact Tom acts on behalf of Anne acting on behalf of Bob, and the delegation certificate is used for that, and with the attribute certificate the server determines that Tom actually was delegated group access on Bob's behalf, and access is allowed. So it's just a slightly more complicated access verification but it's essentially the same idea.

Now let's look at the following situation. Suppose that Bob is actually registered with two CAs, and suppose that further server P accepts authentication from CA1 and CA1', in other words, server P validates and accepts certificates signed by these two CAs. So what happens in this example is that somehow, for some reason, Bob is revoked his certificate by Certification Authority 1. That act in itself would not make Bob, in current systems, lose his accesses to object O, even though the group membership of Bob was determined based on that identity certificate. So we have a dependency between the group certificate issued by CA2 on Bob's being registered and having an identity certificate passed out by CA1. If they intended that Bob should lose access, that intent cannot be satisfied here. Why? Because what happens in this case, is that Bob can construct a perfectly valid request signed with his private key obtained by virtue of his registration with CA1', can use the old attribute certificate which is obtained on the basis of his registration with CA1 and use the identity certificate from CA1'.

So what happens in this case is that server P, which accepts authentication from CA1, validates a request using the identity certificate issued by CA1 (and that validation was passed normally) and then separately and independently validates that this is a valid attribute certificate which it also accepts from CA2. So the question is – if this happens, is this a valid access? Should it be a valid access? Obviously we can take both points of view, namely that this is a valid access and that this should not happen. So if we take the second point of view, as a matter of policy, what we've noticed here is that the scenario gives us an undesirable retention of access by Bob, because the dependency between CA2 and CA1 was not enforced at the revocation of the first certificate.

It turns out that CA1 and CA1′ or CA2 and CA1′, are totally independent authorities, nothing to do with each other. In fact CA1′ may not even exist at the time when this is done. This is exactly the point – that the only dependency that you have when you determine Bob's membership of this group is between CA2 and CA1 and that dependency is not enforced upon revocation; some people argue that it should be, because we know that access control depends on authentication, and that should be enforced. Enforcement in this case would mean that if you revoke the identity certificate, you have to revoke all the attribute certificates depending on that identity certificate.

This certificate never really contains references to identity certificates for the members who are registered. This dependency is actually done when the certificate is created, you check whether or not this particular user was properly registered. If it presents a valid certificate from CA1 to CA2, if they are two different Certification Authorities, then you enroll it because you know that user Bob was in fact properly registered and properly issued a certificate.

Audience: An alternative is to check its dependency at the server P.

Reply: The problem for the two certificates is that the way the certificates are defined and structured gives you no idea at server P that that dependency exists. You have to infer it and check it.

Audience: I think that what we are fundamentally thinking about here is that the names have meaning only in the local scope. So the attribute certificate seems to reserve your name or your identity, but if it's the same code used by CA1 and CA1′, it doesn't work anymore.

Reply: The point is that this notion of scope that you have mentioned is not present in here, and I would agree with you that it should be. My concern here is not resolving this problem because there are ten different ways to solve the problem, my concern is to identify that this is a possible policy option. So the point is that when you have revocation and you introduce attribute certificates, then once you've done that you have to actually introduce the dependencies in the scope of the certificate – which current public key infrastructures do not do. People introduce attribute certificates without really thinking about the implications of what goes on.

Now the same kind of a problem appears if you have delegation. In fact Bob can delegate his attribute certificate to cohort Anne, even after Bob loses his identity certificate through revocation from CA1. It should be fairly obvious that that's the case. There are some additional problems, which I will discuss in a minute, of transitivity of revocation which appear due to some problems of caching the results of certificate validation.

Mike Roe: In this particular scenario, what is in that attribute certificate is a key belonging to Bob, rather than the name Bob?

Reply: Basically the attribute certificate is a group membership certificate, and all it says is that Bob belongs to this group which is managed by CA2, and that membership is signed by CA2.

Larry Paulson: How does that identify Bob?

Reply: That certificate identifies Bob by its ID, by its name if you want.

Mike Roe: That's what you described as independent. In the case where the name of Bob is actually in the attribute certificate, I would expect that to carry on working even if Bob then goes and gets himself an identity certificate. The case I thought was of more concern is where Bob uses an identity certificate, he just gets an attribute certificate with another key in it and says this key is mine.

Reply: That may very well also happen, but the point here is that even if he is just an identity, remember that this a registered identity, and we established this group membership based on that registration. And in fact if Bob registers the same name independently with a second certification authority that's also trusted, if you want, by this server, and on the ACL that group name with Bob's membership appears, then (unless the server starts checking these dependencies) this server should not know whether you are talking about the same or a different Bob.

Ross Anderson: We have a critical problem here, in that in X.509 you're not using the person's name but you're using the hash of the certificate.

Reply: The question is what ID do you use here on this ACL. If again you present the same ID and it's in a different certificate, that's perfectly fine. Since these two certificates are totally independent of each other, that's a perfectly legitimate problem that may appear.

Mike Roe: I talked about naming yesterday; if you've got two different Bobs, one of whom is talking to CA1 and one who's talking to CA2, but they are both on the same ACL, then that is a problem.

Reply: If they are both issued group certificates by CA2, you'd have the problem.

Mike Roe: You need unique names within that context. If they are not unique, you have a problem.

Reply: Right, you use keys, but even then, if you have two independent CAs, you have independent registration.

Audience: The fact that the identity certificate doesn't have the CA1, means that the certificate doesn't tell you that Bob is Bob but says that this key is Bob.

Reply: Associated with Bob, yes, but hold on there's more to it than that since Bob is registered. Remember that CAs have a registration process.

Audience: But it is the key that is registered, not Bob.

Reply: Even Bob is registered with that CA. Ultimately you have to have a registry, Bob is just a principal. [laughter]

The main point is that we added this attribute certificate and these attribute certificates are essentially based on those identity certificates and the user registration. Once you've done that, you have a dependency there that's lost when in fact the same user registers with a different CA and gets a different identity certificate.

John Ioannidis: I may have missed something, but why do you need to keep Bob's name in the attribute certificate?

Reply: You don't necessarily keep Bob's name, you have to keep Bob's membership of that group.

John Ioannidis: Well you don't have Bob's membership, you have Bob's key's membership.

Reply: It depends how you do this attribute certificate. SPKI determines groups exclusively on keys and not on identities and thus solves the problem by definition. In a minute I'm going to come to that and see what other problems SPKI introduces by solving this problem.

Mike Roe: If the CA was actually assigning names, rather than the names being pre-existing and then merely being authenticated by the CA, then in most situations the names aren't really Bob, they're some string that starts out with the name of the CA and ends with this component that distinguishes separate users registered by that CA. So the problem doesn't arise in this case because you can't get clashes on the names.

Reply: Possibly, yes. That's a solution but that's not necessarily done. As a matter of fact I can register myself with a name that I choose myself.

Mike Roe: For example if you get a certificate for VeriSign, then the real name you get back will start off with VeriSign although the final components have in it your personal name, and that is precisely so that certificates issued by different CAs end up with different X.509 names, because they might refer to different people.

Reply: Yes, but suppose that I registered with a CA where in fact the registration process is totally independent of the first CA, there is nothing to guarantee that I get a different name.

Mike Roe: If you're accepting both those certificates, your name just doesn't help either. You've taken two different sets of identifiers which may overlap, but are totally different things, and you said right I'm going to merge them. But then you've got something that you just can't use anymore, you can't work out what it refers to because you've got two strings both of which are Bob.

Reply: Yes, that's true, and if these are independent CAs (in fact they may be CAs that belong to totally different certification authority companies), there is nothing to guarantee that that's the case. For example, if you go through the registration process for Yahoo, and through the registration process for say Excite, or some other service provider, you may in fact register your name so that it collides with another name that you have, or somebody else's name. There is absolutely no guarantee that that will not happen.

Remember I am not talking about solutions, there are zillions of solutions to this. I'm talking about whether we worry about the dependencies that may exist or whether we ignore them, whether this is considered to be a problem or not. And if this is considered a problem, then there are ways to solve the problem. One of them might be to say whenever you revoke this identity certificate, just go and revoke all the attribute certificates depending on it[3] – a perfectly reasonable solution. The problem may be defined away, which is another solution. SPKI defines the problem away by saying – we don't have this thing, we don't have associations between IDs and keys, we only have keys, signed keys – in which case this goes away completely. On the other hand what I mentioned earlier is also true – the SPKI folk decided that they have to introduce, at least at the transition period, identity certificates. In which case this problem may reappear at least in the transition period.

Now another inconvenience may appear, even if Bob's attribute certificate is actually revoked at the time when the identity certificate is revoked. If we allowed transitive delegation of certificates and if the server P caches the result of certificate validation for a long time, which may very well happen, then what will happen in that case (since this change was cached and the result of the delegation was cached) is that until server P decides to re-validate the entire delegation chain, the fact that Bob lost his identity certificate and attribute certificate will have no effect.

So how do you solve that problem? Again there are ten different ways to solve the problem, some are worse than others. One of the obviously impractical solutions might be not to do caching, to just validate all the changes of certificates all the time. Obviously this would be a ridiculous solution and wouldn't work in practice. Another solution might be, when you do a delegation, say when Anne delegates to Tom, to re-validate the entire delegation chain. That may or may not be practical. Another solution might be where Bob loses the attribute certificate, just make sure that all the delegation chains become invalid by generating this additional revocation certificate that you push onto other CAs that Anne and Tom may use.

So solutions exist to this problem, if there is a problem here. The question is which ones do we choose and whether we believe that the addition of this type of certificate causes a problem.

There is also an immediacy problem that appears as well. What happens if Bob's key is in fact revoked because Bob's key is compromised, not because Bob is a bad guy. Bob's compromised key obviously does not lose access, primarily because of the caching problem that we discussed earlier. So in this case, the intruder can use the attribute certificate which is issued to Bob, can sign the request with Bob's stolen private key, and so long as that validation of those certificates is cached, the intruder has access on Bob's behalf. So here is a question of immediacy, not from the point of view of how fast Bob loses access, but how fast the intruder that compromised Bob's key loses access. There are no good solutions to the immediacy of revocation.

Here is what SPKI does and how SPKI solves the problem of selective revocation, namely having to revoke group membership at the time when you revoke identities. Eliminating the identities obviously solves the problem, however two things happened with SPKI. First SPKI still doesn't support transitive revoca-

---

[3] Or you can include the signature of the relevant identity certificate in the attribute certificate, *c.f.* Christianson and Low, IEE Electronics Letters **31**(13) (1995) p. 1943.

tion, so transitive revocation remains a potential problem with SPKI because of the way SPKI supports delegation chains. Furthermore, the way SPKI does groups is quite simple. The manager of a group delegates group certificates to other principals that can further delegate group certificates, SPKI certificates or attribute certificates to other parties. So you belong to a group in SPKI by virtue of having been delegated one of these attribute certificates or authorisation certificates. Here keys are associated with privileges just like capabilities would be, or as group memberships. So now if you have one of those delegated certificates, you belong to the group. But there is no central place where you can tell who belongs to this group, in other words this is a very fluid group. Consequently the problem that we now have is one of access review. You can no longer go to a place to find out who belongs to this group, which was determined fluidly by transitive delegation of attribute certificates. So if you want to have a policy that's based on groups or even further if it's based on rôles, you have lost this per object review facility which is considered by some as fundamental to access control.

If we solve the selective revocation problem by doing away with groups and those identity certificates, then the groups become something very fluid and we have lost this review possibility. Again there are ways to compensate for this loss, but those ways would have to be explicitly implemented.

So my conclusion, or a conclusion that one might reach, is that lack of support for explicit selective and transitive revocation, may lead to a potential access control exposure. The scenarios that we did here were those in which we had multiple signing keys from independent CAs offered through identity certificates. Caching of credentials can cause a problem in a large distributed system. SPKI does solve the selective revocation by eliminating identity certificates. However, user names cannot be completely eliminated even in SPKI. Even though the SPKI authors claim that user names are only for lawyers and that associations between names and keys are only a concern for lawyers, at some point you have to make those associations, you have to commit on some sort of an association. Once you commit on that association you might have reintroduced this selective revocation problem, depending upon how you do access control. And also SPKI introduces an access review problem that has to be solved in any case.

Audience: Suppose that CA2 not only issues attribute certificates, but also issues identity certificates.

Reply: Now that's a different story, because CA2 may issue two different types of certificates with that dependency not enforced. In other words, the enforcement of this dependency is independent of whether CA2 issues both types of certificates or whether or not you have two CAs. The conclusion is that that dependency has to be enforced in one type of solution, and it doesn't matter if CA2 issues both identity and attribute certificates, provided that it enforces the dependency. It doesn't matter whether CA2, or CA1, or any other CA does it. For that matter Bruno's suggestion would also hold – by finding a way to enforce the dependency, or the potential dependency, between, CA2 and CA1'. If you have of a way of doing that, you've solved this problem.

The dependency can be enforced elsewhere, namely later in the server P. In other words, that dependency could be maintained among the CAs *or* may be maintained at server P. Server P may be the ultimate arbiter of those dependencies because server P actually ultimately produces the authorisation. That's a perfectly reasonable approach to enforcing the dependency. The point is that that dependency should be enforced somewhere.

Mike Roe: Suppose that revocation hasn't happened, but it's just that two different Bobs go to two different CAs and get associated with the same ID. One of them gets put on an access control list and the other one magically gets the same access because he has the same identity.

Reply: Sure, sure, very much of a problem, the same idea. Somehow we have to make sure that that wouldn't happen if we want to prevent it. Definitely. Now how do you do it in PKI is unclear to me – because you have independence of certificates and independent registries associated with certification authorities.

Bruce Christianson: Suppose you bind attributes to the identity certificate itself, and you have a rule which says that the identity certificate must contain Bob's public key. What is the problem then?

Reply: Essentially SPKI does that and there is no problem with selective revocation. There is only a transitive revocation problem that still remains, due to caching, and an active review problem which SPKI introduces. Agreed, that's one of the conclusions here, that SPKI solved this problem, but by the way they reintroduced it because they claim that they still need this association between names and keys, this signed association, simply for backward compatibility.

Bruce Christianson: Yes, that was a failure of nerve.

Reply: Well failure or not, this is how they solved the problem. I thought that they had a very elegant solution not only to this problem but to a host of other problems, yet they go backwards and say well we need this for backward compatibility.

Bruno Crispo: You have used SPKI as your reference, but there are other models such as ECMA – what happens with those?

Reply: I haven't looked at ECMA-138 in a very long time.

Matt Blaze: I just want to point out that in PolicyMaker, which pre-dates SPKI, and KeyNote, we don't have this problem because we were never tempted to introduce names in the protocol.

Reply: Great, yes, but most other people do – because not only do they introduce names, but they introduce independent registries.

Audience: I think that the same problem arises in other places. It's not only for names and identities, but for membership generally.

Reply: Membership assignment is really what we have here in this part and it could be rôles not just groups.

Audience: Why not just go back to using capabilities?

Reply: That would solve the problem in a different way but still by enforcing the dependency. So for example in this case, suppose that we no longer have attribute certificates, this is the scenario proposed here, and we just do revocation of identity certificates in the traditional way. Then obviously the dependency between the access control and identity certificates would have to have been done at the last point, namely server P, and server P would know that he would have to go and check the validity of the identity certificate at the time of access. Definitely that would solve it, but again the dependency between access control and authentication is enforced.

I'm not particularly interested in proposing a specific solution to the problem. In fact, as I mentioned, there are several solutions to this problem and some are more practical than others. I am interested in pointing out what happened when we introduced this additional concept in PKI. This is part of a larger project that I'm involved in and this is just a small component but maybe at some other time we'll talk about the other components.

John Ioannidis: Something I just wanted to point out is that if you have short-lived certificates, and you can do away with CRLs[4], some of these problems go away. Of course other problems are introduced.

Reply: Yes, actually one thing that I failed to point out at the beginning is that this talk is independent of whether you use CRLs or on-line authorities, or a hybrid form. In other words, we are not particularly interested in this piece of work in how revocation is actually implemented. You might get some benefit from some implementation.

Matt Blaze: With short-lived certification, you don't have revocation.

Reply: Oh, yes, absolutely, as a matter of fact some problems may go away by default in some implementations. Revocation has a totally different aspect to it and I want to make it very clear. One is this aspect of managing the mechanics of revocation with on-line revocation authorities or CRLs, there is also some very good work on how to minimise communication and how to minimise storage in certificate revocation. These are very important topics, equally important as this one. This talk deals with the kind of policies that you may want to have, how you support them is a different matter.

Ross Anderson: I think it is important, because if you follow the exclusiveness principle of the revocation authorities then you should have a doctrine, which says that whenever anybody certifies anything they must write into the certificate the name and address and so on of the revocation authority for that act of certification. So when CA2 certifies a name that it gets from CA1, it must say so in the certificate. In every certificate there must be a revocation authority's name with a URL, service level agreement, and the works. Then whenever anybody certifies a group membership or delegation or whatever, they must name the revocation authority, and then it's up to the revocation authority and the mechanics to ensure this happens.

Reply: My preference would be exactly that. As a matter of fact one of the things I've advocated for at least ten years now, is that when you design any of these schemes or mechanisms or policies, you have to be very explicit about the dependencies that arise. In fact I made sure I put that case whenever I could, for example, in the US federal criteria (which got propagated into the common

---

[4] Certificate Revocation Lists

criteria[5]). All those dependencies were things that I beat people over the head with for many, many years. Finally there is a recognition of the fact that when you design a policy, you have to be very explicit about the dependencies among the policy components. As a matter of fact you may recall the talk here from two years ago[6] about the dependencies between various management aspects of policies and authorisation aspects of policies, and this again strikes back in this example. Very important. Whether this is going to be explicitly put in as part of a certificate such as, in this case, Ross advocates and as certain patent authors advocate, it's a matter of good design choice.

---

[5] ISO IS15408
[6] LNCS 1550, 67–82

The Correctness of Crypto Transaction Sets

Ross Anderson

Cambridge University

In this talk, given in April 2000, I introduced the topic of the correctness of the sets of transactions supported by cryptographic processors.

There has been much work on verifying crypto protocols, which are typically sets of 3-5 transactions exchanged by two principals. Yet when we look at actual implementations, there are typically 50 transactions supported by each principal's cryptographic facility (which might be a smartcard, cryptoprocessor, cryptographic service provider or security software library). Just as there are failures in which an opponent can achieve an undesired result by cutting and pasting valid transactions, so also there are failures in which an opponent uses cryptographic transactions in an order that was not anticipated by the facility's designer.

I can make this clear using an example I discovered shortly after this talk was given, and which is discussed in some detail in my book [1]. It works against many of the *security modules* – hardware cryptoprocessors – used by banks to manage ATM networks in the 1980s.

One of the security modules' principal protection goals was to ensure that no single employee of any bank in the network could learn the clear value of any customer's personal identification number (PIN). If PINs were simply managed in software, then any programmer with an appropriate level of access could learn any customer's PIN, and could therefore masquerade as them. As banks connected their ATMs together into networks, there was not just the risk that any bank's programmers might in theory masquerade as any other bank's customers, but also that a customer might falsely dispute a transaction he had actually made by claiming that some bank insider must be responsible.

So the cryptographic systems used to compute and verify PINs had to support a policy of dual control. No single member of any bank's staff should have access to the clear value of any bank customer's PIN. So key management involved hand carrying two or more *key components* to each ATM when it was initially brought online. These were combined together by exclusive-or to create a *terminal master key* (conventionally known as KMT), and further encryption keys would then be sent to the device encrypted under this master key. The higher-level management of PINs and keys relied on the tamper-resistance properties of the security modules to prevent programmers getting hold of PINs, or of data used to protect them such as the master keys in ATMs (and of course the PIN keys used to derive PINs from account numbers in the first place).

The upshot was that most bank security modules had a transaction to generate a key component and print out its clear value on an attached security printer.

B. Christianson et al. (Eds.): Security Protocols, LNCS 2133, pp. 125–127, 2001.

They also returned this value to the calling program, encrypted under a master key KM which was kept in the tamper-resistant hardware:

SM $\longrightarrow$ printer: KMT_i
SM $\longrightarrow$ host: $\{KMT_i\}_{KM}$

and another which will combine two of the components to produce a terminal key:

Host $\longrightarrow$ SM: $\{KMT_1\}_{KM}, \{KMT_2\}_{KM}$
SM $\longrightarrow$ host: $\{KMT_1 \oplus KMT_2\}_{KM}$

To generate a terminal master key, you'd use the first of these transactions twice followed by the second, giving $KMT = KMT_1 \oplus KMT_2$.

The protocol failure is that the programmer can take any old encrypted key and supply it twice in the second transaction, resulting in a known terminal key (the key of all zeroes, as the key is exclusive-or'ed with itself):

Host $\longrightarrow$ VSM: $\{KMT_1\}_{KM}, \{KMT_1\}_{KM}$
VSM $\longrightarrow$ host: $\{KMT_1 \oplus KMT_1\}_{KM}$

The module also has a transaction to verify any PIN supplied encrypted under a key that itself is encrypted under KM:

Host $\longrightarrow$ SM: *Account number*,$\{KMT_1\}_{KM}, \{PIN\}_{KMT}$
SM $\longrightarrow$ host: Y / N

So the programmer now uses the zero key to encrypt every possible PIN (0000-9999) and supplies them to the security module along with the target account number and the zero key encrypted under KM, $\{0\}_{KM}$. After about 5000 transactions, on average, he finds the key.

Following this attack, Mike Bond discovered a couple of protocol failures with the IBM 4758, then the only cryptoprocessor evaluated to FIPS 140-1 level 4 – the highest level of tamper-resistance available for unclassified equipment. This startling result is described briefly in [1], and in more detail in a forthcoming paper.

Mike's attacks spurred me to look more closely at the old security module transaction set, and I realised that there is an ever better attack. This uses a transaction that will translate data from one key to another, and can be used to translate almost all the interesting crypto keys in the device to the zero key. The manuals for other security module products have yielded yet more sneaky attacks.

To sum up: the security of cryptographic transaction sets is a new and rapidly growing field of research. This is the talk that kicked it all off.

Much of the talk consisted of an explanation of how the IBM 3848, VISA Security Module and IBM 4758 work at the protocol level. This is rather hard to tidy up into a written article, as I used multicoloured slides to convey the concept of key typing by having 'red keys', 'blue keys', 'green keys' and so on, with each type of keys having a particular kind of function within the system. From section 2.2 onwards, for example, I describe the keys used to protect PINs as 'red keys': a red key should have the property that nothing encrypted under it may ever be output in the clear.

The key typing concepts are made more difficult for the beginner to understand because of the mechanism by which they are usually implemented. This works as follows. The security module has a number of internal master keys, and the working keys supplied in a transaction are encrypted under the master key appropriate to that type. (Thus in the VISA security module, for example, key encryption is done by two-key triple-DES, and what we call a 'red' key is actually a key encrypted in this way under master keys 14 and 15.) The various transactions allow a number of 'approved' operations to be conducted on data that is supplied either in the clear, or encrypted under keys of particular types. Thus, for example, to verify a customer PIN received from another bank's ATM through VISA's network, the programmer calls a security module transaction which accepts a PIN encrypted under a key of the type 'working key shared with VISA', and a PIN verification key; it decrypts the PIN from the first key, checks it with the second, and returns either 'Correct' or 'Incorrect'.

The reader wishing to dive into the brutal details of all this should read the CCA manual supplied with the 4758, as this (more or less) contains the two earlier devices via its backward compatibility modes [7]. The reader wishing for a more abstract view of the problem being addressed should read the following transcript in conjuntcion with chapter 14 of my book [1]. For this reason I've only edited the transcript lightly – adding a couple of illustrations, a couple of equations and a table from my slides.

Ross Anderson
Cambridge, 2nd January 2001

The Correctness of Crypto Transaction Sets (Discussion)

Ross Anderson

Cambridge University

This talk follows on more from the talks by Larry Paulson and Giampaolo Bella that we had earlier. The problem I'm going to discuss is, what's the next problem to tackle once we've done crypto protocols? We keep on saying that crypto-protocols appear to be "done" and then some new application comes along to give us more targets to work on – multi-media, escrow, you name it. But sooner or later, it seems reasonable to assume, crypto will be done. What's the next thing to do?

The argument I'm going to make is that we now have to start looking at the interface between crypto and tamper-resistance.

Why do people use tamper resistance? I'm more or less (although not quite) excluding the implementation of tamper resistance that simply has a server sitting in a vault. Although that's functionally equivalent to many more portable kinds of tamper resistance, and although it's the traditional kind of tamper resistance in banking, it's got some extra syntax which becomes most clear when we consider the Regulation of Investigatory Powers (RIP) Bill. When people armed with decryption notices are going to be able to descend on your staff, grab keys, and forbid your staff from telling you, then having these staff working in a Tempest vault doesn't give the necessary protection.

1 Cryptography Involving Mutually Mistrustful Principals

In order to deploy "RIP-stop cryptography" (the phrase we've been using), you need to get guarantees which are mandatory – in the sense of mandatory access control. That is, you need guarantees, that are enforced independently of user action and are therefore subpoena proof, that a key was destroyed at date X, or that a key is not usable on packets over a week old, or that a key is only usable in packets over a week old if it's used with the thumb print of the corporate chief security manager, or whatever. You could do this with something like Kerberos, you just say that tickets can only be decrypted (as opposed to used) if the corporate security manager says so (this is maybe the cheap and cheerful way of getting RIP-stop into Windows). Alternatively, you could impose a requirement that a key should be unusable in the same key packet twice – possible if you've got a device like the 4758 with a reasonable amount of memory – or you could have a key which is unusable without a correct biometric. All of these give you ways of defeating RIP.

B. Christianson et al. (Eds.): Security Protocols, LNCS 2133, pp. 128–141, 2001.
© Springer-Verlag Berlin Heidelberg 2001

Now when we look at the larger canvas, at the applications that really use hardware tamper-resistance, we find that most of them are used where there is mutual mistrust. Often all the principals in a system mistrust each other.

The classic example, that Simmons discussed in the 80's, was the business of nuclear treaty verification, and indeed command and control generally [10]. The Americans don't trust the Russians, and the Pentagon doesn't trust the commanders in the field not to use the weapons, and so you end up with this enormous hierarchy of tamper-resistant boxes.

Pre-payment electricity meters provide another application that we have discussed at previous workshops [3]. There you have a central electricity authority, and you have hundreds of regional electricity vendors who sell tokens which operate meters. How do you balance power and cash, and stop the various vendors running off with the cash – or selling tokens that they then don't own up to? The only known solution is using some kind of hardware tamper-resistance, at least in the vending stations.

Then you've got bank security modules, which are basically used because banks don't want to trust each others' programmers not to get at customer PINs. Matt asked yesterday: "How could you possibly use tamper-resistance where you have got mutual mistrust?" In practice, tamper-resistance is used precisely where there is mutual mistrust, and this is what makes it difficult and interesting.

A brief history of tamper-resistance includes weighted code-books, sigaba cypher machines with thermite charges, and so on – all fairly familiar. GSM is fairly low-level stuff: your SIM contains a customer key K_c, and this key is *you*, for practical purposes, in the network; it is used to respond to random authentication challenges. You have no real motive to break into the SIM; it's just convenient to use a smartcard to hold K_c (although it does prevent some kinds of cloning such as cloning a phone in a rental car).

Pay-TV becomes more serious, and Markus Kuhn has talked about it at some length [4]. There the mutual mistrust is between the pay-TV operator and the customer. The customer has the master key on his premises, and the pay-TV operator doesn't trust the customer not to use the master key. Hence the need for tamper-resistance.

Banking is an issue that I've written about a lot [2], and the kind of security modules that I worked with (and indeed built some of) are basically PCs in steel cases with lid switches. Open the lid, and bang goes the memory. This is a very simple way of building stuff. You can make it more complex by putting in seismometers, and photo-diodes, and all sorts of other sensors, but the basic idea is simple. When you take it to its logical conclusion you get the IBM 4758, where you have got a DES chip, microprocessor, battery and so on, potted in a tamper-sensing core with alarm circuits around it.

What are the vulnerabilities of such products?

Many of the kinds of vulnerability we had in the 80's were to do with maintenance access. The maintenance engineer would go in to change the battery; he could then disable the tamper-sensing; and he could then go back on his next visit and take out the keys. That got fixed. The way to fix it was to take the batteries outside the device, as you can see in the photo of the 4758 in figure 1. Then there is nothing user-serviceable inside the device, so as soon as you penetrate the tamper-sensing membrane the thing dies irrevocably – it becomes a door-stop.

Fig. 1. – The IBM 4758 cryptoprocessor (courtesy of Steve Weingart)

We've more or less got to the point that the hardware can be trusted. We deal with the problem of whether the software can be trusted by getting FIPS 140-1 evaluation done by independent laboratories that sign a non-disclosure agreement and then go through the source code. That may be enough in some cases and not enough in others, but that isn't the subject of this talk.

2   Cryptoprocessor Transaction Sets

What I'm interested in is the command set that the cryptographic device itself uses. We have up till now, in this community, been looking at what happens in protocols where Alice and Bob exchange messages, and you need to contemplate only three or four possible types of message.

In the real world, things are much harder. If Alice and Bob are using tamper-resistant hardware, then they have got boxes that may support dozens or even hundreds of transactions. And we are assuming that Alice and Bob are untrustworthy – perhaps not all the time, perhaps you're just worried about a virus taking over Alice's PC – but perhaps Alice is simultaneously your customer and your enemy, in which case you can expect a more or less continuous threat.

2.1   Early Transaction Sets – CUSP

Let me review quickly how cryptographic processor instruction sets developed. The first one that's widely documented is IBM's CUSP, which came in in 1980 in the PCF product, and shortly after that in the 3848 [8]. This was a device the size of a water-softener that hung off your mainframe on a channel cable. It was designed to do things like bulk file encryption, using keys that were protected in tamper-sensing memory.

What IBM wanted to do was to provide some useful protection for these keys. If you merely have a device which will, on demand, encrypt or decrypt with a key that is held in its memory, then it doesn't seem to do you much good. Anybody who can access the device can do the encrypting and the decrypting.

So there began to be a realization that we want, in some way or another, to limit what various keys can be used for. Although the details are slightly more complex than the subset I'm giving here, the idea that IBM had was that you can divide keys into different types, and some keys can be local keys and other keys can be remote keys. How they did this was to have three master keys for the device – basically one master key and two offsets that would be XORed with it to create dependent master-keys. A key that was encrypted with the main master key, you can think of that as a blue key, and a key that was encrypted with variant KMH_0 you might think of as a green key, and a key that was encrypted with variant KMH_1 you might think of as a red key.

Now few people go through this documentation [7], because the IBM terminology and notation in it are absolutely horrible. But by starting to think in terms of key typing, or key colours, you can start to make much progress.

One of the goals that IBM tried to achieve with the 3848 was to protect for host-terminal communications using a session key which is never available in the clear, and which therefore has no street value. (This was an NSA concern at the time, because of their various staff members who had been selling key material to the Russians.) So how do you protect communication between a mainframe and its terminal?

The implementation was that you had a host transaction ECPH, which would take a green key – that is a session key enciphered under KMH0 – and a message m, and it would, in the trusted hardware, get its hands on this green key by deciphering it under KMH0, and then apply it to encipher the message m.

ECPH: $\{KS\}_{KMHO}, m \longrightarrow \{m\}_{KS}$

So you had a means of using the green key to encipher messages, and 'can encipher with green key' is a property of CUSP. Similarly, you can decypher with a green key, because can supply K_S enciphered under KMH_0 and a message enciphered under K_S and you will get back m.

How do you go about generating keys?

The technique is to supply a random number, or a serial number – or any value that you like, in fact – and use the device to decypher that under KMH0 to get a green key. In other words, the external enciphered keys that you hold on your database are just numbers that you thought up somehow. They are then 'decyphered' and used as keys.

Then you've got a more sensitive transaction, 'reformat to master key' (RFMK), which will take a master-key for a terminal – which is set up by an out-of-band technique – and K_S encrypted under KMH0, and it will encypher the session key under the master-key for the terminal.

RFMK: $\{KS\}_{KMHO}, KMT \longrightarrow \{KS\}_{KMT}$

So we've got another type of key, a red key I've called it, which is assumed to be held in the terminal. At the terminal, which is a different piece of hardware with different syntax, you've got a transaction DMK which will take a session key encyphered under KMT, and the clear value of KMT which is held in the hardware; it will give you a value of K_S which can then be used to do the decryption. (There isn't any hardware protection on the syntax of crypto in the terminal, because it is assumed that if you have physical access to the terminal then you can use the keys in it.)

Now this isn't all of the implementation, because there are other things that you need to do. You need to be able to manage keys, and (most confusingly of all) you need to be able to manage peer-to-peer communication between mainframes, which was being brought in at the time. So you end up having transactions to set up a key that is a local key at one mainframe and a remote key at the other mainframe. The IBM view at the time was that this made public-key cryptography unnecessary, because DES was so much faster and you needed tamper-resistant hardware anyway, so whay not just have local keys and remote keys? They have got the same functionality.

What went wrong with this? Well, it was very difficult to understand or explain, because the terminology they used is very complex. All sorts of implementation errors resulted. People found that it was simpler just to use blue keys which are all-powerful, rather than to mess around trying to separate keys into red and green and then finding that various things they wanted to do couldn't be done.

Nobody really figured out how to use this CUSP system to protect PINs properly as they were being sent from one bank to another. For example, a PIN from another bank's customer would come in from your cash machine, so you would decypher it and then re-encypher it with a key you shared with VISA for onward transmission. There were one or two hacks with which people tried to prevent PINs being available in clear in the host mainframe – such as treating PINs as keys – but for various reasons they didn't really work.

2.2   Banking Security Modules

So the next generation of security hardware to come along. The VISA security module, for example, takes the concept a bit further. They've actually got about five or six different colours of key.

The basic idea is that the security module is generating the PIN for a cash machine, by encrypting the account number using a key known as the PIN key. The result is then decimalised, and either given to the customer directly or added to an 'offset' on the customer's card to give the PIN that they must actually enter:

```
Account number:        8807012345691715
PIN key:               FEFEFEFEFEFEFEFE
Result of DES:         A2CE126C69AEC82D
Result decimalised:    0224126269042823
Natural PIN:           0224
Offset:                6565
Customer PIN:          6789
```

So you start off with keys which *never* decrypt, such as the PIN key KP, and you also have keys which *can* decrypt. Now the PIN key is a 'red key', a key which can never decrypt, and keys of this type are also used to protect PINs locally. (For example, when a PIN is encrypted at a cash machine for central verification, then the key used to perform this encryption is treated as a red key by the security module.) You can pass the security module a PIN which has been encrypted under a red key and it will say whether the PIN was right or not. The green key operates like a normal crypto key; you use it for computing MACs on messages and stuff like that.

So you use a red key to compute the PIN from the primary account number (PAN), and you use a red key to encipher the PIN from the ATM to the host security module. The whole thing works because nothing that's ever been encrypted under a red key is supposed to leak out – except the fraction of a bit per time that comes out from the PIN verification step. Then you add various support transactions, like 'generate terminal master key component', 'XOR two terminal master key components together to get a terminal master key' and so on and so forth.

What's the security policy enforced by the set of transactions that the security module provides? Well, it doesn't quite do Bell-LaPadula, because if you think of the red keys as being High, it allows an information flow from High to Low – about whether a PIN at High is right or not. So you need an external mechanism to track how many PIN retries have there been on an account, and if there's been more than three or 12 or whatever your limit is, then you freeze the account.

It doesn't quite do Clark-Wilson either, because you can generate master key components and XOR them together, and there's no system level protection for separation of duties on these two master key components; that's part of manual procedure. But the security module is moving somewhat in the direction of Bell-LaPadula and Clark-Wilson (although its evolution went down a different path).

Once you network many banks together, you've got further requirements. You've got one type of key used to encrypt a PIN on the link between the cash machine and the security module of the acquiring bank; you've got another type of key being used between the acquiring bank and VISA; another type of key being used between VISA and the issuing bank; then you've got the top level master keys which VISA shares with banks, and so on. You can think of these as being all of different colours.

So you've got all these various types of key, and you've got more and more complex transactions; the VISA security module now has about 60 different transactions in its transaction set. You've got support transactions, such as translating different PIN formats. You also have got potential hacks which I will come to later.

So the concern with something like the VISA box is: "Is there some combination of these 60-odd transactions, which if issued in the right order will actually spit out a clear-text PIN?" The designers' goal was that there were supposed to be one or two – in order to generate PINs for customers and keys for ATMs, for example – but they all involve trusted transactions that involve entering a supervisor password or turning a metal key in a lock. So the issue of trusted subjects is supposedly tied down.

2.3   The IBM 4758 Security Module Product

Now we come to the more modern IBM product, the 4758. There's another picture of a 4758 in figure 2 with the shielding slightly removed. You can see a protective mesh here, a circuit board inside it behind a metal can, and the sensors here will alarm if you try to cut through (you can see the little sensor lines there). So what does this actually achieve? Well, assuming that the tamper-protection works (and it appears to), the software most people run on it – IBM's Common Cryptographic Architecture (CCA) – introduces a quite general concept of typing, namely control vectors.

A control vector can be thought of as a string bound to each key. The physical implementation of this is that you encipher the key under a different variant of a master key, but that's irrelevant at the level of abstraction that's useful to think about here. You can think of each key as going into the machine with a little tag attached to it saying, "I am a green key", "I am a red key", "I am a key of type 3126", or whatever. By default, CCA provides ten different types: there is a data key; there's a data translation key; there's a MAC key; there's a PIN generation key; there's an incoming PIN encryption key; and so on. There are somewhat over 100 different transactions supplied with CCA that operate using these key types. In addition, you can define your own key types and roll your own transactions. You can download the details from the Web, all 400 and whatever pages of it [7], so the target is public domain.

Even if you use the standard default types, there are some very obscure issues that are left to the designer. There are some possible hacks, or at least unclear

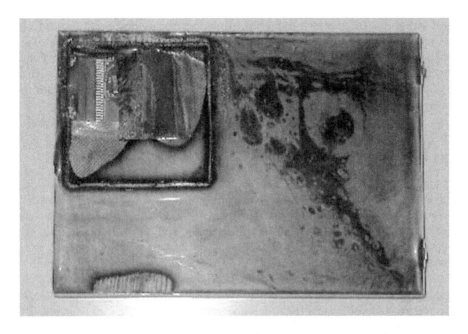

Fig. 2. – The 4758 partially opened – showing (from top left downwards) the circuitry, aluminium electromagnetic shielding, tamper sensing mesh and potting material (courtesy of Frank Stajano)

things, such as if people decrypt rubbish and use it, or if people use the wrong type of key, then can you gain some kind of advantage? Well keys supposedly have parity, so you have to decrypt on average about 32,000 'wrong' keys before you get one that works, but there have been attacks in the past which have used this [6]. Do any of these attacks work on the 4758?

Also, in the typing structure, we find that some of these types have got fairly explicit limitations (such as whether export is allowed or not), and you've got some types of types. But there's also a load of stuff that appears to be left more or less implicit, or at the very least has no supplied formal model.

You have got backward-compatibility modes. The 4758 will do everything that the old 3848 would do: it will do the ECPH, DCPH, re-format to master key, all that stuff, so you get free documentation of the obsolete equipment in the new equipment. You have things that approximate to the VISA transactions.

You also have a claim that the instruction set is comprehensive. Now this makes me feel rather uneasy, because the whole reason that I'm paying out all this money for a security processor is that its instruction set should *not* be comprehensive. There should be some things that it is simply not possible to do with it, and these things should be clearly understood.

So how did the current design come about? Well it should now be clear. We started off with the 3848, and that was not enough for banking so someone (actually Carl Campbell) invented the VISA security module. Then IBM saw itself losing market share to the VSM, so it does the embrace-and-expand play and incorporates the VSM functionality in the 4753. This evolves into the 4758, which was then used for things like prepayment electricity meters [3]. People then invented i-buttons and smartcards, yet more applications with which IBM's product line had to be compatible. Roger's phrase, "the inevitable evolution of the Swiss army knife", is very appropriate.

3   Verifying Crypto Transaction Sets

So how can you be sure that there isn't some chain of 17 transactions which will leak a clear key? I've actually got some experience of this, because with a security module that I designed there was one particular banking customer who said, we need a transaction to translate PINs. They were upgrading all of their customers to longer account numbers, and they didn't want to change the customers' PINs because they were afraid that this would decrease the number of people using their credit cards in cash machines. So they said, "We'd like to supply two account numbers, an old account number and a new account number, plus a PIN, and you return the difference between the old PIN and the new PIN so we can write that as an offset onto the card track."

So I said, "Fine – we'll code that up. But be warned: this transaction is dangerous. Remove this version of the software as soon as you've done that batch job." Of course they didn't, and about a year and a half later one of their programmers realised: "Hey – if I put in my account number and the MD's account number and my PIN, the machine then tells me what I've got to subtract from my PIN in order to get the MD's PIN!" Luckily for the bank, he went to the boss and told all; to which our response was, "We told you, why didn't you do as you were told?" (This episode is described in [5].)

So managing this kind of thing isn't as straightforward as you might think. As I mentioned, we have got no proper formal model of what goes on in a device like this. Although it has some flavours of Bell-LaPadula and some flavours of Clark-Wilson, it doesn't really behave according to either model; there are leaks at the edges. This brings us to all the research opportunities, which aren't necessarily 'insurmountable' but are, I suspect, a step change more difficult than the attacks on protocols that people have being doing up to now.

The first opportunity is to find an attack on the 4758. Find some property of the manual which even IBM will be forced to admit was not something they had in mind when they designed it. Alternatively prove that it's secure (though given the history of provable security, that's perhaps just as damning). Or, more practically, provide a tool that enables the designer to use the 4758 safely. Up until now, the IBM philosophy appears to have been: "We're selling you an F15 and you had jolly well better let us sell you a pilot and a maintenance crew and all the rest of it at the same time." They are not alone in this respect; BBN and all the other vendors appear to take the same view.

So you find that you can go and buy a set of tamper-resistant hardware boxes for maybe $2,000 each, but if you are a bank and you are building an actual installation using them, such as a certification authority, the outlay at the end of the day is more likely to be a quarter of a million dollars. By the time you've paid for the all the consultancy, and the machines they security modules will be attached to, and the firewalls to protect these machines from the network, and the procedures, and the training, and all the rest of it, the cost of the tamper-resistant box itself is essentially trivial.

So if anybody else is interested in getting into the systems integration business and getting that $240,000 instead of funneling it to IBM, then the competitive advantage might consist in having a suitable tool. Now it's not just the 4758! I use that as the target because we don't know how to break its physical tamper resistance, but there are many other architectures where you get a defined set of crypto transactions that may in fact be quite extensible. Those that come to mind are Microsoft CAPI, Intel CDSA – there's dozens out there.

This is definitely more difficult than doing verification of crypto protocols – and more interesting I think – because this is the real world problem. Somebody who has got a penetration of your corporate network is not trying to attack Kerberos, he's trying to attack the boxes that contain the Kerberos keys. Those boxes will do 50 transactions, of which you might normally use only three or four. But the others are there and available, unless you find some way of switching them off in a particular application, which again brings together a whole new set of design issues. So what's the nature of a crypto transaction set in general, and how do you go about verifying it?

Next question: how do you relate its properties to a higher level security policy model, such as Bell-LaPadula? And where this I suppose leads to, from the theory and semantics point of view, is whether you can get a general theory of restricted computation of computers that can do some things but cannot – absolutely, definitely, provably, cannot – do other things. Is there such a language that is complete in the sense that you can express any worthwhile crypto transaction set in it? What do you have to add to mathematics in order to get the expressiveness of metal? In the RIP-stop application it may very well be that provable destruction of a key is all you need, and anything else can be built on top of that given various external services such as perhaps secure time. But provable destruction of a key doesn't seem obviously related to what's going on in banking, because a typical bank is still running with the same ATM keys that they set up in 1985 when VISA set up the ACDS network. Key expiration just doesn't come into their universe.

And finally, if you're going to develop such a language, it would be useful if it could deal with public key stuff as well, such as homomorphic attacks, blinding, and so on. Because if you're going to build a machine which will, for example, not decrypt the same PGP message twice, then you have got somehow to make sure that the bad guys don't send you a message which is an old message which has been blinded so it looks like a new message.

Matt Blaze: I was surprised by your early comment – which I realise was a throwaway – that tamper-resistant hardware appears to be almost done, so let's move on to the next thing. It seems to me that tamper-resistant hardware if anything has become increasingly tenuous of late, particularly with respect to the use of out-of-band attacks such as power analysis and timing attacks. Things have been made even more difficult by putting the power supply outside of the box. Do you think once Paul Kocher gets his hands on one of these IBM boxes and hooks up his spectrum analyser to it that that's the end?

Reply: In the case of the IBM product I don't think so, because they've got a reasonably convincing proof (in the electrical engineering sense) that this can't happen. They filter the power lines into the device in such a way that all the interesting signals, given the frequencies that they're at inside the box, are attenuated more than 100 dBs. I agree that there is a serious problem with smartcards, but we've got a project going on that, we believe it to be fixable. We discuss this in a paper at a VLSI conference recently [9]. What we're proposing to do is to use self-timed dual-rail logic, so that the current that is consumed by doing a computation is independent of the data that is being operated on. You can do various other things as well; you can see to it that no single transistor failure will result in an output, and so on. In fact the NSA already uses dual-rail for resilience rather than power-analysis reasons. So there are technologies coming along that can fix the power analysis problem.

When I say that hardware tamper-resistance has been done, what I'm actually saying is that we can see our way to products on the shelf in five or seven years time that will fix the kind of things that Paul Kocher has been talking about.

John Ioannidis: The kind of tamper-resistance you seem to analyse here is not the sort of tamper resistance I'm likely to find in my wallet or my key-ring. It's more like the sort of tamper-resistance you find in a big box somewhere. Maybe that big box is sitting on my desk, or under my desk, but it's not going to be sitting on my person.

Reply: Wrong. The logical complexity that I've described here is independent of the physical size of the device. You consider the kind of SIM card that's likely to appear, with added-on transactions to support an electronic purse, and you're already looking at the same scale of complexity as a VISA security module. You're looking at much more difficult management problems, because you have got independent threads of trust: the phone company trusts its K_c and the bank trusts its EMV keys, and how do these devices interact within the smartcard itself? It suddenly becomes very hairy and we don't at present have the tools to deal with it.

Virgil Gligor: How many 4758s did IBM sell, do you know what proportion were penetrated relative to NT or Windows 98, or any of the things that you have on your desk?

Reply: They're selling of the order of a couple of thousand a year, I'm aware of only one penetration which occurred – during testing as a result of a manufacturing defect.

I assume that an NT box, or for that matter a Linux box, can be penetrated by somebody who knows what he's doing, and so you must assume that the host to which your security module is attached belongs to the enemy, even if only from time to time.

(Indistinct question)

Reply: It's useful in security to separate design assurance from implementation assurance and from strength of mechanism. Now the strength of mechanism of the tamper-resistance mechanisms in 4758s are very much higher than a smartcard, and a smartcard is very much higher than an NT server, but that's a separate lecture course.

What I'm concerned about here is the logical complexity of the set of commands which you issue to your tamper resistant device, be it a smartcard, or an NT server, or a 4758, because if you screwed up somehow in the design of those, then it doesn't matter how much steel and how many capacitors and how many seismometers and how many men with guns you've got. You're dead.

(Indistinct question)

Reply: We brought the designer of the 4758 over and we grilled him for a day, and we've looked at the things partially dismantled, and we've got one or two off-the-wall ideas about how you might conceivably, if you spent a million bucks building equipment, have a go at it. But we don't have any practical ideas that we could offer to a corporation and say, "Give us a million bucks and with a better than 50% chance we'll have the keys out in a year." The 4758 is hard!

John Ioannidis: What kind of primitives am I going to be offloading on to tamper-proof hardware so that no matter what kind of penetration my NT box has, there won't be an order for a billion dollars to be transferred from somewhere else to my account without my consent, so I can't get framed for fraud.

Reply: The sort of thing that hardware boxes are traditionally used for is to protect the PIN key, the key that generates all the PINs of the eleven million customers in your bank, because if a bad guy gets hold of that you've had it, you have to re-issue your cards and PINs. The sort of thing that you can use a 4758 for in a high-value corporate environment is to see to it that a transaction will only go out signed with the great seal of Barclays Bank (or whatever) provided – let's say – in the case of a $100m transaction, at least two managers of grade 4 or above have signed it using the signing keys and their smartcards. You can set up a system involving the 4758 and the smartcards which will distribute the keys, manage the certificates, and then will basically enforce your Clark-Wilson policy.

John Ioannidis: I'm not a grade 4 manager at Goldman Sachs, or whatever they're called, Suppose I'm a poor AT&T employee, and I have a box on my desk and I do my banking transactions over it, and I have somewhere a key given me by the bank, or I created my own, or both, and I have a tamper-resistant device which I want to use to secure my transaction. Now the question is, what kind of operations should that thing support, and what kind of interface to me, that does not go through NT or Linux, so that a transaction could not be made without my personal, physical approval – not my electronic approval. This is also a hard problem.

Reply: Agreed. But it's not the problem I'm addressing. Many people have talked about signature tablets that will display text; you put your thumb print, for example, to OK this text and this is supposed to give you a high degree of non-repudiation. But that's a different problem; it's not the problem that interests me in the context of this talk.

Michael Roe: What Ross is deliberately ignoring is the effect of successful tamper-resistance. If you have a very secure transaction in a very physically secure processor then the attacker is going to attack the software that goes in between the user interface and the secure box.

Reply: In this talk what I'm interested in is the command set that you use to drive a tamper resistant device and how you go about defining that in a way that's sensible – and assuring yourself that the design holds up. (I'm talking about design assurance not about the human computer interface aspects.)

(Indistinct question)

Reply: There have been attacks on early pay TV systems where there were protocol failures in the smartcard. Now if you believe Gemplus figures that by 2003 there will be 1.4 billion microprocessor cards sold a year (and as the biggest OEM they should know about that) then clearly it is important in engineering and industrial and economic terms, as well as being a problem that's directly related to protocol verification. That's the reason why I bring it to this audience. It is a protocol problem; but it's the next step up in difficulty. And it's sufficiently different that there's an awful lot of new research for people to do, and, hopefully, new theories to discover.

(Indistinct question)

Reply: I'm interested in Clark-Wilson-type objects and Bell-LaPadula-type objects, because that's where the real world is. The usual objection to Clark-Wilson is, "Where's the TCB?" Now as an example application, banking security modules are 90% of the way towards a Clark-Wilson TCB, so this should also be of scientific interest.

(Indistinct question)

Reply: An awful lot of design effort is believed to be about to go into multi-function smartcards, where you've got a SIM card sitting in your WAP device, and into which signed applets can be downloaded by your bank, by your insurance company, by your health care provider, etc.

(Indistinct question)

Reply: Now separability is not the only issue here, there's the correctness of the transactions that people can issue, and whether the applications themselves can be sabotaged by somebody just issuing the right commands in order.

(Indistinct question)

Reply: Even if you can download these applets safely, the applets will have to talk to each other in many cases for it to be useful. For example, if you're going to use your WAP device to pay for hospital treatment, by transferring money from your electronic purse to your health card, then that involves having interfaces that allow transactions between the two, and that's hard to do.

References

1. RJ Anderson, *'Security Engineering – a Guide to Building Dependable Distributed Systems'*, Wiley (2001) ISBN 0-471-38922-6
2. RJ Anderson, "Why Cryptosystems Fail" in *Communications of the ACM* vol 37 no 11 (November 1994) pp 32–40; earlier version at `http://www.cl.cam.ac.uk/users/rja14/wcf.html`
3. RJ Anderson, SJ Bezuidenhoudt, "On the Reliability of Electronic Payment Systems", in *IEEE Transactions on Software Engineering* vol 22 no 5 (May 1996) pp 294–301; `http://www.cl.cam.ac.uk/ftp/users/rja14/meters.ps.gz`
4. RJ Anderson, MG Kuhn, "Tamper Resistance – a Cautionary Note", in *Proceedings of the Second Usenix Workshop on Electronic Commerce* (Nov 96) pp 1–11; `http://www.cl.cam.ac.uk/users/rja14/tamper.html`
5. RJ Anderson, MG Kuhn, "Low Cost Attacks on Tamper Resistant Devices", in *Security Protocols – Proceedings of the 5th International Workshop* (1997) Springer LNCS vol 1361 pp 125–136
6. M Blaze, "Protocol Failure in the Escrowed Encryption Standard", in *Second ACM Conference on Computer and Communications Security*, 2–4 November 1994, Fairfax, Va; proceedings published by the ACM ISBN 0-89791-732-4, pp 59–67; at `http://www.crypto.com/papers/`
7. IBM, *'IBM 4758 PCI Cryptographic Coprocessor – CCA Basic Services Reference and Guide*, Release 1.31 for the IBM 4758-001, available through `http://www.ibm.com/security/cryptocards/`
8. CH Meyer, SM Matyas, *'Cryptography: A New Dimension in Computer Data Security'*, Wiley, 1982
9. SW Moore, RJ Anderson, MG Kuhn, "Improving Smartcard Security using Self-timed Circuit Technology", Fourth ACiD-WG Workshop, Grenoble, ISBN 2-913329-44-6, 2000; at `http://www.g3card.com/`
10. GJ Simmons, "How to Insure that Data Acquired to Verify Treaty Compliance are Trustworthy", GJ Simmons, *Proceedings of the IEEE* v 76 no 5 (1988)

Micro-management of Risk
in a Trust-Based Billing System
(Transcript of Discussion)

AT&T Laboratories Research

What I am going to talk about is a micro billing system we've developed at the labs, which uses a trust management system, KeyNote[1], to do risk management in a micro billing application.

Micro billing is one of many ways of getting money for very low value transactions. By very low value I mean things that cost from about a Euro[2] down to a thousandth of a Euro or even lower. There are some problems with very low value transactions which don't exist when you're doing higher value transactions – where you buy $10 worth of petrol with a credit card, or you transfer several billion dollars to your money laundering account in Switzerland. And the constraints are, you have very low margins of profit: something that costs a cent, even if you have 50% profit, it's only half a cent profit.

Now of course you may be selling billions of those, in which case you have billions of those half cents, but still it's an issue. Also because the cost is so low the per transaction risk is low, so you don't really care if you miss a few transactions. If you're providing content over your Web page and you're charging a tenth of a cent for every ten pages, if some of those queries don't actually get paid eventually you may not care all that much, you're making it up in volume. You also have many customers. Newspapers cost half a Euro each or whatever, and these are very low value transactions, but there are lots and lots of customers who buy newspapers every morning. It's also interesting to mention that newspapers don't really make their money from the actual money paid by the customers who buy them, but that's another issue.

And you also may have lots of different policies on how you charge, and how you get paid for, this low value transaction depending on what you're buying: soda[3] from a vending machine, or petrol, or a newspaper, or you're buying content over the Web. We have an easy and very common method for performing low value transactions and I'll give you some examples.

This is an example, this is one penny and I can make a low value, actually I don't know if I can buy anything for one penny but for a few of them I can buy something.

Audience: Can I have the penny to do a field trial?

Reply: No, you can't have it.

---

[1] LNCS 1550, pp 59–63.

[2] Let's be non-nationalistic here.

[3] Soda is what we call carbonated drinks in the north east coast of the United States.

B. Christianson et al. (Eds.): Security Protocols, LNCS 2133, pp. 142–154, 2001.
© Springer-Verlag Berlin Heidelberg 2001

Now, we have a method for low value transactions, it's called cash, and for really low value transactions it's called coins and they have some interesting properties. They have all the nice properties of money which is they are hard to forge and they have intrinsic value and if I give you a one penny coin I transfer value from me to you and now you can use it in any way you want, and there are lots of ways that you can use them to buy stuff. You can give them to a person and they count it, and then they will give you goods, or you can walk up to a vending machine and put them in the slot and goods will be dropped, hopefully. However, you can't really have a coin collection box next to the computer and drop in one penny at a time when you try to buy content. This has been tried in the past where you would buy, for instance, your refrigerator over a period of a couple of years by having a coin box next to it that you would put a dime at a time, and after the refrigerator had been paid off with who knows how many dimes, that would be collected every month by the dime collector, the refrigerator was yours. But this is not a very agreeable thing to have to do when you are buying content over the net, you have to have a box to drop coins in, and the question is who comes to collect the coins? All a problem that you really don't want to deal with.

So we may not want to use cash for some kinds of transactions. Another reason we may not want to use cash is that cash has overheads. It's estimated that the cost of doing a transaction with cash is about 6% of the value of the transaction. That's because cash has lots of handling costs, it may not have handling costs to you when you have £100 in your pocket, but the supermarket that has at the end of the day hundreds, or thousands, or tens of thousands of pounds in its tills, has to have the armoured car come over and carry the money to the bank, and somebody has to count it, and all that process is actually expensive, it doesn't come for free. So even though intrinsic value is transferred when I give you a bank note or a bill or a coin, the transaction that occurs there has a hidden cost for the handling of the cash; so it's not free.

What are some other means of doing transactions? One is cheques, and we'll come back to that in a moment, another one is credit cards. Credit cards are fine and dandy for transactions of about $10 and up, maybe even a little bit lower, but there is a fixed cost in doing a credit card transaction that for very low value transactions is just not worth it. It's not worth going through the hassle of authenticating a credit card transaction to buy a newspaper, or to buy a cookie, or even to buy soda from a vending machine.

Billing systems for small amounts, which is what we call micro billing, are of interest to lots of vendors and clients, especially with the Web being what it is and all sorts of other applications coming up. What we really want to avoid is having to do on-line transactions, or on-line verification of certificates, and with due respect to Ross, we want avoid tamper resistant hardware if we can.

Now that I've set up the stage, here is what I want to present. You all remember KeyNote, at least I will assume this is the case, and we've devised a system we call KeyNote micro-cheques to do our micro billing. The benefits here are that we can have off-line transactions, when I actually buy something with a

KeyNote micro-cheque I don't have to be on the network and the vendor doesn't have to be on the network, it happens completely off-line. However, eventually both I and the vendor, at some point, have to get on the net and transfer data but that can happen when it's convenient for me and when it's convenient for the vendor, and that can be in the middle of the night when network traffic is low. It can happen once a month as opposed to every second. It can happen when accounts are set up, it can happen when bills are cleared and cheques are cleared, it can happen when, for instance, the gas truck comes to fill up to the tanks in the gas station[4], it can happen when the maintenance person comes to refill the vending machine, it can happen whenever you want; the point is it doesn't have to happen on-line.

The idea is that we have the electronic equivalent of a cheque. Now why we chose this model as opposed to something else is a different story and you can ask me in private, but the decision was made to go for the metaphor of a cheque for our micro billing system as opposed to any other metaphor such as anonymous cash or small coins. What these cheques really are is short-lived credentials that I issue to my vendor. When I want to buy something from Matt's vending machine I will write an electronic cheque (we'll see how I actually write this later) that says, pay to the order of Matt the sum of 50p for today's date for a product that he dispensed today. Matt will collect a whole bunch of those and we'll see how he can deposit them, and we'll also see how I can pay for my account. The important thing here is that there is a "bank". We put the bank in quotes because it can be a single entity or it can be a conglomerate of entities talking to each other, which has a relationship with me the payer and all the other payers, and also has a relationship with vendors.

The micro billing system is based on our trust management language and the reasons for that will become obvious further down the talk. The idea is that, because we are basing this on the trust management language, we can control how much risk we put in every stage of the system in a very fine grained way, by changing the precise nature of the credentials we issue.

A rough sketch of the architecture of the system. There are payers and there are vendors who communicate all the time and they communicate off-line. By off-line I mean they communicate without having to talk to anybody else, they only have to be able to talk to each other. And there is this thing I call the bank, which is really composed of smaller entities, it's composed of an agent which provisions the payers and the vendors, and gives them the ability to carry on these transactions in such a way that they will trust each other, or believe each other, I don't want to use the word trust. There is another agent which acts as a clearing house for these micro-cheques and makes sure that they haven't been replayed, that they haven't been forged, that they haven't been copied over and over and sent to all different places. When this clearing happens, as a result of the vendors depositing the cheques to the clearing agent, there is no direct communication from the payer to the clearing agent. The clearing agent will verify these cheques and deposit the relevant amounts in the vendors banks and

---

[4] At the petrol station.

if there is only one bank it's just a matter of transferring accounts; we know how to do this, and we are going to bill the payers.

Now these two steps, which are actually the hardest steps in any kind of billing system, can be piggy backed on existing systems. We know how to debit accounts in other people's banks, and there are lots of companies, my employer being one of them, who have a lot of infrastructure to bill for very small amounts of money. Whenever I get my phone bill there is a detailed list of all the five and ten cent (and sometimes $10 and $100) transactions of these phone calls I have made with my carrier (which happens to be AT&T), and then I write one lump cheque or I can arrange for that money to be transferred directly from my account to AT&T and everything is settled. So another idea here is that we should be able to piggy back on existing billing infrastructures.

A fundamental problem of all these new suggested micro payment systems that have been proposed is that they require new kinds of billing infrastructures and new kinds of payment infrastructures, and this is just not going to happen unless there is a very compelling reason. So I think we can get a large advantage by designing a system that can piggy back on an existing infrastructure, and not requiring a new way of doing business.

I will describe the most interesting part, which is what this transaction looks like, in terms of a prototype, a demo we built in AT&T labs, which involves a vending machine, a soda machine, this monster about yea wide and yea high and yea deep, which sits right behind Matt's chair and annoys him every day for the last two years, right Matt? I built some circuitry to drive the relays and listen to the buttons and it's connected to a Linux box which also talks over an infra-red transceiver to a Palm pilot. One eventual use for this could be for cell phones with an infra-red interface, which most modern cell phones have, because they have a substantial amount of computational power to do all the DSP and crypto already necessary for its day to day operation. Also it's something pretty much everybody carries with them, or will be shortly. Cell phones are the obvious thing to use. If anyone has an API for programming cell phones, we would love to see it.

So the idea is that I walk up to the vending machine, whose diet cola is button number 2, I press button number 2, a little LED flashes, I pick up my Palm pilot or my cell phone, I point at it, and on my screen I get this message that says, you have ordered a diet cola for fifty cents, shall I pay? At that point I can press 1 for yes, or 2 for no. I decide to press 1 for yes, and a few seconds later, a diet cola drops in the collection bucket, I pick it up and I drink it and I'm happy and at the end of the month I look at my phone bill and there is a charge for fifty cents for a diet cola which I bought on 4 April from that vending machine, and I'm happy.

Larry Paulson: I'm not sure the phone bill is the right analogy, the thing about the telephone companies is that you have an account with them and you spend lots of money, even if only five or ten cents at a time, so you have just a few people that you buy things from. I ask whether that model will work if you have somebody who only buys one thing from each vendor, is it worthwhile for that vendor to sell to them this way?

Reply: Presumably that vendor is not only doing business with me, he's doing business with thousands of customers who may only buy one thing from them at a time, but they're still doing business with them.

Audience: Sure they'll be making a lot of business but unless the overhead is small, he'll actually being losing money.

Bruce Christianson: The question is whether there's more overhead per transaction than in the case where all the transactions are with the same vendor.

Reply: The answer is no, there is exactly the same overhead. Anyway the question is not about whether this is a valid business proposal, we have people looking at this.

Ross Anderson: We built a very similar system in 1991. We found that we could not leverage off the existing cheque clearance system because it was too expensive. It was locked into large numbers of contracts between different banks, and you would end up paying several dollars for a cheque at the high end for clearing. We wanted a maximum charge of a few tens of cents, and so we ended up building separate clearing houses, separate buildings, separate machines, a completely redesigned infrastructure from scratch, and I'm not sure if I would leverage off the existing infrastructure.

Reply: Well a leverage of the existing infrastructure for interfacing with a bank. The clearing agent which is receiving all the cheques and cashing them for themselves would have to build infrastructure to actually understand the packets they're getting, and going from that to summing up amounts based on account numbers and debiting accounts and crediting accounts once a month or once every two months, is not a considerable overhead. But the clearing agent is not depositing individual paper cheques to the banks where they originated from, with all the overheads intrinsic in a paper cheque .

Ross Anderson: Sure, so the only way you're using the existing infrastructure is that you're using the facility to send direct debits to people with accounts every month.

Reply: Correct. Also I'm using the infrastructure that already exists in phone companies and other such firms, that have business relationships and – let's say it – trust relationships in the human meaning of the word trust; that they're not going to defraud. It's very easy for me to keep a precise record of all the transactions I make, just like it's very easy to keep a record of all the phone calls I make, but in practice I don't, and I trust that when AT&T says I made this phone call to Greece, I actually did.

Wenbo Mao: But phone companies providing soft drinks ...?

Reply: We don't want to sell soda, we just want to bill you for soda. We want somebody else to sell it to you and we'll arrange for them to get the money. Just like VISA is not selling you computers, VISA is just selling you the facility of being able to pay for a computer you buy, and collecting money for it. How we charge for it is not clear, we leave that for the business people to figure out. The idea is that you either charge by the transaction, and you charge less than VISA would charge because it's sold on, presumably because we have risk management strategies that are better or I don't know what. Or we charge the vendor for having the facility not to have to collect cash. If cash cost them 6% and Amex would cost them 4% maybe we can charge 3.9% and they would prefer us. Or maybe we charge by displaying ads on your cell phone every time you make a purchase. Maybe we should strike that from the record, I don't want to give anyone ideas.

Audience: I don't know about here, but in Finland the phone companies more or less already know. They are becoming banks and they have to face the law that regulates the banks because they are doing this kind of thing, and that might really be a problem for your proposal as well.

Reply: Well I don't want this to be a billing talk, I'd much rather this stay a security talk and there is a lot of security here that I haven't talked about yet. I understand that there is a lot of general interest in this subject but I'd like to go back to the security protocols involved rather than the business applications. There is some early indication that there is a lot of business interest in this.

Virgil Gligor: Actually many of the phone companies are already in the business of marking bills for a lot of other small companies. The question that I have before we move on is, why do you think the banks would be willing to pay a middleman 3.9% if the banks were taking the risks. Are you taking any risks in this transaction? If you charge 3.9% then this system must take some risks off the banks back, to give the banks an incentive to use this system.

Reply: Yes, the risk I'm taking is that after I credit the vendor that the customer is going to default on me and not pay me. But the banks don't enter into the picture of using the system, the banks don't even see the system. What the banks see is that people who hold accounts with them receive money in those accounts and other people who hold accounts with them are debited. The banks don't enter into the transactions.

Bruce Christianson: What happens if I press button one and then I don't get my cola?

Reply: The same thing that happens if you press button one after you've put in a one dollar coin and your cola doesn't come back, nothing: you lose. There is an 800 number that you call and complain and then it's up to the customer care department to see if they believe you or not, and most of the time they believe you, but you can do the same thing here, that just does not enter into the protocol. You can call them on your phone and incur extra income for the wireless provider.

Matt Blaze: Forget for a minute that he works for a phone company, we designed this from the point of view of that this is an interesting way of integrating the concept of risk management and trust management, and we're kind of trying to sell it to our employer as something that we could get involved in and JI forgot that he doesn't work for any of you people.

Reply: Let's get on with the protocol. I used the term bank to make the presentation simpler, but I think it made it more complicated. All right, wait. Suppose we relabel "bank" as "the Mafia", would that be any better?

We all know what an electronic cheque looks like: I, N, must pay to the order of, etc, and then after I press one on my cell-phone (and this is not a transaction that's going over the air, this is just a transaction that's going over the infra-red port), what I'm transmitting to the vending machine is a certificate, a credential from the Mafia, that says that I am good for issuing cheques for today for amounts up to a dollar and only for buying soda, not for buying alcohol or tobacco, and I transmit those two blocks to the vendor. Now the vendor will run this KeyNote micro-cheque and the credentials I send and the master public key it has from the Mafia, in his local KeyNote programme, to verify that what I sent him is actually good, and he will eventually get paid.

So this is the equivalent of verifying that the cheque I gave him is good. But because of the trust management that is in place, he can do that off-line. Why can he? Effectively, the short lived certificate which is good for a day and is refreshed every day is the Mafia's way of saying: 'even if a person defaults to me, I will still pay you because I guarantee the certificate'. The Mafia can mitigate its risks by issuing a certificate to good clients that would be good for two days and to bad clients that would be good for one day and can further mitigate the risk by making sure that the client understands that if they default and don't pay the bill for the certificate which was issued for a day, bodily harm will come to them.

Audience: Or more importantly, they won't get a certificate tomorrow.

Reply: Right. Another thing here is that a lot of policy can be encoded in the payer's credentials, so that if different ways of treating customers have to be encoded, they don't necessarily have to be encoded in every little vending machine or every little acceptor of these cheques. They can be transmitted securely and in a way that cannot be tampered with because it is signed with the issuer's public key. We can encode policy that way. We will see how that happens.

So I made that payment at a vending machine, and I made a payment somewhere else, and other people made payments at the vending machine – how does it all get cleared? Whenever it is convenient, the vending machine, or the vendor in general, will submit those transaction triplets – the offer that was made to the original client, the KeyNote micro-cheque that was issued by the client, and the client credential that accompanied that micro-cheque – to the clearing service. Now the clearing service will run, in its own local KeyNote compliance checker, the same computation that the vendor did when it dispensed the product. And it will see that it was good and proceed to credit and debit the corresponding parties. Here is also the place where the clearing house verifies that the vendor has not cheated and submitted a cheque twice, because it has all the cheques that are good for that billing period, and there is a nonce in each of those micro-cheques so they cannot be replayed. Everything here is signed with a public key, as for KeyNote in general.

Audience: What I am thinking is that it may be OK for amounts of about a pound or a dollar but I then you may find that you need to add other kinds of mechanisms for making smaller payments to the same vendor, for transactions of one tenth of a cent or something like that.

Do I need to sign for each product or do I save all this data and do the signing for one tenth of a cent?

Reply: It depends on the business model as to what they do for one such transaction. They may enter several transactions at once or each individually. The clearing house has the key recorded for all the players. The data has to be collected somewhere.

How much does a signature cost today and how much will it cost in eighteen months? The answer is that unless we have a very clear understanding of what the business models are, what the precise costs are, how much we are charging for it – we cannot just say a cent or a tenth of a cent or a pound. I have some back of the envelope calculations which show that this is profitable for a thousandth of a dollar but this is an order of magnitude calculation, this is not something that I would put in a business plan. So with 1999 technology, this is profitable for writing cheques for at least a thousandth of a dollar if not smaller.

Audience: I suspect from experience with UEPS that a limiting factor isn't going to be cryptography, it's going to be the cost of doing the on-line transaction processes.

Reply: Unfortunately the numbers are propriety but there was somebody in the lab who was trying to figure out the cost of billing somebody for a phone call, down to the cost of the addition on your phone bill and the additional activity in your disc drive. People have calculated this.

Let's go back to the protocol. I am very interested in the business issues but let's see if there are any security problems with the protocol which will make all the business questions obsolete.

Audience: No, they would make them more interesting [laughter].

Reply: Remember when a client first signs on to the system and agrees to use it, they have to get credentials from the Mafia. And just like every other transaction component in this system, these are KeyNote assertions; they are written in KeyNote. In fact they specify under what conditions – time restrictions, money restrictions, type of product restrictions – the bank will honour a micro-cheque written by this payer. These are very short-lived messages, they can be good for as little as a day and they are refreshed very frequently. If they live on my cell phone, they can arrive as Short Message Service messages if I am using GSM. They can arrive as other kinds of message for other kinds of cell phones. They can even have their own message type, it doesn't have to be SMS. They are sent whenever you walk into a cell for the first time in the morning and turn on your phone or they can be issued more frequently.

Let us see what one of them looks like. This is KeyNote syntax. It says that the authoriser is the bank's public key which is well known by the vendors and by the clearing houses, that there is only one licensee here in the payer's public key which is used to sign the micro-cheques. The conditions under which these micro-cheques are trusted are the obligations of the soda machine as opposed to drug trafficking, the currency is US dollars. The amount has to be less than two dollars and one cent and the date has to be before October 2001. And if all these conditions are met, then the cheque that has been issued is good and this is signed by the bank's key, or again substitute Mafia for bank.

So this is something that I have on my portable. Now I walk up to the soda machine and I press the button. The soda machine transmits to me over the infra red interface, or some other convenient interface such as a bluetooth interface, an offer which describes the transaction that I want to make. In this particular case, it would be that the obligation is with the soda machine, the currency is US dollars, the amount is 50 cents, today's date is April 4th, here is a nonce and here is the vendor's public key; this need not be secured by anything because if the vendor gives me the wrong public key, then they are just not going to get paid. So it is in the best interest of the vendor to give you the correct public key.

In response to that I will write a cheque which says that the authoriser for this credential is me, the payer's public key, that the licensee for this credential is the vendor's public key which I just got, and that these are the conditions under which it is going to be honoured. If you notice carefully, these conditions are more restrictive than the conditions of my short lived credential in that the amount is exactly 50 cents and the date is exactly today – it is not any date less than some specified date in the future. If these conditions are met, then this is true and this is signed by me and I send this back to the vendor.

So the vendor will take this short term credential that I sent him plus the micro-cheque, and using the bank's public key that he has, he is going to run a compliance check to see if the cheque is good. He is not really interpreting the cheque to see what to dispense, he is merely running the same check that the clearing house is going to run to verify that he is going to get paid. If he makes sure that he is going to get paid, then he dispenses the product.

Let's see what some of the needs of the players are. It is evident that the vendor needs these things; it needs the bank's public key so that it can verify things, it needs its own long term policy which can simply say ' trust anything that the bank has authorised' or it can have some more restrictive policies, for instance it can keep its own counters and count how many times a particular public key has asked for products and not dispense more than twenty products in the same day.

What the payer needs is a long term secure channel to the bank so that he can get fresh certificates and he needs a secure channel so that the bank can sign the payer's public key whenever the payer's public key changes.

Audience: Is that a name or a public key?

Reply: It's its public key, there are no names involved.

Audience: Could the soda machine service engineer steal the public key?

Reply No. The service engineer can steal the cheques but he cannot deposit them to his own account, because the micro-cheques have been issued to the vendor's public key not to the engineer's public key. So the signature will not compute.

Audience: He can see what the public key is before hand. So he goes to the vending machine, changes the key and then comes back two weeks later and changes it back to the original one.

Reply: The service person who comes to fill up the soda machine may not fill it up and just steal the soda. This is a system management issue: how much do you trust the delivery person who goes there and makes the delivery? But if a person is sophisticated enough to change the public key, they probably won't be working as a delivery person for a soda machine company.

Audience: A lot of these small payment systems do not accumulate large values.

A basic principle says that you can always loose in small ways but you make it up on volume.

Reply: In the computer science department in Columbia we once ordered pizza for fifty or sixty people. About two hours later the pizza delivery place called us up and said 'have you gotten your pizza yet?' and we said 'yes, thank you very much, why?'. Apparently the delivery person delivered the pizza and then ran off with the money. This is all about reducing risk, but some risks you decide you have to take. At least he did not run off with our pizza.

Audience: So none of this scales for large transactions.

Reply: This is not a replacement for VISA. This is a replacement for nothing that currently exists.

Ross Anderson: Curiously enough, the COPAC system has a maximum value per transaction of about $100,000 or so. They use the moderate tamper resistance available with smart cards rather than refreshing credentials daily, but otherwise it is a very similar system. It doesn't freak people out having $100,000 transactions listed, because it is rare that somebody comes along and spends that much money; and if you do get ripped off and it does get stamped by crooked shop staff, then that's life.

Reply: Some more remarks need to be made. The payer's hardware does not store any value, this is not a wallet in the Mondex sense or in the Proton card sense or even in the phone card sense. The credentials issued to the payer by the bank effectively encode the bank's risk strategy or the provider's risk strategy. For instance the credential may say – this credential is good for purchases up to 2 dollars up to tonight and then only half a dollar up to tomorrow night. So if I fail to renew this credential, because I am a good customer the company will still allow me to buy things tomorrow but at a reduced risk. It can also encode things such as – 'oh, you switched on your phone today and it is very hot' so today we will have a field in there that says 'the price of soda should be at least 60 cents'. So if I try to buy 50 cent soda, I will fail. In fact, I think one soft-drink manufacturer threatened to do that by implementing its vending machines to update the cost of product on a daily basis for precisely that reason – when it is very hot, the price of soda goes up[5].

When I, the payer, transfer value to the vendor, the vendor cannot transfer value back to me, they cannot give me change. So this cannot be readily used for money laundering, or I hope not. Of course I can be both a payer and a vendor if I have two different agreements with my bank and somebody else can be the same thing and we can exchange value that way – maybe that is more

---

[5] I don't suggest that people should be doing this sort of thing, of course not.

traceable. The other thing which I glossed over is that there is nothing magical about this, there is really no tamper resistance necessary in the actual storage of credentials because it is in my best interests not to touch that. There is no value stored so I don't gain anything by tampering with it. There is some concern about somebody else tampering with it and causing me to get things just out of sheer malice but again, this is for small value transactions and it is not clear how much the damage is going to be. There is no reason why this cannot be implemented as a browser plug-in; the only reason it has not happened yet is because I do not have the time and I do not have the necessary slave labour[6] to do it.

Some more remarks. We believe that it is important for these micro billing protocols not to hard code any payment policies or vendor policies. The policies should not be in the protocol, they should be in the actual credentials used so that they can change without changing all the underlying infra-structure and also so they can change on a per user basis, you don't have to change the entire system. There is no need for a global PKI because we are not certifying that I, JI, can pay for things. All that it is being certified is that this public key can pay for things and this can happen just on a purely local basis with people I already have a business relationship with, such as my phone company. There is no business defining any encoding mechanisms, let the appropriate agencies define that. Right now everything is transmitted in ASCII text. This is not an anonymous cash mechanism, it is very traceable; it is about as traceable as credit cards and people are very happy to be using credit cards. Besides, I don't think we have any privacy anyway so why bother trying to pretend[7].

Here are my conclusions and yours may be different from mine and we can discuss them. This is effectively a cheque based system, it has similar properties and risks to cheque based systems. Maybe we are doing better than real cheque based systems but I have not seen the statistics. Cheque based systems are implemented by humans, this is implemented by machine so it has the potential of being cheaper. We have user trust management systems to implement risk management and so the buzzword content of this sentence is pretty high and I should be happy. I already mentioned the last conclusion which is that the attributes are encoded in the individual credentials, not in the entire system. We have a patent on this but don't kill us for that, we are just following orders.

Audience: Have you any data on the time it takes from when you press a button to the authorise of the transaction – is it done within seconds?

Reply: Yes. Right now it takes about 10 to 12 seconds because it is not very well programmed. The current implementation is written in C using open SSL ported to the Palm pilot. It does, I think, a 384 bit RSA signature in about 10 to 12 seconds. The 384 was chosen solely because if we put on anything more, we would have to wait half an hour for the pilot to decide.

---

[6] I mean graduate students.

[7] Apologies to Scott McNealy who said something similar.

If we were using the next generation of hardware, whatever that is, there would almost certainly be an elliptic curve and we could optimize these figures. No-one wants to wait 10 seconds to be served.

Matt Blaze: Even if it is free. The soda machine currently dispenses bizarre drinks.

Reply: That is the other way we looked at to minimise the risks – it was to dispense drinks that nobody really wants.

There are a lot of business questions but I brought this here because there is a protocol involved, and that's the feedback I am really looking for.

Audience: If you think about that replacing your Infra-Red with a radio link, or even if you are using an IR ring, you have a possible problem. You have to really make sure that you are talking to the right cash machine, the one of the right colour. And then you have the problem that somebody might implement the wrong colour or something like that. So you are in a way assuming that you will always get the key for the right window of the product.

Reply: OK let us see what the risks are. The risks are that this conversation is going to be overheard – well, there are no secrets being transmitted, there are just things being signed. If an offer is for a larger amount than I think you should be paying, I am already seeing the sum on the display of the till[8]. So what my device is going to tell me is – shall I pay 214 dollars to this till or 14 cents to this till and then I will say yes.

Audience: The real problem there is that if you have that kind of rogue vendor, he can randomly send sale messages to the customer and let us say that every tenth customer or so gets a fake key and pays for the wrong window and then they might try again and then they get the soda billing. If you go there often enough, you will notice that something is wrong with this vending machine but by the time that the service person comes, you can take your fake sender to the next soda machine and continue with it like that.

Audience: Because you have got encrypted authorisation, I have to supply your phone with the public key of the product that I want to sell. At the end of the day, I have got to get the cash out of the system somehow.

All the messages are signed, what you are suggesting is that it is a given that there are some risks with the signatures and that that is acceptable. Why not take the cryptography out entirely and just do it 'no crypto'?

Reply: Oh, oh, oh. The answer to that question depends on whether or not the crypto actually costs too much and we don't know the answer to that.

I sort of believe that it is possible to implement a system like this with secure crypto by optimising carefully.

The novelty of this system is that it is a micro payment system and it is both off-line and it does not involve secure hardware. When you get your hardware, you have the ability to pay for only one-at-a-time transactions. Whether you need elaborate security on top of that, given that you are limited in what you can buy, is not entirely certain.

---

[8] The cash register.

George Danezis: You have a maximum sum of money that you can spend per transaction. But if your card is stolen ...

Reply: Here is where risk management comes in once again. If my phone is stolen, what do I do now? People are going to make phone calls until I report it and the agreement I have with my provider is, that if I report that my phone has been stolen within some time from when I lost it, then I am only liable for up to so much money. Just like I am only liable for so much money if I lose my credit card, even though thousands may have been charged on it.

Audience: The point is that somebody who steals this can go and buy lots of newspapers.

Reply: So they are going to buy 10 newspapers, 20 sodas, and 100 gallons of gas for their tractor trailer but so what?

Audience: They could buy 10 million Web pages.

Reply: That is a more interesting risk. But part of the beauty of this is that the credentials are very specific – what each user is allowed to do is heavily tailored to the individual user and the type of transactions. What I might say is that for Web transactions, if people are on-line, then I can make these things much shorter lived. So if it is for Web pages, the certificate is only good for three hours instead of a day.

Or for five minutes. There is an interesting system issue of how do you select the right certificate to send along, and this is a totally different protocol.

Broadening the Scope of Fault Tolerance within Secure Services

Geraint Price[*]

University of Cambridge
Centre for Communications Systems Research
10 Downing Street, Cambridge, CB2 3DS
G.Price@ccsr.cam.ac.uk

Abstract. We believe that to date the use of fault tolerance within secure services has been limited to the scope of replicating services. We demonstrate that controlling state within a protocol execution can be a useful abstraction of fault tolerance within a secure environment, and this can lead to more widespread use of fault tolerance within secure services.

1 Introduction

In the past there has been much made of the similarity between fault tolerance and security, in terms of their aim for continued service in the face of adversity.

Most of the existing work done to merge the two fields concentrate on using fault tolerant mechanisms and models as a means of increasing the resilience within servers.

The main problem we face when merging the two fields is the dichotomy that exists when it comes to the implementation of their techniques. Fault tolerance relies heavily on using replication, whereas security is primarily concerned with reducing the scope – and subsequently any replication – of data within the system.

A prominent theme in fault tolerance is control of information, with different checks on various actions and data items being used before the effects of such information is allowed to filter to other parts of the system.

Such mechanisms that are currently used within secure environments are concerned with the limitation of the scope of this control to existing Trusted Computing Base strategies. By looking at the fundamental principles that underly fault tolerance we aim to demonstrate in this paper that such control can – in some cases – legitimately reside with the client in a client-server model of security.

In section 2 we look at some existing work in the field. Section 3 gives an overview of why we believe state to be a useful abstraction in our environment. Sections 4 and 5 give some examples of the use of our abstraction of state, and we draw our conclusions in section 6.

---

[*] An early version of part of this paper is contained in my PhD dissertation [14].

B. Christianson et al. (Eds.): Security Protocols, LNCS 2133, pp. 155–164, 2001.
© Springer-Verlag Berlin Heidelberg 2001

2   Background

The primary work done to date on incorporating fault tolerance and security is the work on *Rampart* by Reiter [17,16,15]. It uses a secure group broadcast primitive in order to allow a replicated service to continue correct execution in a byzantine faulty environment. It provides a very robust environment in which a service which requires both security and high availability can reside.

It does highlight that using a fault tolerant mechanism can be useful, but trying to provide a generic environment for such processing to take place can be prohibitively expensive, especially when it comes to scalability.

Another drawback of this model is that it re-enforces the Trusted Computing Base (TCB) view of security and doesn't allow the client to take greater control in the situation reflected by his security policy.

Given the security community's concern with the ultra-paranoid, most existing work uses a byzantine threat model. Syverson [19] calls for a relaxation in the worst case scenario when it comes to applying fault tolerant mechanisms within security[1]. He discusses the use of a probabilistic method of surviving an attack on a communication channel[2]. His argument then centres on viewing the correct processes and attackers as a pair of competing networks, and places the discussion within a game-theoretic model in order to try and calculate the processes' advantages in co-operating in groups against each other. While little is offered in the way of providing a realistic measurement of the applicability of such a model, we are not concerned with the implementation, but agree that models for computation, other than worst case scenario, can be sought to improve upon the application of fault tolerance within secure services.

3   Faults and Protocols

To gain some more insight into how else we could use fault tolerance in secure services, we try to answer the question: "What does fault tolerance mean in terms of security protocols?". Our aim is to get a better understanding of where the core notions of fault tolerance affect existing work in security.

We explore what constitutes a fault, and how we can this map this to a setting which uses secure protocols.

Our modifications draw upon the terminology proposed by Anderson et al. in various places [3,2,4] which is used almost universally within the fault tolerant literature.

3.1   Fault, Error & Failure

We work backwards through the terminology chain defined in the literature. The final stage of error is referred to as a **Failure**. The definition as given in the literature [3] is:

---

[1] A similar argument is made by Meadows [11,10].
[2] This is an extension of the *two generals problem* [9, pp. 465–472].

Failure A failure of a system is said to occur when the behaviour of the system first deviates from that required by the specification of the system.

This definition relies on the notion of a specification for system behaviour. What exactly are we looking for in the specification of a security system? Taking a security protocol as an example, it has been noted in the literature [5] that the function of a protocol is to allow its participants to achieve certain goals. In particular, we note that security protocols are generally designed with the goals of specific principals in mind.

Using a two-party authentication protocol [13] as an example, we note that A and B view the successful completion of a protocol as meeting certain goals upon completion of the protocol. Conversely S has no goals to fulfil by running the protocol. In this sense S is benign as far as the goals of the specification of the protocol are concerned. We introduce the term **Beneficiary** to describe A and B in relation to specification of the protocol, as they are the participants who aim to achieve the specified goals by running the protocol.

With this in mind we amend the definition to apply to a security protocol as follows:

Protocol Failure A failure of a security protocol is said to occur when the beneficiaries do not achieve the goals stated in the protocol specification.

In order for the system to fail there has to be an action prior to the failure, which the failure can be attributed to.

The system is defined to be encapsulated by a set of states which are modified by transitions. Both states and transitions are said to be either *valid* or *erroneous*, with the set of states represented by $\mathcal{S}$ and transitions by $\mathcal{T}$, then the state transition graph flows as shown in figure 1. An erroneous transition is one that moves the internal system state from a valid state to an erroneous state. An erroneous state is one which, if not transformed back to a valid state will result in the failure of the system.

Re-defining these in terms of a security protocol, we define the message content to encapsulate the **state** within the cryptographic protocol, and a **transition** is subsequently the movement at a participant from and incoming message to an outgoing message.

The terms used to describe the system prior to a failure are **Fault** and **Error**, and are defined are follows [3]:

Fault A fault is said to occur in the system, when an internal state is transferred from a legitimate state to an erroneous state.
Error An error is said to be when some internal system state is defective.

In the case of valid states and transitions, they are transitions which follow the protocol specification. In our analogy which uses messages and transitions, then a **fault**, as defined in the fault tolerance literature, is synonymous with a transition that produces an erroneous message. The following definitions provide a more concrete view of the secure counterparts of the above definitions:

Valid States

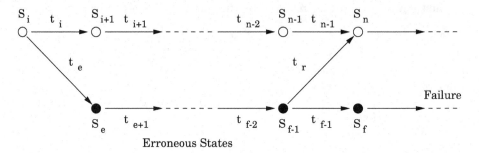

t_e = Erroneous transition

t_r = Recovery transition

Fig. 1. State transitions

Erroneous State A message, which could possibly allow a legitimate participant to make a transition, and, if not detected would allow a beneficiary to
derive false goals.

Erroneous Transition A transformation from a valid message to an invalid
message, taking the system into an erroneous state.

In order for the constituent parts of fault tolerance to be achieved (e.g., fault
diagnosis) there are some scenarios where it is only the beneficiary is able to
ascertain an erroneous state. Therefore in those circumstances there is a requirement for the beneficiary to be in control of the fault recovery decisions
within the protocol.

4   Choice and Denial of Service

How can using this notion of controlling state help in a secure environment? Here
we will demonstrate an example of a new attack model, and that by allowing
the client to control parts of the state which we would not normally attribute to
its control in this environment, then we can circumvent the attack.

Little has been written on the subject of denial of service, with the notable
exception of work done by Needham [12] and Gligor [8]. Currently, the major
concerns within Denial of Service are maintaining availability of the server (especially Needham's work concerning the vault) and maintenance of fair play
between users of a service. Little is said with regard to the problem of the server
itself launching a denial of service attack.

Consider a system providing a service to a set of users. We are concerned
about a variant of denial of service, where the service can selectively deny service

to some portion of the users with a high degree of accuracy. We coin the phrase **Selective Denial of Service** to describe this scenario.

More formally: A system is resilient to a **Selective Denial of Service** attack if it consists of a service S (potentially a set of services $\mathcal{S}$), and a set of users $\mathcal{U}$, where the service should not be able to selectively deny service to any particular member A within the set of users $\mathcal{U}$ with greater probability than random choice.

We do note two exception to the above definition:

- It its possible for S to deny service to A by denying service to all members of $\mathcal{U}$ simultaneously, by closing down completely, but this goes outside the bounds of selectivity used in our definition.
- It is also possible for S to deny service to A if it can manipulate the group membership properties of $\mathcal{U}$, such that A is the only member of the group. Again, we consider this threat scenario beyond the scope of our work.

An example of where such a threat might be encountered could be in a stock trading service. If an application for processing by a particular client was delayed for a certain length of time, then there could be a negative impact on the result of the request from the client's point of view.

4.1   Building a Solution through Anonymity

Our solution to this problem draws upon the use of an anonymity mechanism built for different requirements. In his work on digital cash, Chaum [7] proposed a mechanism that allowed a user to generate electronic cash in a manner that preserved the user's anonymity during spending.

The building block of the system is that of *blind signatures*, where the use of a *blinding factor*, chosen randomly by the user provides a means for anonymity.

While we originally described two solutions to this problem, we only cover one here for brevity.

Before describing our protocol we first of all define the players involved in our scenario:

Z The Authorisation server : Provides the users with the tokens that allow them to use a service S.

N The Authentication server : Checks the authenticity of the users with regard to their membership of the system.

S Server : Any of a set of servers $\mathcal{S}$.

A User : A uniquely identifiable member of the set of legitimate users $\mathcal{U}$.

G Group : A non-empty, identifiable subset of the legitimate users $\mathcal{U}$, to which A is a member.

In our protocol, A wishes to receive some service from a provider S. The protocol is organised into three rounds. In each round the user A communicates with N, Z and S in turn. We also highlight the fact that A is potentially a member of a number of various groups, and indicate this through explicitly adding a second group G' into the description.

In the first version of our protocol design, the client contacts the Authorization server before the Authentication server. This is reversed in the version of the protocol we describe here.

The protocol proceeds with a three round structure and we describe each of the rounds below:

Round 1 : A to N

The reason we highlight the difference between G and G' in this section is that A needs to carry out each section of this protocol separately for each group of which A is a member and for which she wishes to use the associated "right" incorporated within the group at any given time period.

Thus $\forall G : A \in G$, A generates m_i (where $i = 1 \ldots j$) of the form "As a member of G my pseudonym is 'Fred' ". A then generates a set of j random numbers (K_i), and then computes:

$$A : t_i = m_i K_i{}^e \; mod \; n$$

The set of all t_i's is then sent to the authentication service. N requests that A un-blinds all except one of the set to verify the integrity of the request, and signs the remaining request. Again, for brevity we omit the part of the protocol which reveals the blinding.

$(1) A \rightarrow N : A, < t_1, \ldots, t_j >$
$(2) N \rightarrow A : t_r^d \; mod \; n$

The main difference between this and the other protocol is that in this protocol we make explicit use of a pseudonym[3].

Round 2: A to Z

To reveal which pseudonym A has been left with, she then performs the calculation:

$$A : m_r = t_r^d / K_r \; mod \; n$$

A then sends this signed pseudonym, along with the name of the service S she wishes to use to the authorisation server. Z then checks that a member of G is able to use S and generates a valid token for A by signing the request and sending it back.

Again, even if Z and N collude at this point they cannot recover any useful information because of the blinding mechanism.

$(3) A \rightarrow Z : S, m_r$
$(4) Z \rightarrow A : \{S, m_r\}_{K_Z^{-1}}$

Round 3: A to S

To use the service, A sends the valid token to S, along with any request specific information (Q). Note that, to secure any request specific information

---

[3] Although we use a name here for illustrative purposes, a 128-bit random number could be used in practice.

(T) in the reply, A has to include a session key for S to use in order to encrypt message 6, because A's own public key cannot be identified by S at this point.

$(5) A \rightarrow S : \{\{S, m_r\}_{K_Z^{-1}}, k, Q\}_{K_S}$
$(6) S \rightarrow A : \{T\}_k$

5   Servers and State

In this section we briefly cover how we see the allocation of control of state can be used in balancing trust in a replicated server. In existing work on replicated servers [17] which use the State-machine [18] approach to replication, there is no interrogation of how the replicated state can affect the client's view of the trust model. When we looked at adopting the Primary-backup [6][4] approach to replication we noticed that the variation of state replication was a means by which we could allow the client to control the reliance inherent in his security policy with regards to the replicated server.

We include here our notion of stateless and semi-stateless servers to highlight our discussion on state and its effect upon the use of fault tolerance in secure services.

5.1   Stateless and Semi-stateless Servers

The cryptographic means by which most protocols are secured do not lend themselves to sharing information between many communicating hosts – i.e., if we use a shared secret key to keep a channel between two communication parties confidential, then it is not reasonable to share the key with other parties.

In order to circumvent this constraint, we need to apply the securing mechanisms in an orthogonal manner to the information being manipulated by the servers in order to provide service to their clients.

To avoid the corruption of any global request specific state via a single faulty server, the individual servers which make up the replication group should in theory not share this state. We define this property below:

Stateless servers A stateless server is one whose replication mechanisms and use of state to provide the functionality of the group service is not shared by other members of the group. This allows them independence from each other, leading to a scenario where a malicious server can reveal all his information to the world without compromising the ability of other group members to continue delivering service.

It is clear to see from the above definition that it is going to be difficult to implement such mechanisms in practice, as the limitation of information flow

---

[4] The Primary-backup approach to replication was first discussed in the literature by Alsberg and Day [1].

between servers deprives us of much of the functionality of the backup mechanism.

In order to impose less stringent constraints on the replication mechanism, we define a less stringent property which we term *Semi-stateless servers* which allows limited information sharing between replicas. We define this property below:

Semi-stateless servers A semi-stateless server is one who shares a limited set of information with other servers in the group, and whose shared information is necessary to allow the replication procedure to provide a richer set of operations. This shared information does not extend to the state necessary to carry out the security critical section of the application. This allows a bad player to broadcast all his secrets to the world without compromising the ability of the other replicas to provide a secure service.

We clarify these differences to demonstrate that services can be replicated in a manner that does not jeopardise the security of the service being provided. An instance of this might be a server replicated purely to avoid a denial of service attack, where the threat model does not include the compromise of the server and its secrets, but an attack on the communication infrastructure which can lead to a loss of service.

What we aim for with the second scenario is that the state shared between the servers is relevant to the requests of a particular client (i.e., a client's public key deposited with a key server) and that, while this state needs to be replicated between the servers to achieve a richer functionality set between the servers, the client can in some way dictate the amount of independence that each replica has in the state transitions made on this data. This can lead to scenarios where the control of replicated state dissemination is carried out by the client. Therefore allowing for the client to increase or decrease the reliance it has in the replication mechanism according to its own security policy.

6   Conclusions

What we hope to have demonstrated in this paper is that controlling the state in a protocol (particularly by the client) can help expand the use of fault tolerance as a principle within secure applications.

We look at the very principles underlying fault tolerance from their notions of fault, error and failure, to how managing state is part of this strategy. Then we adapt these notions to the scenario of a secure protocol and how translating that state control is important to the beneficiary in a protocol. This extends past the initial work done in this field of using existing fault tolerance mechanisms.

Our example which defines a new class of denial of service attack uses control of the information (and hence system state) that the server uses to verify a client's identity. What we find interesting with regard to this solution is that the client is in control of information that is of no use to him at all. It is the server that is interested in the integrity of the information, but having the client control the flow of this information does not change the server's ability to carry out its task correctly at all.

This demonstrates quite clearly that sharing this sphere of control can be of benefit to both parties.

Our aim with the future of this work is to build on the notion of "control of information" and apply it to existing formalisms. Using some type of process logic should allow us to understand more clearly how moving the design from a traditional TCB model to a shared control model can aid such emerging security concerns such as e-commerce, where mutual distrust seems to be the prevalent design criteria.

References

1. Peter A. Alsberg and John D. Day. A principle for resilient sharing of distributed resources. In *Proceedings of the 12 th International Conference on Software Engineering*, pages 562–570, October 1976.
2. T. Anderson and P.A. Lee. *Fault Tolerance: Principles and Practice*. Prentice-Hall International, 1981.
3. T. Anderson and P.A. Lee. Fault tolerance terminology proposals. Technical Report 174, University of Newcastle upon Tyne, Computing Laboratory, University of Newcastle upon Tyne, Computing Laboratory, Claremont Tower, Claremont Road, Newcastle upon Tyne, NE1 7RU, England., April 1982.
4. T. Anderson, P.A. Lee, and S.K. Shrivastava. *System Fault Tolerance*, chapter 5, pages 153–210. Cambridge University Press, 1979.
5. M. Burrows, M. Abadi, and R.M. Needham. A logic of authentication. *Proceedings of the Royal Society of London*, 246:233–271, 1989.
6. Navin Budhiraja, Keith Marzullo, Fred B Schneider, and Sam Toueg. *Distributed Systems*, chapter 8, pages 199–216. Addison-Wesley, 1993. 2 nd Edition.
7. David Chaum. Blind signatures for untraceable payments. In *Proceedings of Crypto '82*, pages 199–203, 1982.
8. Virgil D. Gligor. On denial-of-service in computer networks. In *Proceedings of the International Conference on Data Engineering*, pages 608–617, February 1986.
9. J. N. Gray. *Notes on Data Base Operating Systems*, volume 60 of *Lecture Notes in Computer Science*, chapter 3.F, pages 393–481. Springer-Verlag, 1978.
10. Catherine Meadows. The need for a failure model for security. In *Proceedings of the 4 th International Workshop Conference on Dependable Computing for Critical Applications*, 1994.
11. Catherine Meadows. Applying the dependability paradigm to computer security. In *Proceedings of the 1995 New Security Paradigms Workshop*, 1995.
12. Roger M. Needham. Denial of service: An example. *Communications of the A.C.M.*, 37(11):42–46, November 1994.
13. Roger M. Needham and Michael D. Schroeder. Using encryption for authentication in large networks of computers. *Communications of the A.C.M.*, 21(12):993–999, December 1978.
14. Geraint Price. The interaction between fault tolerance and security. Technical Report No. 479, University of Cambridge, Computer Laboratory, December 1999.
15. Michael K. Reiter. The rampart toolkit for building high-integrity services. In K. P. Birman, F. Mattern, and A. Schiper, editors, *International Workshop on Theory*

and Practice in Distributed Systems, volume 938 of Lecture Notes in Computer Science, pages 99–110, September 1994.

16. Michael K. Reiter. Secure agreement protocols: Reliable and atomic group multi-cast in rampart. In *Proceedings of the 2 nd A.C.M. Conference on Computer and Communications Security*, pages 68–80, November 1994.

17. Michael K. Reiter. Distributing trust with the rampart toolkit. *Communications of the A.C.M.*, 39(4):71–74, April 1996.

18. Fred B. Schneider. Implementing fault-tolerant services using the state machine approach: *A tutorial. A.C.M. Computing Surveys*, 22(4):299–319, December 1990.

19. Paul F. Syverson. A different look at secure distributed computation. In *Proceedings of the 10 th I.E.E.E. Computer Security Foundations Workshop*, pages 109–115, June 1997.

Broadening the Scope of Fault Tolerance within Secure Services (Transcript of Discussion)

Geraint Price

University of Cambridge

I seem to have landed myself in the denial of service section of this workshop. I *have* got something that has to do with denial of service but it's a piece of a larger two way discussion that I'm going to branch into. I'm going to talk about using fault tolerance within secure services, particularly looking at trying to broaden the way it's used currently. I will provide some formal discussion of why I believe that what I'm trying to do is a viable alternative to what's being done at the moment, provide a concrete example of what's going on which includes denial of service (and I'll try and talk more about that than I had initially planned to), ask some fairly open questions, and hopefully provide ample food for discussion.

So if we look at both fault tolerance and security we can fairly easily understand that both fields are trying to do a similar sort of thing: they're trying to stop bad effects from spreading out throughout the system and corrupting the system. These bad effects are obviously different in the two cases: fault tolerance is looking at just trying to contain crashes – sort of random occurrences that might go wrong – whereas security is looking towards trying to stop bad people from doing bad things, so you've got the next level up of what's going to go wrong. But there is this dichotomy between how fault tolerance uses replication and how security uses replication: one of the most general approaches to fault tolerance is to replicate the system in some way, so that you can make checks and comparisons between the replicas. But in security you go back to a trusted computer base, you want to limit the amount of replication, you want everything to be nailed down into one place if possible.

The initial work done in trying to use fault tolerance principles within secure services is based on server replication, primarily work that came out of Cornell with the Isis system providing a non-secure version of a replicated server which got beefed up by Reiter. Along with Rampart there's some more recent work that he's done on Phalanx, which looks at using database quorum systems in order to replicate the server in a manner that a client can have some form of guarantee that, if a portion of the server breaks down in some way, then the answer that he's going to get from the server is still correct.

All this work so far has given rise to a lot of good questions about what's going on when things go wrong with your server, but at the end of the day it's still trying to promote the trusted computing base model of security. The client still has to trust the server implicitly. What's going on is, you're using fault tolerance as an abstraction layer over the replication mechanism, and you're not

B. Christianson et al. (Eds.): Security Protocols, LNCS 2133, pp. 165–169, 2001.
© Springer-Verlag Berlin Heidelberg 2001

really trying to get at reducing this trusted computing base model. I want to look at ways in which we can use fault tolerance in a more general way within security, and with this I'm going to look at an abstraction of fault tolerance where controlling the state within the system can be used to try and model what goes on within other fault tolerant systems apart from server replication.

In the early work done in fault tolerance, everything looked at trying to categorise what was going on if you've got a failure within the system; so you start off with definitions of faults, errors and failures within a system. What goes on in a system when the system fails is that the system cannot provide the specification that it was designed to provide. So if we try and translate that into what we believe to be security goals, if we look at the BAN logic, then we see what would be the specification of the goals (taking protocols just as an example here) that the client wishes to see achieved by the end of the protocol run; for example that A and B believe that they're sharing a secret key together. So a failure of the security protocol is said to occur when the beneficiaries do not achieve the goals stated in the protocol specification. I think that's quite simple.

Within the fault tolerance community, before the failure occurs they pin down the state the system is in when an error occurs to which you can attribute the failure. And the translation is that the error propagates through to the system until the failure occurs. We have modified a state transition diagram of what goes on within the system, so if we look at this diagram then there needs to be an erroneous transaction to which we can attribute the point where the system first deviated into what was going wrong, and if we want to recover the system then we have to have a recovery transition. To monitor the state and control this recovery transition fault tolerance goes through its primary aims, which are the error detection, the damage assessment and the error recovery parts of the system. So controlling the state then becomes inherently part of controlling the fault tolerance.

So if we go back to looking at the definition of protocols, then what is the state within a protocol? Well, I've tried to argue that any state within the protocol is basically just messages. Transitions on these messages happen at a client when somebody reads in a message and then spits out a different message. That's a state transition, so the message encapsulates the state. So if we want to control the constituent parts, then we need to be able to monitor what's going on within the protocol; and if we go back to our statement at the start of looking at protocols, then it's the client, in not being able to achieve his goals, who is the one who is most concerned about the protocols completing successfully. And in some cases, it's only the client that's going to be capable of carrying out the constituent parts of fault tolerance in order to recover the system into a state where he can carry on and eventually achieve his goals. So this is why I think that controlling state is a viable alternative to what is currently done with server replication and that it is a means of being able to provide the client with an ability to control the security within some sort of fault tolerance sense.

Now I'm going to provide a simple example of controlling state as a means of providing better control for the clients over making sure that the goal of the protocol is achieved. And this is where the denial of service attack comes in. There's not a lot written currently about denial of service and there's at least one person in the room who has written about this, so I'd better be extremely careful about what I say. Virgil has written some work which equates any denial of service to an increase of the maximum waiting time that clients have to wait and the trade off between different clients, playing each other off, trying to achieve a sort of one-upmanship on the rest of the legitimate clients in the system. And then there's Roger's work which looks at possible attacks from the outside, and his example of the bank vault. What I want to present here is what I believe to be a new form of denial of service attack, where the user is concerned with the possibility of the service itself actually denying him service but in a very specific sense. This is what we term the selective denial of service attack – the service should not be able to selectively deny service to a particular user within the system within a greater chance than random choice. Say if I want to go to a file server and then for some reason the system that I'm using decides that it doesn't want me to be able to complete a transaction, because it's beneficial for the system to make me wait until the close of trading for the day or whatever. So in any position where it's beneficial for the system to not allow me to complete transactions, maybe even for a short period of time, then I don't want it to be able to do that. In this case with trading, if I'm only denied service for five minutes then that's enough to . . .

Virgil Gligor: Is this really denial of service or is it some sort of an unfulfilment of an agreement? If there is an implied agreement between the user and the service regarding what the service puts out to the user and what the user pays for, if anything like this happens then the agreement is violated and this is not, in my opinion, a denial of service problem but is an integrity problem.

Reply: But if it still allows the service to deny the ability for me to carry out what I want to, I can only retrospectively demonstrate that the service contract has been violated.

Virgil Gligor: You can, and then you complain that this is an integrity violation. But it's a nice problem anyway, call it whatever you want.

Reply: I've been able to construct a solution to this problem, whether it be a denial of service attack or not, by allowing the client to control the state within the system over and above what is generally thought to be his means of controlling the state. By extending this model of controlling the state, we're able to afford a higher degree of protection to the client than is usually evident in the system.

We build a system on top of the blinding signatures method generated by Chaum for electronic cash giving the client the ability to control his identity within the system in order to close down the threat.

Matt Blaze: So this is denying the ability of the server to deny service to a particular user, not for a particular type of transaction. The server may know what the transaction is but not who asked for it.

Reply: Yes. As I said, the point that stops this from becoming trivial is the fact that the user will be a member of a group, so all members of the group can produce the same transactions. But it's to stop the server from picking on one member of the group and denying it from producing the same set of transactions as another.

Bruce Christianson: Equivalently, the protocol allows the server to defend itself from an accusation that it is playing favourites.

Reply: Yes, right.

In the protocol, you've got the user who generates a set of these messages. Now the client picks a pseudonym at the start of the session, he multiplies it by some random number which he thinks up, and sends the set of messages to an authentication server. Now what this says is that I am providing this pseudonym as Alice, as a member of the group. Then the server picks out which ones it wants to be unblinded. It can then check that all these are valid pseudonyms for groups containing Alice and the one it then signs (which Alice then unblinds), is one that the authentication server doesn't know about. Then Alice says to the authorisation server – I want to use service S, here is my authenticated pseudonym for today, the server signs that, and then the rest is standard stuff.

So using this sort of an extension of controlling the state is viable. And what I think is more important here is that in traditional systems it's the authentication server or the authorisation server that's interested in Alice's identity for the day. Traditionally Alice would have no need to control her identity from the authorisation point of view, but in taking control over her identity by providing the pseudonym, she becomes capable of side stepping this attack.

So if we accept that providing them with some form of control of state is useful for clients within client server systems, can we extend this backwards to server replication mechanisms? The current use of server replication is generally a state machine approach, where, the abstraction layer provided gives the client the same view as if he's interacting with a single processor. All the server replication happens underneath the abstraction layer, so it looks to the client as if he's talking to a single state server. So if we look at state replication in servers, then the replication itself hampers both the cryptographic means by which we keep the security – but this has been solved to date – and it also provides some difficulty with controlling the primitives of chains in the transitions and the application state. So if we open this up, can we look at mechanisms that allow the client to control more of the state transition that's happening underneath the application layer, in a way that allows the client to control the correctness of the application state? If we step back from this, having to monitor the state allows the client to control the fault tolerance within the system. If we allow the client, in some sense, to join forces in the transactions that are happening in a replicated server, then instead of having the current mechanism where using server replication is a means of enforcing the trusted computing base, using server replication allows the client to interactively talk to the different servers and reduce the trust inherent in its policy.

Coming back to this notion of sharing, by sharing we're controlling the state which in the client server leads to a reduction of trust. Unfortunately, we do also have a negative impact on the functionality which can be applied within the replication mechanism: if we allow the client to get involved then it's going to slow down transactions, it's going to make it more difficult for the server to take steps independently.

So in the end what I would like is that if we allow the client to get involved in sharing the control of the transactions of the state within the system, then we're allowing the client to have some sort of volume knob on how much she trusts each replication server, according to what set of transactions. And then by providing some sort of rich set of interactions with the server, the client can have more control over, and reduce, the amount of trust that her policy has within each server replica.

Also I hope to show that by allowing the client to get involved in this process, we can move away from the standard state-machine approach of replication, towards the primary-backup mechanism where the client can control the progress of the group through some sort of nominated client. Suppose you're looking for a replicated server purely to stop a denial of service attack If I'm using a key server, and one of them gets bombed out, I can go to the next one. I can help control the way in which my primary server replicates my state throughout the system, so through normal transactions I am capable of taking more control over updating the state within the system, and I still have this option of going to a backup if things don't work, but maybe I then have to accept a reduced functionality within the replica system.

So, hopefully I've been able to demonstrate that by abstracting the state from initial work done within fault tolerance, we can fit this into the security model, and provide for a better understanding of using such things as fault tolerance within security. By sharing the control of the two security domains, the fault tolerance can effectively be used in order to reduce the amount of trust that a client has to have in the server. And as Bruce said, the server is then able to defend itself more vigorously in cases of malpractice.

Bruce Christianson: I think that this could actually be pushed a bit further because it means that even if you can have clients who are in different security policy domains and who want a different service, that service can still be provided by a single set of physical resources that is effectively shared between mistrustful domains by an untrusted server.

Reply: Controlling the actual functionality of the state transitions should be able to provide the client with a greater degree of control of what it wants the server to do, rather than just hitting a certain number of options on an API. It can decide in a more interactive manner not only about what sort of physical transactions happen on the state of the system, but also how much trust it is willing interactively to give to each transaction as it goes through the system. The more interactive you force the system to be, the greater the penalty of cost of course.

Bruce Christianson: But the ability to share expensive resources is potentially a huge saving in cost.

DOS-Resistant Authentication
with Client Puzzles

Tuomas Aura[1], Pekka Nikander[1], and Jussipekka Leiwo[2]

[1] Helsinki University of Technology
P.O.Box 5400, FIN-02015 HUT, Finland
{Tuomas.Aura,Pekka.Nikander}@hut.fi
[2] Vrije Universiteit, Division of Sciences
De Boelelaan 1081A, 1081 HV Amsterdam, The Netherlands
leiwo@cs.vu.nl

Abstract. Denial of service by server resource exhaustion has become a major security threat in open communications networks. Public-key authentication does not completely protect against the attacks because the authentication protocols often leave ways for an unauthenticated client to consume a server's memory space and computational resources by initiating a large number of protocol runs and inducing the server to perform expensive cryptographic computations. We show how stateless authentication protocols and the *client puzzles* of Juels and Brainard can be used to prevent such attacks.

1   Introduction

Denial-of-service (DOS) attacks that exhaust the server's resources are a growing concern on the Internet and other open communications systems. For example, in the SYN attack, a client floods the server with the opening messages of the TCP protocol and fills the space reserved in the server for storing half-open connections.

A solution to such threats is to authenticate the client before the server commits any resources to it. The authentication, however, creates new opportunities for DOS attacks because authentication protocols usually require the server to store session-specific state data, such as nonces, and to compute expensive public-key operations. One solution is to begin with a weak but inexpensive authentication, and to apply stronger and costlier methods only after the less expensive ones have succeeded. An example of a weak authentication is the SYN-cookie protection against the SYN attack where the return address is verified not to be fictional by sending the client a nonce that it must return in its next message. This strategy is not entirely unproblematic because the gradually strengthening authentication results in longer protocol runs with more messages and the security of the weak authentication mechanisms may be difficult to analyze.

In this paper, we advocate the design principle that *the client should always commit its resources to the authentication protocol first and the server should*

B. Christianson et al. (Eds.): Security Protocols, LNCS 2133, pp. 170–177, 2001.
© Springer-Verlag Berlin Heidelberg 2001

be able to verify the client commitment before allocating its own resources. The rule of thumb is that, at any point before reliable authentication, the cost of the protocol run to the the client should be greater than to the server. The client's costs can be artificially increased by asking it to compute solutions to puzzles that are easy to generate and verify but whose difficulty for the solver can be adjusted to any level. The server should remain stateless and refuse to perform expensive cryptographic operations until it has verified the client's solution to a puzzle.

2   Related Work

Classical models of denial of service by Gligor and Yu [6,17], Amoroso [1], and Millen [13] concentrate the specification and design of fair multi-user operating systems. They assume that all service requests are arbitrated by a trusted computing base (TCB) that enforces the policy set by a single security officer. Their ideas do not extend well to open distributed systems like the Internet where there is no central trusted administration and no global policy or means for enforcing one, and there are too many simultaneous users to theoretically guarantee the availability of any service.

Graph-theoretical models of network reliability by Cunningham [4] and Phillips [14] assess the vulnerability of a communications network to the destruction of nodes and links. These models are useful in the design of network topologies on the physical layer but their applicability does not easily extend to higher protocol layers.

The SYN attack against the TCP connection protocol on the Internet was reported e.g. in [3]. The attack and possible remedies were analyzed in detail by Schuba et al. [15]. Cookies have been previously used in the Photuris protocol by Karn and Simpson [11] and in the Internet Key Exchange (IKE) by Harkins and Carrel [7]. Criticism of the latter [16] shows that the gradually strengthening authentication is not straight-forward to design and a careful analysis of the server resource usage is needed.

Meadows [12] formalized the idea of gradually strengthening authentication. The design goals of a cryptographic protocol should specify how much resources the server may allocate at each level when its assurance of the client's identity and honest purposes step by step increases. This assurance is measured by the resources the client would need to mount a successful attack.

The advantages of statelessness in the beginning of an authentication protocol were recognized by Janson & al. [9] in the KryptoKnight protocol suite. Aura and Nikander [2] generalized the cookie approach to create stateless servers that maintain connections by passing the state data to the client. The paper also gives examples of authentication protocols where the server avoids saving a state until the authentication of the client is complete. Hirose and Matsuura [8] applied these ideas to a DOS-resistant version of their KAP protocol. In addition to remaining stateless, the server in their protocol postpones expensive exponentiation operations until it has verified that the client has performed similar operations. This way, the server commits its memory and computational resources only after the client has demonstrated its sincerity.

The idea of requiring the client to commit its resources first was described early by Dwork and Naor [5]. They suggested increasing the cost of electronic junk mailing by asking the sender to solve a small cryptographic puzzle for each message. The cost would be negligible for normal users but high for mass mailers. Juels and Brainard [10] recently presented a simpler puzzle that could be sent to TCP clients during a suspected SYN attack. If the server thinks it is under a denial-of-service attack, it can ask clients to compute the reverse of a secure one-way function by brute force before they are allowed to carry on with rest of the protocol. The cost of the brute force computation is parameterized by revealing some input bits to the client and letting it find the remaining ones.

However, Juels and Brainard concentrate on the SYN attack and don't consider DOS attacks against authentication protocols. They, in fact, suggest that a certificate-based client authentication solves the DOS problem and, hence, would not benefit from the puzzles. We disagree with this and use the client puzzles to generalize the design principles of the DOS-resistant KAP to any authentication protocol. We also improve the efficiency of the client puzzles by reducing the length of the puzzle and its solution, by minimizing the number of hash operations needed in the verification of the solution (at the cost of slightly coarser puzzle difficulty levels), and by observing that the puzzles can in some networks be broadcast to the potential clients.

3   Client Puzzles

The server in an authentication protocols can ask the client to solve a puzzle before the server creates a protocol state or computes expensive functions such as exponentiation.

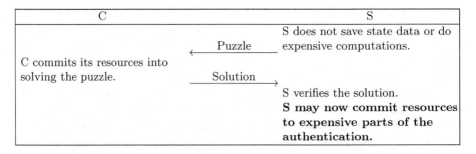

Fig. 1. Server suspecting a DOS attack sends puzzles to new clients

A good puzzle should have the following properties, the two last of which are new in comparison to [10]:

1. Creating a puzzle and verifying the solution is inexpensive for the server.

2. The cost of solving the puzzle is easy to adjust from zero to impossible.
3. The puzzle can be solved on most types of client hardware (although it may take longer with slow hardware).
4. It is not possible to precompute solutions to the puzzles.
5. While the client is solving the puzzle, the server does not need to store the solution or other client-specific data.
6. The same puzzle may be given to several clients. Knowing the solution of one or more clients does not help a new client in solving the puzzle.
7. A client can reuse a puzzle by creating several instances of it.

The puzzle we use is the brute-force reversal of a one-way hash function such as MD5 or SHA. This is a practical choice because the hash functions are computable with a wide variety of hardware and the brute-force testing of different inputs is likely to remain the most efficient way for computing the inverse of these functions. (The difficulty of solving number-theoretic puzzles like factoring may depend heavily on the sophistication of the algorithms used by client.)

To create new puzzles, the server periodically generates a nonce N_S and sends it to the clients. To prevent the attacker from precomputing solutions, the nonce needs to be random and not predictable like, for example, time stamps. (About 64 bits of entropy is sufficient to prevent the attacker from creating a database of solutions from which it could frequently find a matching nonce. Birthday-style attacks that may result in occasional matches will not do much harm here.) The server also decides the difficulty level k of the puzzle. N_S and k together form the puzzle that is sent to the client.

To solve the puzzle, the client generates a random nonce N_C. The purpose of this nonce is twofold. First, if the client reuses a server nonce N_S, it creates a new puzzle by generating a new N_C. Second, without the client nonce an attacker could consume a specific client's puzzles by computing solutions and sending them to the server before the client does. (About 24 bits of entropy is enough to prevent an attacker from exhausting the values of N_C given that N_S changes frequently.)

The client solves X (and Y, which will be discarded) from the following equation by brute force and sends the solution X to the server.

$$h(C, N_S, N_C, X) = \overbrace{000\ldots000}^{\text{the } k \text{ first bits of the hash}} \underbrace{Y}_{\text{the rest of the hash bits}}$$

h	=	a cryptographic hash function (e.g. MD5 or SHA)
C	=	the client indentity
N_S	=	the server's nonce
N_C	=	the client's nonce
X	=	the solution of the puzzle
k	=	the puzzle difficulty level
$000\ldots000$ =		the k first bits of the hash value; must be zero
Y	=	the rest of the hash value; may be anything

The server changes the value of N_S periodically (for example, every 60 seconds) to limit the time clients have for precomputing solutions. As long as the server accepts solutions for a certain value of N_S, it must keep book of the correctly solved instances so that the solutions cannot be reused.

The above puzzle satisfies the criteria for good puzzles. The server only needs to generate a single random nonce to create a new puzzle. The only efficient way to solve the puzzle is to try values of X by brute force until a solution is found. The cost of solving the puzzle depends exponentially on the required number k of zero bits in the beginning of the hash. If $k = 0$, no work is required. If $k = 128$ (for MD5), the client must reverse the entire one-way hash function, which is computationally impossible. Reasonable values of k lie between 0 and 64. The puzzle can be solved on a wide range of hardware because the hash functions are one of the simplest cryptographic operations.

We believe the exponential scale for puzzle difficulty is sufficient for applications. That way, the server can verify the solution in a constant time with a single hash. A more accurate scale could be achieved by combining several puzzles with varying size k. This would, however, increase the cost of verification. (Combining puzzles of varying size would achieve the same granularity of puzzle difficulty as the sets of equal-size subpuzzles in [10] but at a slightly lower cost to the server.) The parameter k should normally be set to zero and increased gradually when the server resources are close to being exhausted. Later, when the server again has free capacity, it is time to decrement k. This way, the correct value is found dynamically and we do not need to know the exact cost of the brute-force computation for the range of parameter values.

The solutions cannot be precomputed because the same N_S is used only for a short time. The client identity C is used as a parameter in the puzzle so that solving the puzzle for one C does not help in finding solutions for another C. This means that it is expensive for one client to impersonate several clients because the solution must be recomputed for each client. The client may reuse the same N_S by solving the puzzle with a new N_C.

Finally, it is feasible to use the above puzzle in the stateless phase of the protocol because the same periodically generated N_S may be used for all clients. This makes it also possible to broadcast the puzzle.

4   An Authentication Protocol

We will now look at how the client puzzles are used to improve the DOS-resistance of an authentication protocol. In the protocol of Fig. 2, C and S authenticate each other with digital signatures and nonces. The protocol can easily be extended into a key exchange by including encrypted key material in the messages.

The protocol normally begins with a broadcast message from the server. In a non-broadcast network, this message may be sent individually to clients that greet the server with a Hello message. The server broadcast consists of a random nonce N_S and a parameter k that determines the difficulty of the puzzle. The

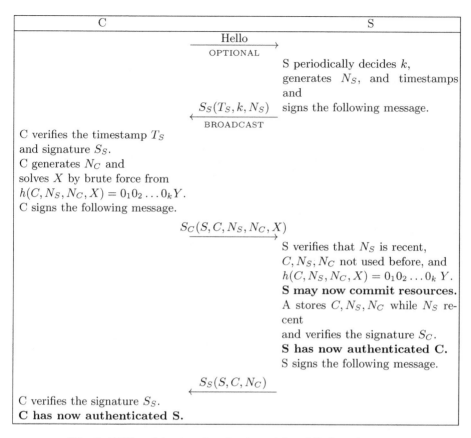

Fig. 2. DOS-resistant authentication with public-key signatures

server generates a fresh nonce periodically and sends the same values N_S, k to all clients during that period. The message may timestamped and signed to prevent an attacker from broadcasting false puzzles. The timestamp T_S and the signature can be omitted if the potential DOS attacks againts the clients are not a concern. The client then generates a nonce N_C, solves the puzzle, and returns the signed answer to the server. The client may reuse a recent puzzle by generating a new nonce N_C.

The server first checks that the same client C has not previously sent a correct solution with the same N_S, N_C. Replayed solutions are ignored. The server verifies the client's solution to the puzzle by computing the hash and, only after seeing that it is correct, verifies the signature and continues with the last message of the authentication. The server stores the values C, N_S, N_C as long as it still considers the nonce N_S recent. If an attacker wants to induce the server to store false values of this kind or to verify false signatures, it must compute a solution to a new puzzle for every stored data item and verified signature.

The puzzle increases the length of the messages only minimally: one byte for k and up to about 8 bytes for the solution X. The nonces are needed in any case for the authentication. Puzzles should only be used when the server suspects it is under an attack and its capacity is becoming exhausted. Otherwise, the server can set $k = 0$. This means that there is no puzzle to solve and any value of X is ok.

5   Conclusion

We showed how the robustness of authentication protocols against denial of service attacks can be improved by asking the client to commit its computational resources to the protocol run before the server allocates its memory and processing time. The server sends to the client a puzzle whose solution requires a brute-force search for some bits of the inverse of a one-way hash function. The difficulty of the puzzle is parameterized according to the server load. The server stores the protocol state and computes expensive public-key operations only after it has verified the client's solution. The puzzles protects servers that authenticate their clients against resource exhaustion attacks during the first messages of the connection opening before the client has been reliably authenticated. It should be noted, however, other techniques are needed to protect individual clients against denial of service and to prevent exhaustion of communications bandwidth.

Acknowledgments

Tuomas Aura was funded by Helsinki Graduate School in Computer Science and Engineering (HeCSE) and by Academy of Finland projects #44806 and #47754.

References

1. Edward Amoroso. A policy model for denial of service. In *Proc. Computer Security Foundations Workshop III*, pages 110–114, Franconia, NH USA, June 1990. IEEE Computer Society Press.
2. Tuomas Aura and Pekka Nikander. Stateless connections. In *Proc. International Conference on Information and Communications Security (ICICS'97)*, volume 1334 of LNCS, pages 87–97, Beijing, China, November 1997. Springer Verlag.
3. TCP SYN flooding and IP spoofing attack. CERT Advisory CA-96.21, CERT, November 1996.
4. William H. Cunningham. Optimal attack and reinforcement of a network. *Journal of the ACM*, 32(3):549–561, July 1985.
5. Cynthia Dwork and Moni Naor. Pricing via processing or combatting junk mail. In *Advances in Cryptology - Proc. CRYPTO '98*, volume 740 of LNCS, pages 139–147, Santa Barbara, CA USA, August 1992. Springer-Verlag.
6. Virgil D. Gligor. A note on the denial-of-service problem. In *Proc. 1983 IEEE Symposium on Research in Security and Privacy*, pages 139–149, Oakland, CA USA, April 1983. IEEE Computer Society.

7. Dan Harkins and Dave Carrel. The Internet key exchange (IKE). RFC 2409, IETF Network Working Group, November 1998.
8. Shouichi Hirose and Kanta Matsuura. Enhancing the resistance of a provably secure key agreement protocol to a denial-of-service attack. In *Proc. 2nd International Conference on Information and Communication Security (ICICS'99)*, pages 169–182, Sydney, Australia, November 1999. Springer.
9. P. Janson, G. Tsudik, and M. Yung. Scalability and flexibility in authentication services: The KryptoKnight approach. In *IEEE INFOCOM'97*, Tokyo, April 1997.
10. Ari Juels and John Brainard. Client puzzles: A cryptographic countermeasure against connection depletion attacks. In *Proc. 1999 Network and Distributed Systems Security Symposium (NDSS)*, pages 151–165, San Diego, CA, February 1999. Internet Society.
11. Phil Karn and William A. Simpson. Photuris: Session-key management protocol. RFC 2522, IETF Network Working Group, March 1999.
12. Catherine Meadows. A formal framework and evaluation method for network denial of service. In *Proc. 12th IEEE Computer Security Foundations Workshop*, pages 4–13, Mordano, Italy, June 1999. IEEE Computer Society.
13. Jonathan K. Millen. A resource allocation model for denial of service. In *Proc. 1992 IEEE Computer Society Symposium on Security and Privacy*, pages 137–147, Oakland, CA USA, May 1992. IEEE Computer Society Press.
14. Cynthia A. Phillips. The network inhibition problem. In *Proc. 25th Annual ACM Symposium on the Theory of Computing*, pages 776–785. ACM Press, May 1993.
15. Christoph L. Schuba, Ivan V. Krsul, Markus G. Kuhn, Eugene H. Spaffold, Aurobindo Sundaram, and Diego Zamboni. Analysis of a denial of service attack on TCP. In *Proc. 1997 IEEE Symposium on Security and Privacy*, pages 208–223, Oakland, CA USA, May 1997. IEEE Computer Society Press.
16. William A. Simpson. IKE/ISAKMP considered harmful. *;login;*, 24(6):48–58, December 1999.
17. Che-Fn Yu and Virgil D. Gligor. A formal specification and verification method for the prevention of denial of service. In *Proc. 1988 IEEE Symposium on Security and Privacy*, pages 187–202, Oakland, CA USA, April 1988. IEEE Computer Society Press.

DOS-Resistant Authentication
with Client Puzzles
(Transcript of Discussion)

Tuomas Aura

Helsinki University of Technology

What I am going to talk about is denial of service resistant authentication protocols. I will extend some existing ideas to improve the resistance of authentication protocols to denial of service attacks.

First I will consider denial of service attacks and network denial of service in general. Traditional models of denial of service and availability started with Virgil's work in the early 1980s. All the security research at that time considered the security of multi-user operating systems, and from that came some limitations of the models. One thing is that a multi-user operating system is a closed system. You have a certain number of principals or subjects acting there, and that's it. If a new one comes in, it *has* to go through the security administrator. Secondly the whole system is controlled by a single trusted computing base, there is a reference monitor that can monitor all the actions and allow or deny them.

Even for a distributed system, if you have a trusted computing base, someone can decide what sorts of access you allow and what you do not. Then you can do a calculation to make sure access is guaranteed to certain priority class subjects, and you can define availability in terms of maximum waiting time. Also you can prove the availability, and prove the maximum waiting time, to be true, assuming there are enough resources in the system to go round for the normal case. Only if one of the users makes a malicious attack only then can you have an over demand of resources in the highest priority class.

On the other hand, in an open system, like the Internet, anyone can join in. There are lots of crazy people out there; insecure machines, insecure sites. There are lots of insecure people who feel they would like to attack other people's machines. You have no control over these people and it is possible for them to attack you in a coordinated way from many different directions simultaneously. You definitely do not have a trusted computing base. As a consequence, you can never guarantee the availability of service in terms of maximum waiting time for all the clients. There are no priority classes usually for the services.

Sometimes you authenticate your clients but sometimes you want to allow clients from all over the world: you want to allow new customers to come in, you definitely don't want to keep strangers away.

In this case it is obvious that all these clients, from all over the network, can flood you with access requests, can flood you with traffic, and can mount a coordinated attack on you and consume your resources. So we cannot prevent denial of service in the way that a classical denial of service model would want

B. Christianson et al. (Eds.): Security Protocols, LNCS 2133, pp. 178–181, 2001.
© Springer-Verlag Berlin Heidelberg 2001

to do – that is prove mathematically under some formal model of the system that it is not possible for resources to run out. Here it is always possible.

So what do we do? Can we prevent this denial of service, or do we throw our hands up and say it's not possible? At the least we would like to make it more difficult to mount this denial of service attack. How much resource does an attacker need to take down a server? How many different places on the network does a coordinated attack need hosts in order to succeed? How much traffic does an attacker need to be able to send from different directions? How much computation does an attacker need to do to cause a certain amount of damage?

It is no longer a question of whether availability is guaranteed, but what is the likelihood (in our social environment of the Internet) that an attack will occur, that someone malicious enough has the resources to do it.

Virgil Gligor: Do you agree that in an open network fundamentally denial of service cannot be prevented, but that if the attack cost exceeds the gain from the attack it is unlikely that a denial of service attack would take place?

Reply: Yes. That is precisely the goal here, that the cost of the attack should be greater than the damage caused.

Ross Anderson: Presumably this does not apply to an attack for glory or revenge?

Reply: There are some things we can do to make attacks more difficult, and at least we should do that if nothing better is available.

I am not interested in attacks where with constant effort you can take the server down (*e.g.* by exploiting bugs in the networking software). The attacks of interest are those where the attacker uses an increasing number of resources to consume an increasing number of resources at the server. At a certain point the level of service to normal users becomes low enough that this can be considered denial of service.

Examples of these kinds of denial of service attacks on the Web include the SYN attack, where you open TCP connections faster than the server can deal with them, leave them all in half-open state and let the server's memory suffer with lots of half-open connections. This works especially in the earlier implementations of the TCP protocol where there are limited size kernel tables for state for 100 connections and no way of purging them fast. Now this has improved and there are some other counter-measures to that.

Other things that an attacker can try to consume are: memory, disk space, kernel table space, processing power and communications bandwidth. That last is probably the nastiest thing because I don't see any way of preventing that – recently we have seen SYN flooding attacks at some Web sites, and maybe there is no easy way to correct that.

It has been suggested that to prevent denial of service in this kind of environment we should authenticate the clients. In some cases yes, you can authenticate the clients but then you get additional problems: authentication usually involves public key cryptography which is computationally expensive and in fact these protocols can be used to consume the processing power of the server – you get a new attack that is caused by the authentication protocol. Someone can send you lots of false certificates and let you verify them so that all your time goes into verifying certificates.

So authentication is not the solution, but there are some solutions that have helped: the SYN attack has been effectively stopped by SYN cookies, where the first thing the server does when a new client wants to connect is to send it a pseudo-random number to the client and then wait until the client returns that, which proves that at least the client IP address is valid, in effect providing a very weak level of authentication before getting into anything that is more expensive for the server. During the time in the cookie exchange when the server is waiting for the response, if the system is designed well, the server can remain stateless. It does not need to save any information about that particular client or connection request.

Round the same time when people are looking for defences like cookies against the SYN attack, Pekka and I did some work on stateless servers. We had the idea that by making the server completely stateless you can make it more resistant to denial of service attacks where someone opens more connections and stops them in the middle or just floods you with lots of requests, because you are pushing the task of storing the state to the client.

There are examples of completely stateless protocols – ways of maintaining connections between the client and the stateless server – but the most useful part of the paper was about authentication protocols. The authentication protocol, just like the cookie exchange, should remain stateless at least until it has authenticated the client reliably. That way the server does not commit memory resources to the client before the client has been authenticated. Maintaining a stateless connection requires some crypto, so it does cost something.

Ideas from our paper were taken by Matsuura and Hirose[1] and they modified their key agreement protocol to be denial of service resistant, so that it remains stateless during the first message exchange. Their protocol had the additional nice property that the client has to do the first exponentiation. So the client has to do the expensive operation and the server can verify at low cost that the client has done the exponentiation.

We'd like to generalise this idea to any authentication protocol. Meadows, at last year's Security Foundations Workshop, generalised the cookies in another way where the server will only commit more resources when the client has been weakly authenticated. Our system will be just one step, but at any point in the protocol the server will have done less work than the client.

So what is the way to make the client do work? This relates to a Crypto92 paper about the prevention of junk mail. Before being allowed to send a message, the sender is required to solve a puzzle, say factoring a moderate sized number. The receiver should be able to verify the solution to this puzzle at low cost.

The same idea has been suggested by Jules and Brainerd for preventing the SYN attack. In the beginning the client contacts the server. At that stage, the server will not save any data about the client. It will simply send a puzzle to the client. Now the client solves the puzzle, and sends the solution (with the

---

[1]   Information and Communication Security, ICICS'99, LNCS 1726, pp.169-182

hello data again) to the server. After verifying the solution, the server can safely create state for the client.

Here are the requirements for a good puzzle: Creating and verifying the puzzle should be inexpensive, the cost should be adjustable (exponentially with the security parameter k), the puzzle should be solvable on any type of hardware, it should not be possible to pre-compute solutions, and the server should not need to store client state. We also introduce two new requirements: The same puzzle should be able to be given to many clients, and the same client should be able to create many instances of the same puzzle (for use in broadcast networks).

Our puzzle is a little bit simpler than that of Jules and Brainerd, and it has additional properties. What we have is a one-way hash function with constant data as arguments, and X that the client must find. By trying about 2^k values, the client finds an X such that the first k bits of the hash value are zero (or some other constant). The security parameter k is the number of zeroes that must appear. Hash functions have the nice property that, unlike factorisation, the algorithms for breaking them don't improve every day. Another field is the client name or IP address, there is a nonce from the server, and there is a counter which can be increased by the client each time.

Matt Blaze: How does the server remember the client counter value?

Reply: Once the server has verified the puzzle it *has* to create state. It needs to maintain the last counter number for the same nonce for any client.

The client has to do brute force search for X, but the server has to calculate just one hash value to verify that the solution is correct. After verifying the solution the server has to commit some computational resources to this client to validate the signature on the authentication message. And secondly, it has to create some state for the client – as long as the nonce is valid it has to remember the last puzzle the client has solved.

The same thing can be plugged into almost any authentication protocol, I think. At any point the cost of processing to the client is greater than the cost to the server. Any denial of service attack has a cost greater than the damage it will cause. The security parameter, k, can be increased to make the puzzle harder if the server is under heavy load (and so suspects that a denial of service attack may be taking place). The drawback is that there is more work for the client to do, but no more than in other approaches.

Bruce Christianson: How can a client defend itself against a denial of service attack by someone masquerading as a server? The client has to do the first exponentiation.

Reply: By signing the first message, which contains the puzzle and a timestamp, that will reduce the risk.

Virgil Gligor: This is effective against attacks on CPU and memory resources, but not against network traffic. But I think it may be the kind of thing one should look for in the future.

Matt Blaze: I'm going to argue shortly that everything is hopeless [laughter] – the network denial of service problem is much worse than we think.

Public-Key Crypto-systems
Using Symmetric-Key Crypto-algorithms

Bruce Christianson, Bruno Crispo, and James A. Malcolm

The prospect of quantum computing makes it timely to consider the future of public-key crypto-systems. Both factorization and discrete logarithm correspond to a single quantum measurement, upon a superposition of candidate keys transformed into the fourier domain. Accordingly, both these problems can be solved by a quantum computer in a time essentially proportional to the bit-length of the modulus, a speed-up of exponential order.

At first sight, the resulting collapse of asymmetric-key crypto-algorithms seems to herald the doom of public-key crypto-systems. However for most security services, asymmetric-key crypto-algorithms actually offer relatively little practical advantage over symmetric-key algorithms. Most of the differences popularly attributed to the choice of crypto-algorithm actually result from subtle changes in assumptions about hardware or domain management.

In fact it is straightforward to see that symmetric-key algorithms can be embodied into tamper-proof hardware in such a way as to provide equivalent function to a public-key crypto-system, but the assumption that physical tampering never occurs is too strong for practical purposes. Our aim here is to build a system which relies merely upon tamper-evident hardware, but which maintains the property that users who abuse their cryptographic modules through malice or stupidity harm only themselves, and those others who have explicitly trusted them.

We mention in passing that quantum computing holds out the prospect of devices which can provide unequivocal evidence of tampering even at a distance.

This talk addresses three issues. First, we review the differences between symmetric and asymmetric key crypto-algorithms. Advantages traditionally ascribed to asymmetric-key algorithms are that they:

- scale better than symmetric-key, and solve the key-management problem
- allow local generation and verification of credentials, avoiding the need for servers to be on-line
- prevent servers from masquerading as their clients
- provide locality of trust and allow the consequences of key or hardware compromise to be confined
- provide attributability, preventing clients from masquerading as one another or from repudiating commitment.

We explain in detail why these advantages actually result from system-level assumptions about the hardware or application architecture, rather than from the choice of crypto-algorithm.

Next, we consider the problem of constructing security protocols based upon symmetric-key algorithms embodied in tamper-evident hardware, under corre-

B. Christianson et al. (Eds.): Security Protocols, LNCS 2133, pp. 182–183, 2001.
© Springer-Verlag Berlin Heidelberg 2001

sponding system-level assumptions. The protocol building-blocks which we use are all well known:

- private key certificates for on-line introductions
- hash chaining for forward secrecy
- key-mapping for unforgeable attribution
- capability conversion across domain boundaries to prevent theft
- explicit delegation certificates to avoid key-movement
- secrets hashed with identities to provide public keys

and so on. However by combining these elements together with tamper-evident hardware, we obtain a novel system infrastructure which allows the properties desired of a public-key crypto-system to be achieved when the underlying crypto-algorithm is symmetric. In particular, our proposals allow explicit *lack* of trust to be exploited systematically as a lever so as to make the system more secure.

Finally, we turn our previous arguments inside out, and observe that existing public-key crypto-systems – where the underlying crypto-algorithm is asymmetric – can also be made more robust by deploying the new infrastructure and the associated tamper-evident hardware.

Public-Key Crypto-systems
Using Symmetric-Key Crypto-algorithms
(Transcript of Discussion)

Bruce Christianson

University of Hertfordshire: Hatfield

Mike has told me that I must finish on time, so I'll try not to say anything un-controversial[1].

Many of you will have seen the recent announcement that the number 15 has been factorized at Bletchley Park by a quantum computer. The timing of the announcement[2] is significant, but given all the public money that's being pumped into quantum computers, it's worth considering the implications for us if this effort succeeds.

Discrete logarithm and factorization both succumb to an attack by a quantum computer in a time that's essentially linear in the length of the modulus. The reason for this is that, in the Fourier domain, you're looking for the period of a particular sub-group, and you can do that by a single measurement on a superposition of states. You transform the states into the Fourier domain, which takes $N \log N$ multiply operations, and by superposing you can do N of those in parallel. So it's $\log N$ time, and then you do a single measurement.

You don't get exponential speedup on every problem, only on those where you are essentially making a single measurement in the Fourier domain. On general sorting or matching or searching problems you get quadratic speedup, but that's enough to destroy Merkle-puzzle type key algorithms.

On the other hand, symmetric ciphers are alive and well. You need to double the block length and double the key length, but apart from that you can carry on as before. And it's actually easier to produce tamper-evident devices, in fact now you can even tell remotely whether they've been tampered with, which you couldn't before.

So what are the implications of this for crypto-systems or crypto-protocols, rather than just for the algorithms people? It's been known for a long time that you can do public key cryptography using symmetric key algorithms and tamper-proof boxes. For example, Desmedt and Quisquater have a system[3] where essentially you get the public key K^+ from the private key K^- by applying a symmetric algorithm to K^- using a master key M that is known only to the hardware, so that $K^+ = \{K^-\}_M$. The problem with this is that drilling into one verification box blows the whole crypto-system, because the master key is

---

[1] Because that would waste time.

[2] 10:59 GMT, Saturday 1 April 2000AD.

[3] Y Desmedt and J-J Quisquater, 1987, Public Key Systems Based on the Difficulty of Tampering: Is there a Difference between DES and RSA? Advances in Cryptology – Crypto86.

B. Christianson et al. (Eds.): Security Protocols, LNCS 2133, pp. 184–193, 2001.

a global secret. And it doesn't just blow the entire system, it does it retrospectively: it's always been the same secret so you can go back and tamper with event logs and things like that.

So the first thing we want to see is how far we can get with merely *tamper-evident* hardware. This is hardware which has the property that you can tell whether or not somebody has drilled into it: you can't get the secret out without leaving some physical evidence. Of course, the physical matrix within which tamper-evident hardware is deployed must be irreproducibly unique: someone who gets the secret out of one box mustn't be able to blow the secret into another box and pass the second box off as the first. And so it also has to be possible to verify that the physical matrix matches the secret inside, as well as being physically intact[4]. But all of this is still a weaker requirement than tamper-proof, which says you can't get the secret out at all.

We want to retain all the good things that we associate with public key crypto-systems, like confinement of trust, localization of operation, containment of partial compromise, retrospective repair; this general instinct that we have about public key, which says that malice or stupidity harms only the person who misuses their crypto-module, or people who explicitly trust the misuser's honesty or competence.

Let's start by reviewing the well-known advantages that asymmetric algorithms allegedly have over symmetric key. I want to convince you that these advantages are to a large extent mythical. The first claim is that asymmetric key supposedly scales better than symmetric key and solves the key management problem. Well no, not really. Asymmetric key does use N keys rather than N^2 keys in total for N people, but each individual user still needs to manage N different keys. They need one key for everybody they're actually ever going to talk to.

The only way to reduce the total number of keys to N is by forcing everyone to use a single public key. Each public key is used by N other people. This is exactly what makes the revocation problem hard in the asymmetric case.

Revocation with symmetric key is relatively straightforward: you tell the person with whom you share the secret that the secret is blown. There are protocol implications where Bob doesn't want to hear what Alice is telling him, for example, because Bob in the middle of trying to rip Alice off, or where Alice wants to pretend to have told Bob because she's in the process of ripping Bob off, but it's an end-to-end, one-to-one problem, it's not one of these dreadful things requiring revocation authorities to do fanout.

The initial key distribution requires the same effort to bootstrap whichever algorithm you use, because you've got N people who have to register with some central authority. To make the cost scale linearly with the system size, you need some kind of third party. Everybody has got to register with the third party, and registration requires some sort of real world artifact, no matter how you do it. You can't register by electronic means to do the initial bootstrap, the initial bootstrap requires some sort of tamper-evident token. This token might be a

---

[4] See LNCS 1550, pp157, 166-167.

letter on company letterhead signed in blood by various people, or it might be a tamper-evident device. Asymmetric key doesn't require confidentiality of the real world artifact, just integrity, but if you've got a tamper-evident token then that's not an issue anyway. So there's not a lot of difference there.

But we do need some sort of third party, a trusted third party, or better, several mutually mistrusting parties, which I'll call either a CA or an AS depending on whether the algorithm is asymmetric key or a symmetric key. Of course what these actually are, whether they're really certification authorities or authentication servers or not, depends on the application. When I say CA I just mean a third party in an asymmetric key world, I don't necessarily mean an actual certification authority.

The second myth is that asymmetric key allows local generation and verification of credentials. This is a big advantage, it means you don't have to support on-line checking of credentials. So that means the CA can be off-line, which means it's more secure, and it also means the protocol is more efficient and more convenient. But the way we use asymmetric key cryptography at the moment, the revocation authority has to be on-line, and misbehaviour of the revocation authority is a show-stopper. So the advantage claimed for asymmetric key becomes illusory as soon as you have revocation.

After you've introduced yourself to somebody for the first time, once you've established a relationship with somebody and you're doing business with them, there's very little difference between asymmetric and symmetric. Because if you make your server stateless, which you probably want to do anyway, then you can just push out the credentials that the client needs in order to reintroduce themselves. The client is told, this is part of your state, you've got to present these credentials in the next message that you send.

You almost certainly need to log transaction order whichever world you're in, because there are disputes about whether a transaction occurred before or after a particular key had been revoked, or a particular certificate had been revoked. And there's the old push versus pull debate, the transmitter needs to log that they've revoked a key, the receiver needs to log that they have done a check to see whether a key has been revoked or not. There's a slight tendency to use push technology with asymmetric key and pull technology with symmetric key. But if you say, look I want to design a push protocol, and you sit down and you do it, it's really spooky that the difference between an asymmetric key version and a symmetric key version is so very slight. You are not only writing down the same messages but you're actually putting the same fields in them, it's quite macabre.

At introduction time – now I've never met you before but I want you to store my files for me – there still isn't a vast amount of difference at the system level. In the asymmetric case, if we were being sensible, the first time I did business with Mike I would get the fact that my public key certificate was being issued to him registered somewhere. Because that way the revocation problem becomes straightforward. Either there's a single authority that Mike knows he has to go to to check whether the certificate has been revoked, or the revocation authority knows that when that certificate is repealed it should tell Mike about it. In fact, you can make a good argument that there should be a separate instance of the certificate for each user to whom it's issued, and that the capability should be bound to those instances, harping back to Virgil Gligor's talk earlier[5].

Alternatively, we can use introduction certificates with symmetric key, tokens like $\{A, B, S, Kab\}_{Kas}; \{A, B, S, Kab\}_{Kbs}$ etc. You don't have to do the introduction while the AS is on-line, you just at some previous point have to have indicated that you will wish to engage in transactions with the other person. This is a requirement which you usually have to satisfy anyway at some point well in advance, regardless of which algorithm you're using, it's a systems issue.

So we get onto the third reason that asymmetric key is alleged to be better: it prevents authorities from masquerading as their clients. This is where asymmetric key appears to have a genuine advantage over symmetric key. Well of course a CA *can* masquerade as a client, but the point is that it will get caught. You can break into a CA and issue false key certificates, but when you're challenged you can't produce the real world artifact that goes with the electronic certificate, and then people can go back and they can work out which transactions were committed with those false credentials, and then they can undo those transactions. Or you can have some other protocol that says what to do when you discover this. Provided it didn't involve confidentiality because then the undo involves shooting people. And provided the provenance of the real world artifact is secured.

Under all these conditions it's clear that a CA with asymmetric key doesn't allow *retrospective* breaks. You can't go back and alter the history of which certificates things were signed with, provided people kept careful logs – which is a point I'll come back to later – and didn't just verify the credentials and then throw them away. You can go back and you can work out which transactions are suspect. You say, oh look, there's some sawdust and a little drill-hole in the CA, let's find out which transactions we need to roll back.

But you can also do forward secrecy using symmetric crypto-algorithms. Alice has a secret s_0 that she shares with the AS authority S, and at each step she uses the key $k_i = h(0|s_i)$ which she gets by hashing that secret with a zero, and then she replaces the shared secret by $s_{i+1} = h(1|s_i)$ which she gets by hashing the shared secret with a one, and then she carries on. Now if someone drills into the authority, then the authority is compromised from that point on, but it doesn't get the attacker access back into the past. Everything up to the last point at which the authority was physically secure, is still secure.

And if we always put protocols in these outer wrappers, just as was being suggested in the previous talk by Tuomas Aura[6], then we have gradually increasing authentication, gradually increasing certification. If you receive credentials and the outer wrapper is broken, that's the point at which you say, I want an integrity check now please. This box is using the secret one ahead from me, somebody has done an extra transaction, let's have a look and see whether this is just a failure of the outer protocol or whether there's sawdust on the floor.

---

[5] Khurana and Gligor, these proceedings
[6] Aura *et. al.*, these proceedings

If you've issued false key certificates, you've got to prevent the person whose real key certificate you've replaced from seeing the false one. And that means that following a CA compromise, you need an active wiretap in the asymmetric case. In the symmetric case you can force the situation to be that you still need an active wiretap following AS compromise, and you've got the same time window in which to do it[7].

The fourth myth about asymmetric key is that it gives locality of trust. Except that if you're crossing multiple security domains, which is the only case in which locality of trust is any big deal, you've got to have a separate authentication channel to begin with, because the global hierarchy of trust is never going to happen, see previous talks. And when you think about it, the integrity of your verification key requires tamper-evident hardware local to the verifier anyway. Otherwise how do you know what your hardware is doing, how do you know it's got the right verification key in it, and how do you know it's actually applying that key to the credentials and not just saying "OK". You've got to have some guarantee that what's in the hardware is what you thought it was when you put it in there, and since you've got to have that mechanism anyway, you might as well use it.

So all this third party stuff is really a red herring. The advantage claimed for asymmetric key reduces ultimately to the assertion that asymmetric key makes signatures unforgeable. The people who share a key can't masquerade as each other, because they don't have the same secret. But you need to log transactions to establish time order relative to events like revocation of a key, or of a certificate or a capability or a rôle or something like that. You need to keep a log at each end, and anything that keeps a log can do key mapping.

Matt Blaze: Are there any events like revocation other than revocation? If you design systems that don't have revocation, then is it important to allow revocation?

Reply: A lot of people say, I don't have revocation in my system. When I probe a little deeper, it usually turns into a push *vs* pull debate, a debate about whose responsibility it is to get a freshness certificate. I can say, you have to send me a freshness certificate or I don't believe your key, or I can say, I have to get a freshness certificate from someone or I don't believe your key, or I can say, I will conditionally commit your transaction, and then I will go and get a freshness certificate that was issued after the commit point and then I'll believe it was your key. Now if you want to say that those systems don't have revocation then I claim there are things like revocation that aren't revocation, but for which my argument applies.

John Ioannidis: It's a fine point between needing a freshness certificate or having a short term certificate.

Reply: Sure, and I'm not trying to say that revocation is an issue in every system. There are shades of grey, and eventually you get to the point where you

---

[7] For details see Bruno Crispo, 1999, Delegation of Responsibility, PhD thesis, Computer Laboratory, University of Cambridge.

can say, I don't have revocation, or at least I'm happy for it to take a month to revoke things.

Sometimes the thing you're trotting off to isn't a revocation authority or a freshness certificate server, sometimes it's a time authority, or sometimes it's actually a logging authority: part of the credentials you have to present to commit this transaction is evidence that your intentions have been logged for the purpose of recovery or whatever. The point is that you're going off somewhere, and something is happening in an environment which facilitates key mapping. But I agree that while you can stretch this argument out in various directions, it doesn't apply to everything.

So the point about key mapping is, that Alice sends her token, encrypted with the key that she shares with Bob, but also with the key that she shares with the port S that the token is going through.

$$A \longrightarrow S : \{X\}_{Kab}; \{X\}_{Kas}$$

The port does the key-mapping and appends the token encrypted under the key that Bob shares with the port.

$$S \longrightarrow B : \{X\}_{Kab}; \{X\}_{Kas}; \{X\}_{Kbs}$$

Bob can't forge all the tokens that are logged, because he doesn't know the key that Alice shares with the port. But Alice can't forge the credentials that are presented to Bob either. Neither can the port.

More generally, if you're communicating between domains, security policy is typically enforced by firewalls, which may be internal to the domain. It's not the case that every message has to go through the firewall, but typically setting up an association requires some sort of policy approval, and firewalls do protocol mapping anyway, firewalls keep logs anyway, and firewalls apply security policies anyway, and the two firewalls at either end of a pipe tend to be mutually mistrusting, and therefore they're good pieces from which to build a system like this.

There are considerable merits in forcing tokens to have different bit representations in different security domains. So the idea is to have border controls. You have to change your money as you go through the firewall, and if you present money that you've received from another domain by a covert channel, it won't work. If someone's rung you up and dictated the bit pattern of a capability down the phone, it won't work, because it didn't go through the appropriate security policy.

Li Gong's ICAP mechanism[8] can readily be made to be like this. ICAP actually had a central server and application of authentication to individual users using shared keys and hash functions. But if you put this server in the firewall, in the gateways instead of in the middle of the domain, and you put domain-based secrets into the authentication code, then you can build capabilities which have

---

[8] Li Gong, 1990, Cryptographic Protocols for Distributed Systems, PhD thesis, Computer Laboratory, University of Cambridge.

a different form in the different domains, but which can be checked by the policy servers in the host domain. The authenticator is

$$h(\text{Object} \mid \text{Subject} \mid \text{Rights} \mid \text{Domain Secret}).$$

So modifying Li Gong's ICAP gives you another valuable building block.

The next building block is the use of hash chaining, which you can use to take the mutually mistrusting parties off-line. The MMPs have to be involved when you first set up the association, but the firewall typically has to be involved then in any case. After that the MMPs can go off-line until there's a dispute. The general hash-chaining technique here is a very standard one. We authenticate a shared secret X_0 at the beginning, verify that this really is the shared secret, then I choose a successor secret X_1, hash it, hash that together with X_0 and the signature S_1 of the thing I'm about to commit to.

$$A \longrightarrow B : h(X_0|h(X_1)|S_1)$$

I then get a commitment from you, confirmation that this intention has been logged at the far end. Then I reveal the signature, the current secret and the hash of the next secret, and on we go.

$$A \longrightarrow B : X_0, h(X_1), S_1, h(X_1|h(X_2)|S_2)$$

This is one brick, it's not the wall. What we do is to take this and put it into a Desmedt and Quisquater type box, but one where there isn't a global secret. Instead, the secret depends on the different certificates are that are involved in the transaction. These are symmetric-key certificates, not asymmetric-key certificates, so parts of the certificates are secret. But the key you end up with can be made public. In the event of a dispute you say to everybody, OK produce your tamper-evident token, together with a log book that includes the hash chains and the signatures and so forth[9].

Although you have control of the token, it may actually be the property of the other domain. The other domain has given you this token and said, keep this token safe because otherwise disputes are likely to be resolved against you.

The log book you can keep on a piece of paper or on a write-only optical disk, but it's your responsibility to keep it. If you can't produce it, or if the transaction done by the verifier doesn't tie the current value of the hash in the token with the end value of the log, the last entry on the log, then the dispute is likely to be resolved against you. So you have the same incentive to keep this stuff secure that you have to not blurt out your private key in the asymmetric case.

Now we come to the first set of conclusions. Users shouldn't know the bit-values of the secrets that they control. And it's a very bad idea to share all of the secret information that you need to commit a transaction with any one other party, it's a particularly bad idea to share it all with an arbiter. You should

---

[9] For details see chapter 8 of Bruno's thesis, cited earlier.

divide pieces between enough mutually mistrusting parties to ensure compliance with the protocol.

In other words, lack of trust makes the system more secure. Isolate the mutually mistrusting parties, or isolate the parts of them that do this bit of the protocol. Putting them in the middle of a firewall is a very good way to isolate them from things you don't want them to see. Isolate them in such a way that it is very hard for them to agree upon anything other than what the protocol says should be the agreed story.

We're not talking about what actually happened here, we're talking about institutional truth, what we're all going to claim happened given the state of the logs. You impose a heavy penalty on being the odd one out and you make it very difficult to agree on anything else, the prisoners' dilemma type of thing.

The tokens which a user "controls" may be part of another domain, because the controller doesn't have access to their internals. The idea is that you bind things that look like capabilities – I don't want to get into the theological dispute about what they're called, I can't keep up with recent fashion – you bind things that look like capabilities to things that look like certificates, and then you revoke the certificates or the capabilities forward to the point of use, rather than back to the issuer.

In fact if you think about what a key certificate should really look like in the asymmetric key world, it should say, "I, the certification authority for domain A, assert that this key for Alice can be used by Bob in domain B, provided that Alice wants me to certify this, and provided that the domain B is willing to receive this certificate, and provided Bob said he actually wants to use it to bind something to."

$$T = Ka^+, Kas^+, X, Kb^+, Kbs^+; \qquad S = \{T\}_{Ka^-}, \{T\}_{Kas^-}, \{T\}_{Kbs^-}, \{T\}_{Kb^-}$$

In fact this looks just like a delegation token, a point that Mike Roe made a couple of years ago[10].

So we come to the final conclusions. I started in a somewhat fanciful way by saying, let's see what happens if asymmetric key doesn't work anymore. What would we do if we had to rely on tamper-evident hardware and symmetric key algorithms? Thinking about this suggests a number of things which it would be sensible to do differently, and these changes to how we currently do things still appear remarkably sensible even when the underlying algorithm remains asymmetric. There are differences between symmetric and asymmetric algorithms from the point of view of the resulting crypto-system, but they are very subtle, and they are not at all the differences you find described in books suitable for children.

Any questions or heckling?

John Ioannidis: I suppose if an AS is compromised then whether a signature is subsequent to the compromise cannot be resolved.

Reply: You can't use signatures ad infinitum even now, unless they've been logged or archived or put into something that gives you assurance that they

---

[10] LNCS 1550, pp168–176.

existed prior to the key being revoked or compromised or the certificate expiring, or some other thing that would have violated your policy if you had checked it.

Otherwise you can't know which happened first, even in the asymmetric case.

Ross Anderson: You assume that publication of a secret key compromises part of the system, but the existence of an append-only file makes it trivial to use one-time signatures.

Reply: That's true. The question that needs to be addressed there is the issue that Matt Blaze raised last year[11], which is the need to layer confidentiality servers on top of the event logger, so that people can't see bits of the log that they mustn't see, whilst still having an assurance that the chain is intact for the bits that they are allowed to see. But again, that's a problem now, it's not a problem that comes about from the fact that asymmetric key stops working.

Mark Lomas: How can I make backups of my private key?

Reply: You make backups of your actual private key? Shame on you.

Mark Lomas: The reason I make backups of my private key is because my machine might be unreliable.

Matt Blaze: But if you had a good public key infrastructure you'd simply create new keys.

Reply: Exactly. What you actually have is a requirement to be able to transfer your rights to a different key in a controlled way under certain circumstances, or equivalently here to a different physical token, without having a period of a month while you can't access your system.

There are two arguments for never moving private keys around. The first is that if it's physically possible to move a private key from one place to another, then someone is going to do it when you don't want them to, or make a copy while it's in transit. It's usually when keys are moving around that they get filched.

I agree that you can make the process of moving them safer, but what I'm saying is that it's possible to give an excellent solution to the wrong problem and very often moving a private key is the wrong problem, it doesn't need to be solved.

The second reason is that very often when we run a protocol, one of the things we want to authenticate is that a particular specific piece of hardware, say a particular hand-held device, was involved in the protocol. Then it's very important that we satisfy ourselves that it wasn't some other piece of hardware that had the same noughts and ones in it. The easy way to do this is if there *is* no other piece of hardware with the same noughts and ones in it. And in those cases you have to be able to guarantee not simply that you didn't move the keys around, but that it wasn't possible for you to move the key, you could not have done it.

How can we meet this requirement? We tend to think that binding and unbinding capabilities from certificates is really hard, and revoking certificates is a real pain, and certifying things is really difficult, and it's a rare event anyway, so let's try and avoid doing this as much as possible. What I'm suggesting is

---

[11] LNCS 1796, p46.

a world view where these things actually happen all the time. Whenever you want someone to use a public key that *they* haven't used before, that's a certification transaction. When they say "I've finished using it", that's a revocation transaction. What we need is an infrastructure that deals efficiently with these events, and then you can just put keys in one physical place and bind them there for life. Then all your bindings between bit patterns and real world entities are happening at the edge of cyberspace instead of in the middle. The last thing you want to do is to bind two bit patterns to each other via a real world entity because then you can't verify the binding remotely[12].

Matt Blaze: I guess the major reason for not revoking secret keys is that it's psychologically a bit embarrassing to have to revoke one. Revoking a key is a very public event.

Reply: You're absolutely right, we have to take the social stigma out of revoking your key. We need a sort of revocation pride march or something. Reclaim the night, revoke the right.

John Ioannidis: It's not too wise to say why you revoked your key, because then everyone knows it's lost and that you don't want other people to send you anything.

Reply: I don't have to say why I revoked a key. Maybe the session ended, or maybe I'm just bored with it. All I'm going to say is, my name is Bruce and I just revoked this key.

---

[12] For more on this theme see LNCS 1361, pp105–113.

Denial of Service – Panel Discussion

Virgil Gligor, Matt Blaze, and John Ioannidis

Virgil Gligor: I decided to go first, to review a brief history of what I think the denial of service problem was, and the motivation. I started working on this at a time when the denial of service problem was being denied, in fact we were in a state of denial. In particular, this is 1981 to 1983 when the Orange book was being written, and some of us were told that denial of service doesn't exist, it's not a security problem. So by 1983 the tune had changed, it wasn't really that denial of service wasn't a security problem: it was really a subset of an integrity problem, therefore if we address integrity and confidentiality we covered the entire spectrum of security altogether and let's not worry about denial of service.

So by 1985 I had written a second paper on the topic[1] in which I showed that in fact denial of service was a separate security problem, separate from confidentiality and separate from integrity. In the same paper, I showed that in fact it occurred as a problem in distributed systems and networks and network protocols equally well as in operating systems.

By 1988 there was one more realisation which occurred to a couple of us, and this I think is absolutely fundamental: the realisation was that given a service – a generic general service – and given a bunch of users of this service, you cannot prevent denial of service unless you have agreement among the users of the service: agreement that could not possibly be programmed and checked in the service itself[2].

The classic example in this area was actually the dining philosophers problem, in which Dijkstra showed that you had to have agreements among the philosophers so that you could demonstrate that the philosophers would not deny each other service, and these agreements were in fact enforced outside the dining table service. So we generalised that concept. Now the implications of that are absolutely fundamental, which was not realised until later on. What it means is that you could not construct a service outside the participant that could monitor the behaviour of the participant in such a way that denial of service could not happen.

And if you go further you realise that that is a property of a problem which is neither safety nor liveness, so what that essentially means is that if you want to prevent denial of service, not only do you have to look at the services but you have to look at the behaviour of the users of those services.

---

[1] Virgil D. Gligor: On Denial-of-Service in Computer Networks. Proc. Second International Conference on Data Engineering, February 1986, 608-617

[2] Che-Fn Yu, Virgil D. Gligor: A Specification and Verification Method for Preventing Denial of Service. IEEE Transactions on Software Engineering **16** (6), June 1990 581-592. It was a 1988 paper originally published in Oakland, written prior to the massive Internet DOS attack of 3 November.

B. Christianson et al. (Eds.): Security Protocols, LNCS 2133, pp. 194–203, 2001.

Consequently, more recently, we realised that it is futile to talk about prevention of denial of service in an open network when in fact this user agreement could not possibly be enforced. So that's a brief history of what was realised over the course of many years, and it's only now that people are trying to cast various properties of security policies into either safety or liveness, or non-safety and non-liveness. I guess John McLean was one of the first to point that out that information flow, for example, doesn't fall into that and also Stew Lee and Arizankintinos did the same here.

It turns out that denial of service, in a general form, falls into one of those <neither safety nor liveness> problems, although there are instances of the denial of service problem which are purely safety or purely liveness, which of course can be handled in some way. In fact, we should probably look as hard as we can to the possibility of reducing those instances of denial of service problems to either safety or liveness in some sense, so that they can be solved outside the users of services, and some of the things that you heard here today go a long way in this area. In other words, we are trying to solve the problem on a case by case basis with interesting mechanisms that might be construed as safety mechanisms, and we get a lot of mileage in practice if we do that.

So my sense is that our first task in denial of service is, to try to reduce the problem as much as we can, to either a safety or a liveness problem, but I don't think that outside this kind of generic approach there is much hope for prevention. Of course there is always scope for detection and recovery – we shouldn't be greedy and always try to do prevention – and in practice most of the time we do just that, we detect that there is a denial of service problem and we try to recover from it in some way.

Matt Blaze: I'm going to speak briefly about a very practical question. I'm putting on my protecting the Internet hat, for a moment, and taking off my researcher hat. So the problem that I want to solve at the moment and I want to encourage people to think about, is the problem of protecting the Internet against distributed denial of service attacks. The solution space is very, very heavily constrained but also has the property that if something works you've made tremendous progress even if you can't prove that it works. So the theme of this talk is really: this Internet thing had to end sooner or later and it appears, unless we do something soon, that sooner is now.

Just to give you some quick background on what's been going on, the attackers against the Internet, against the major services on the Internet and the Internet infrastructure itself, have gotten considerably more sophisticated, or at least obtained tools that let them behave in a much more sophisticated manner than they've been able to behave in the past.

In the simplest case, we are seeing denial of service attacks that exploit basic properties of the underlying protocols of the Internet, things like the fact that, if you send somebody traffic, the network will route that traffic to their network link and if you can send them enough traffic you'll flood their network link. But that's simply a property of the way the Internet works, it's a very dumb attack which says, send lots of data to the recipients that you want to flood.

We're also seeing things like, there are a limited number of clients that a server can serve at any given time, so if you can essentially fill up all of its available resources by having it do work that may not actually be useful from the server's point of view, you can prevent it from serving, for example, new customers if it's an electronic commerce site.

We can go through a progression of the kinds of attackers that might be present. Initially we've designed protocols and we've worried about making networks robust against one bad guy, we want to design protocols that make it difficult for one bad guy to cause any significant amount of harm. Now typically that's very important because there's very little you can do, as one host on the net, to do very much damage to another host on the net, without at least causing an equivalent amount of damage to yourself, and without attracting a great deal of attention to yourself.

Now, until very recently in most of the Internet it's very easy to forge your source address. Internet Service Providers are getting a little bit better about having source address filtering, to prevent their clients from forging addresses so as to make it difficult for the recipient even to know where attacks are coming from. This has improved things considerably. So now if you see somebody using up too much of your bandwidth you can simply stop talking to them.

So that raises the question, what if you have a conspiracy of bad guys. You convince lots of your friends to run programs that attack a particular target. We've started to see attackers, using an attack tool, that have behaved in a much more conspiratorial way. Most recently we've seen an even more worrisome kind of attacker model on the Internet which was where we have perhaps one bad guy, but that bad guy isn't actually initiating the attack. Instead we have a bad guy who is breaking into insecure operating systems, some of them maybe even produced by the company who also provided us with this coffee, on machines that are spread out over the net. The proliferation of things like cable modems means that there are a large number of non-professionally administered computers sitting out on the net with high bandwidth links. So a distributed attacker simply, at leisure, breaks into lots of these machines, and installs software that sits dormant waiting for the command to go and attack a particular target.

John Ioannidis: Because they're on a dedicated link they're on all the time which complicates the problem.

Matt Blaze: That's right. So the analogy that I like to draw when I am talking to reporters about this, is that the Internet is like a giant water distribution system and the machines that are attached to the Internet are like toilets. Now if you flush your toilet, no matter how often you flush it, it's very difficult to have any effect on the amount of water pressure available, or to affect anything about the global properties of the water system, or even to deny water to your neighbour. If you can convince a number of people you might be able to have some local effects, but imagine that every toilet in the world were programmable and the attacker could simply insert a programme that responds to a global command that says, flush.

What you get in water distribution systems is a phenomenon — I did some research on this — known as a water hammer, because you get a drop in water pressure followed by water going down what are now empty pipes, which causes a water mains to break. The Internet is surprisingly analogous to a water distribution system. None of this is pretty when you have programmable toilets.

So what we've seen, and this has gotten quite a lot of press, is the idea of a manually distributed denial of service of attack in which there's one bad guy controlling machines that he has probably broken into over a long period of time in the past.

This raises the possibly of the things the bad guys haven't perfected yet but no doubt will very soon, which is the automatically distributed denial of service attack, which is actually the Internet Worm technique, where one installs software that automatically exploits well known bugs, installs itself and then looks for new targets at each of its sites, and of course you get exponential growth in the number of compromised machines. This is actually even easier to do on a large scale by mistake than it is on purpose.

Based on tools that we've seen, that have been found on compromised machines, it's absolutely clear that the attackers are thinking along these lines. It's very likely we'll see an automatically distributed denial of service attack on the network soon.

Now let's look at another side of the coin which is, who are the targets. Well traditionally, fortunately, and what's kept the Internet going for so long in spite of some fundamental weaknesses, the attackers have not really been very interested in doing much damage that anyone cares about. Traditionally an attacker focuses on one target, who's probably somebody on an Internet relay chat host, that they've had a fight with. So they send denial of service tools from a script towards that user's machine in order to log them off. This is annoying behaviour, it's certainly bad, but it doesn't have any global effect, it doesn't affect anybody except the people involved.

More recently we're seeing, things like Yahoo being the target, services on the net that many network users depend on. Even though the denial of service attack may have the same scope in and of itself, the effect of which machine it's bringing down makes it much more important. And recently we saw the attack against many big targets all at once. There was some evidence that attackers did this manually distributed denial of service attack against many of the major electronic commerce sites.

There's an obvious next step for the attackers who want to do lots of damage, they get their automated attack tools in place over a large portion of the net and use it to attack to the network infrastructure itself, for example, the root DNS servers. If the root DNS servers are taken down, the net is essentially useless. Similarly the underlying routing infrastructure has many of the same properties. This would be enormously disruptive and it's clear that the attackers are thinking along these lines. They're writing their tools now and we as secure protocol designers need to start thinking about the responses.

Now there are a few interesting constraints. First of all the protocols that the attackers are using are not security protocols. The protocols that the attackers are using were not designed to provide security, they're designed to provide communications. This is not a failure of a security protocol, this is a failure of things like TCP and ICMP and Ping and so forth. So what can we do to design systems to support this? Well we've heard a number of proposals along these lines, some here. For example the idea that it should be much more expensive to initiate communication than to cause somebody to use resources to respond to it[3]. This is a very important principle for designing protocols to resist denial of service. One can imagine things like, at every hop along the network, if you send out a message to initiate communication, you have to send out much more traffic and it gets reduced as it goes along to its destination. We could be clever and design things along these lines. The idea of puzzles that you have to respond to before the server will create any state is another thing that will work to do this.

But if you want these ideas to actually be used on the Internet, then there's a constraint, which is that you can't actually change any of the protocols. Not even a little. Really, honestly. You can't change anything. You cannot change TCP. Anything that involved changing the fundamental protocol used by a client to talk to a Web server simply isn't going to be taken seriously.

John Ioannidis: Most of the mechanisms to prevent denial of service are mechanisms to protect against consuming resources that the server owns. They do not protect against consuming resources that the server depends on but does not own, such as their network links, and that's where the big problem is. It's not that I'm going to make the dot com servers do lots of crypto computation, I'm just going to take down their multiple T3.

Matt Blaze: Right, exactly, and imagine compromising one of those sites that has a T3. If you have a T3 connection you can use up your bandwidth to take down a lot of T1 connections at targets that you might be interested in, and this is just how the net works.

It's helpful to use source address filtering, but even if they're using ingress filtering everywhere, the attacker can get around it by just compromising more machines. So there are some hard problems.

To give you an example of some of the solutions that are being put forward, one of the things that's difficult to do in the presence of forged addresses is to know where traffic is coming from, so you don't know who to complain to when you're suddenly being flooded, if the source addresses are forged. This doesn't help with the massively distributed attacks, but in the moderately distributed or non-distributed attacks it would be very helpful to have some indication of where your packets are coming from. One of the proposals that it looks like ISPs and router vendors are likely to adopt fairly soon is this: anytime a router passes a packet the router will flip a 20,000 sided coin, and if the coin comes up heads then the router will send an ICMP packet, that includes the packet headers of the packet that the router saw, to the destination saying, by the way I saw this

---

[3] Aura *et. al.*, these proceedings

packet, here's my address, it came in on this interface for me, just letting you know. Now this will cause a 1/20,000 increase in total traffic but it will provide, at least statistically, information to hosts about where traffic is coming from, so if they suddenly get flooded they'll know where the traffic is coming from.

Now the authentication issues here are hairy, but you at least don't have to do any of the verifications on-line. So as designers of security protocols, this is a problem we need to seriously think about, how do we manage this constraint of being resistant to denial of service when we can't actually change the end-to-end protocols that are being used to send the traffic.

Virgil Gligor: I think this is an interesting problem, where the compatibility with existing systems, or existing mistakes, is important. So for that reason I think we need to focus on detection and recovery, and even denial of service detection and recovery is not an easy matter. Let me give you an example.

The target was the Bureau of Labour Statistics, which was about to release the unemployment data for the previous quarter in 1997. Now the unemployment data nowadays in the US is a very sensitive type of figure, because if you get prior knowledge that unemployment went down, there is an implication of increased inflation, which affects the stock market. So what happened was, somebody flooded the Bureau of Labour Statistics. They got the data, they flooded their site and the flooding of the site caused a secondary effect that their telephone lines became flooded, in other words, everybody who couldn't get to their site started calling. For a number of hours, about half a day, the unemployment data, could not be released. So essentially what has happened in this case was, not only there was a possibility of denial of service attack, but recovery from the denial of service attack caused even more denial of service on a different communication channel.

So that basically says that we have to be able to design systems to recover some guaranteed way, or even a probabilistic way, from denial of service instances, otherwise there is no particular hope of anything. And perhaps this mechanism which was proposed, sending out packets about the route of some packets, might help in identifying the source and might be a first step towards recovery.

John Ioannidis: The situation is even more hopeless than has been presented. One reason is: assuming we find a way of doing something about the problem, the question is, who pays for it?

Until we are in the position where the people who are in the position to deploy countermeasures are the ones who are going to profit from them, it's hard to do anything about it. Fortunately the larger ISPs are recognising the fact that it is to their best interest, they think it's the best interest of their biggest clients, to deploy such a thing, they are starting to do something about it but it is not clear exactly who is going to have to pay what it costs.

Virgil Gligor: The bigger ISPs — in particular phone companies — are actually building secondary channels for offloading traffic by agreement with other service providers. For example, BT has agreements with AT&T and with

Sprint, and with some of the others, so that if some of their links are flooded then automatically their traffic gets routed through some other provider.

Matt Blaze: Fortunately it is extremely difficult to flood the backbone links, which are on the order of T48s. The recent denial of service attacks that occurred, that got all the press in the US, apparently weren't even a blip on the backbone traffic. So it's going to take one level beyond even what I described before the attackers are going to be in a position to flood those.

Virgil Gligor: So what this shows is that at some level service providers recognise that there is a problem, and found some way to cope with it, but whether that's sufficient is unclear.

John Ioannidis: Well for instance if a major site has five links to five service providers, and because of the distribution of the hacked sites which are contributing to the attack, all five links are being shadowed, it's the links close to the edge that are most vulnerable, and it's there where agreements between the service providers aren't going to help much.

Virgil Gligor: Well here is a potential solution to some aspects of denial of service. Remember what the military does in communication, they do something called spread spectrum, and have all sorts of techniques for frequency hopping. Now suppose that this major service provider will be allocated a lot of addresses, chunks of IP addresses, maybe not in the millions but in the ten thousands. And suppose that there is a way to randomly pick the IP address to which you respond at any one time, and suppose that there is a way to inform everybody else about it. That means that essentially your attacker, once he goes up to your IP address, will have a limited chance to flood all your links completely.

John Ioannidis: That doesn't work in the presence of address aggregation. If we solve denial of service by taking out address aggregation, we've actually complicated the problem.

Virgil Gligor: Possibly, but in some sense this is the kind of measure we have to have if we really want to detect and recover fast.

John Ioannidis: The more traditional approach to attacks on the system is redundancy, and spread-spectrum can sort of be viewed as redundancy in an Information Theoretic way. Now spread-spectrum is not just for preventing jamming, it's also for preventing tracing of where you're coming from. So there is no reason to assume that the same tactics won't be used by the hackers to hide where they're coming from. And if for some reason some group of hackers decided to take down enough machines around the network, they could easily bring the entire network down and ....

Ross Anderson: Consider the following scenario. Suppose that twenty million Greenlanders all at the same time send a very large word attachment to the e-mail address of a well known political figure. This doesn't involve any automation, it just uses twenty million angry people. That causes something to break. How you stop it — and you have to because it's causing things to break in America — is by not providing an enormously fast satellite link to Greenland. Now is there a useful analogy here?

Matt Blaze: But here's what the Greenlanders do. They get accounts on US ISPs from which they actually send these e-mail messages, so all they're doing over the link are low bandwidth operations to set up the attack, then hitting return.

Michael Roe: The problem where's there's a large number of people who are really upset with you is fundamentally unsolvable. Particularly if they're in the same country as you.

Matt Blaze: But the problem is that "you" might be the root DNS server, in which case we're all dead.

Michael Roe: If there's a conspiracy amongst a large proportion of Internet users to cause the Internet structure itself to stop working, then yes, we're in deep, deep trouble.

John Ioannidis: In the case of root DNS servers and top level domain servers, which are (but should not be) the same machines, the big ISPs are already trying to figure out how to effectively make some duplicated addresses, with each ISP replicating the top levels of domain servers. Unfortunately this has some additional political problems when you consider the last couple of years, and the war concerning top-level domains.

The other comment I want to make that BCP, which was released a couple of months ago, was actually written five years ago. It took five years for somebody to decide to make a best current practice server. Actually it's not even the best current practice, it's the best practice that we hope to have sometime in the future, but that doesn't make for a good TLA[4].

Virgil Gligor: That's essentially what I was going to say next, that even sometimes when we have solutions they are very difficult to deploy in the Internet because of the size, because of compatibility, because of the fact that people don't patch things.

Matt Blaze: Frequently also because of perception – take a look at the authenticated DNS, it's like carphone proposal, what ever happened to that? There's nothing hard about it, it would have solved a large number of problems, not all of them, but where is it?

John Ioannidis: The question here is, what does it buy me to set up security? It doesn't by buy me anything unless everybody else sets it up.

Virgil Gligor: Precisely. It's the infrastructure that is not a profit making proposition, and this is part of the problem.

Matt Blaze: In any event, I would encourage people to think about the problem. Think about the problem of taking down the Internet, and think about how you might change the network infrastructure — without changing the network protocols — to be resistant to denial of service attacks. We as protocol designers like to think in terms of changing the protocol itself, but we're constrained in ways which mean we can't. We have to think of ways in which to change the network infrastructure so that the behaviour of the protocol is better against this kind of attack.

---

[4] Three Letter Acronym.

Ross Anderson: Conspiracy theorists might consider the following scenario. Suppose you work in the Information Warfare department in Greenland and your mission is to bring down the Internet. You could use the kind of techniques that we are currently talking about. Now if your job is actually protecting information against this kind of warfare then you might start thinking in terms of vaccination. But the only way to get ISPs and Microsoft and so on moving is to go and shoot Yahoo and half a dozen others and hope that this will cause the necessary momentum in motivational terms.

Virgil Gligor: The best motivator was the Internet Worm attack which took down 60,000 computers. That was a sizable fraction of the Internet at that time.

Matt Blaze: Those 60,000 computers have learned their lesson, unfortunately they are now a tiny fraction of the net.

So that's the real point, we've already had that attempt at inoculation and it didn't work.

Bruce Christianson: Denial of service is just a special case of a more general misappropriation of resources. Even if you have an agreement that it's OK to do something that you want to do, expensive resources are always shared and if everybody wants to do it at once, then there isn't enough to go around. So appropriation is a protocol for how you decide who gets the resources in a particular context.

Now there are two cases to denial of service, one is where somebody else is using your resources that you're entitled to, and the other is where they are using your resources and actually they are entitled to do that under the appropriation protocol.

It would be useful to work out the implications of a protocol which users could use after the event to say, here's my bandwidth requirement, here's my buffer requirement, should I have got it? I don't like the term quality of service, it isn't quite the right concept.

John Ioannidis: The problem with quality of service type solutions is that – fortunately – most applications we have on the Web today couldn't care less about quality of service, all they need is to get service eventually. So to put in place a mechanism for everybody to have to use is going to be extremely expensive, and nobody is going to want to pay for it.

What contributed to the success of IP is precisely the fact that it does not require service to the seller.

Michael Roe: And all these attempts to put in resource reservation end up reintroducing virtual circuit.

I think that quality of service isn't going to work because of the issues Matt talks about. We can't dictate to everybody that they all change the protocol they're using. But I almost felt if you were able to redesign the Internet from scratch you'd do something like circuit switching, resource reservation.

Matt Blaze: Right. But look, how to redesign the Internet from scratch to solve this problem is a hard problem that we could all probably solve, it's hard enough but it's interesting and so it's very tempting to go off and do it but that's not going to have any impact.

Michael Roe: It's irrelevant to the real problem.

Markus Kuhn: Another denial of service attack is based upon the problem that TCP/IP depends upon voluntary cooperation for connection control, and I have no reason to actually implement exponential back-off.

Matt Blaze: People are doing that. You see those banner ads that say your Internet connection is not optimised? What they're selling you is a tool kit that will replace your client TCP, with a greedy one that will give you better performance of the expense of the net as a whole. Not only did they already think of it, they're making money on it.

Ross Anderson: There's one attack being alleged that I'm not sure really is happening. The people who are running the anonymous re-mailers alleges that the encrypted messages between their re-mailers get lost far more frequently than normal mail messages.

I think what's really happening here is that the infrastructure is a lot flakier than people are prepared to admit, and because they've got an end to end integrity check they're spotting it.

Virgil Gligor: It's very likely that you get more denial of service if you use encryption. All you need to do is to flip a bit and the integrity checks won't pass at the other end. They actually might pass the usual checksum but now they won't because they have too good a detector.

Michael Roe: There are lots of good reasons that putting in either a signature or encryption will cause a simple error to make the whole transaction fail, rather than the error just being ignored.

It goes back to the Second World War, the attack against the Siemens and Halske T52 machine was to crank up the level of the noise on the telegraph lines as they went across Sweden, increasing the number of retransmits. With that cipher a retransmit is the same message with a different initialisation vector which was very bad news indeed.

The Resurrecting Duckling — What Next?

Frank Stajano

AT&T Laboratories Cambridge
http://www.uk.research.att.com/~fms/
and
University of Cambridge Computer Laboratory
http://www.cl.cam.ac.uk/~fms27/

Abstract. In the context of the security of wireless ad hoc networks, we previously explored the problem of secure transient association between a master and a slave device in the absence of an online authentication server. We introduced the *Resurrecting Duckling* security policy model to address this problem.

Master-slave relationships, however, do not exhaust the range of interesting interactions. We therefore extend the Duckling model to also cover relationships between peers.

1 The Duckling: Why, What, and What's Missing

The range of devices that contain a microprocessor is continually expanding in every field — from consumer goods to office equipment, "white goods", vehicles and medical and scientific instrumentation. Looking ahead, the next development after endowing every device with a processor is going to be to allow all these computing nodes to communicate with each other, enabling them to co-operate and take advantage of each other's services. For convenience, in many cases this connectivity will be wireless: devices will be able to talk to each other as required by forming short-lived *ad hoc wireless networks*.

One respect in which such networks are fundamentally different from their well studied more traditional cousins is the absence of online servers for functions such as authentication. Your digital camera and your electronic organiser may spontaneously decide to communicate at any time, for example while you are taking pictures in the middle of the desert, and the ad hoc network they establish will be completely local, with no backbone infrastructure to connect it to the Internet or to anything else. This means that the problem of authentication can no longer be solved in the traditional way. The symmetric cryptography solutions in the tradition of Needham-Schroeder, Otway-Rees, Kerberos etc. explicitly require an online ticket-granting server; and even the solutions based on public key cryptography and signed certificates eventually fail if the certification authority is not online, due to the difficulty of performing timely revocation[1].

---

[1] Certificates may certainly be marked with an expiration date, and the interval between renewals may be made sufficiently short that timely revocation becomes pos-

B. Christianson et al. (Eds.): Security Protocols, LNCS 2133, pp. 204–214, 2001.
© Springer-Verlag Berlin Heidelberg 2001

In a previous work [7,8] we highlighted *secure transient association* as the fundamental authentication problem in this scenario: one principal, for example the universal remote control of your electronic house, needs an association with another principal, for example your garage door or your hi-fi (or indeed both, and more). This association needs to be *secure*, in the sense that you don't want anybody else with the same type of controller to be able to open your garage door or turn on your hi-fi from the street in the middle of the night, but it also needs to be *transient*, in the sense that you want to be able to undo it when you decide to resell your hi-fi to buy a better one, without for that being also forced to resell your garage door, your television and your refrigerator.

The solution we proposed is formalised in the *Resurrecting Duckling* security policy model, which we shall now summarise. The slave device is the duckling, while the master controller acts as its mother duck. The duckling may be in one of two states, imprinted or imprintable, depending on whether it contains a soul or not; it starts (pre-birth) as imprintable, becomes imprinted at birth when a mother duck[2] gives it a soul, and it becomes imprintable again on death, when the soul dissolves. The soul is a shared secret that binds the duckling to its mother: as long as the soul is in the body, the duckling will stay faithful to the mother and obey no one else. Resurrection is allowed, as the name of the policy suggests, but the duckling's metempsychosis works in reverse: instead of one soul inhabiting successive bodies, here we have one body hosting a succession of souls. The soul is originally transferred from mother to duckling over a non-wireless channel[3] (e.g. electrical contact) in order to bootstrap the rest of the protocol. Death, which makes the duckling imprintable by a new mother, may be triggered by the conclusion of the current transaction or by a deliberate order from the mother duck ("commit suicide now!"), but not by one from an outside principal[4]. The mother duck should backup the soul with local escrow parties since, if the soul is lost (for example because your dog chews on the remote control), the duckling will be unresponsive to any other principal and it will be impossible to reset it to the imprintable state.

This model expressively describes a great variety of interesting situations, not just the relationship between a remote control and an array of household appliances. It describes, for example, the bond between a wireless thermometer and the doctor's PDA that records graphs of the temperatures of the various patients; there, death of the thermometer duckling occurs at the end of the

---

sible, but the cost of this strategy is indeed in the necessity for frequent renewals of the certificates, which must be propagated to all the devices in the field — an expensive proposition if, as we assumed, the devices have no online connection to the server. And we haven't even mentioned the subtle issues to do with the requirement for secure clocks.

[2] *Any* mother duck, actually. That's the point of imprinting: any entity the duckling sees at birth is taken as being the mother duck, even if it looks like Konrad Lorenz.

[3] This is an informal way of saying "over a channel whose confidentiality and integrity are axiomatically guaranteed".

[4] This is to say that attempts to kill the duckling should damage its body or otherwise be uneconomical compared to buying a new, imprintable duckling.

transaction, when the thermometer is returned to the bowl of disinfectant. It even describes a possible mode of interaction between an e-wallet and an e-ATM: as the banking customer gets near the e-ATM, she wants the machine to imprint itself to her e-wallet and no one else's; but at the end of the transaction, the e-ATM duckling dies and is again imprintable to any other customer. It is also a representation of the relationship between a computer and its superuser, the soul being here the superuser password: when the computer ships, it is imprintable, in that anyone can become its superuser by installing the operating system and supplying a master password; but, once that is done, nobody can become mother duck unless the current superuser voluntarily relinquishes control[5].

There are however a number of other equally interesting situations that the model so far described does not adequately cover. All the above cases involved a definite master-slave relationship between the mother and the duckling, but we can envisage cases of ad hoc networks between devices that it would be more natural to consider as peers. If the components of your hi-fi and video system talk to each other, for example because the timer wants to start the satellite TV tuner and the DVD writer in order to record something off air, or because the DVD player wants to tell the TV that it should set the aspect ratio to widescreen for this programme, does it make any sense for the DVD player to become the mother duck of the television?

The new work presented here extends the Resurrecting Duckling model to cope with such peer-to-peer cases.

2   The Many Ways of Being a Master

2.1   Human or Machine?

The first interesting remark concerns the nature of the principals. The master-slave model so far presented seems to make sense primarily when the mother duck master is a person and the duckling slave a peripheral that the person wishes to use. The master initiates imprinting of the slave (including the physical contact step) and then starts giving it orders. This pattern tends to suggest that the master, even though it is a physical device (the remote control), is actually only the cyber-representative of a sentient being (the person who owns the remote control, the television, the fridge and all the rest of the equipment).

Blurring the distinction between the person and the computer that represents it is a common sin, which may sometimes have unexpected consequences.

---

[5] There is a noteworthy subtlety here: if we consider the duckling to be just the hardware of the computer, then this system does not properly follow our security policy model, because it is trivial for a thief to kill the duckling by taking out the hard disc and reformatting it in another computer, thereby returning the duckling to the imprintable state. If however we consider the installed software to be part of the duckling, i.e. if the value of the computer is more in its software, configuration and data than in its hardware, then a computer with encrypted file system does follow the policy, because reformatting the disc will damage the duckling's body — here taken to include the data and installed software.

We shall remedy by being more precise and identifying two separate interactions: the one between the remote control as master and the DVD as slave is one where the principals are both computing devices; but on top of that there is another relationship between the owner as master and the remote control as slave, in which one principal is a human and the other is machine. The interesting point is that this second relationship, too, can be modelled with the Resurrecting Duckling: the virgin remote control gets imprinted to its owner on purchase when the owner types in a PIN. We thus have a hierarchy of master-slave duckling relationships: the human is mother duck to this remote control and possibly other cyber-representatives (for example the e-wallet, to use another one of our previous examples), while the remote control is in turn mother duck to a number of devices (DVD, hi-fi, garage door etc.). Each principal (whether man or machine) has control over all the principals in the subtree of which it is root[6] — but such control can only be exerted with the co-operation of all the principals down the relevant chain of command: I may be the mother duck of my remote control, in turn mother duck of my DVD player, but if I break the remote control I will not be able to play any DVDs despite being the grandmother duck of the player (unless I restore the relevant imprinting keys from the local backups).

2.2 Smart Dust

Before going any further we should introduce the application scenario that originally inspired me to extend the Duckling model.

Take a wireless network not of a few nodes but of several thousand; scale the nodes down in volume from 10,000 mm^3 (i.e. a few cm across) to 1 mm^3; throw in some extra science fiction such as laser-based optical communications between those microscopic gizmos; what you get is a rough approximation to what the wizards at Berkeley are developing under the heading of "smart dust".

The system [6] consists of autonomous millimetre-sized sensor nodes, the "dust motes", that can be scattered in great quantities over the area to be monitored. Each dust mote consists of battery, solar cell, sensors, micromachined catadioptric mirror (which can reflect or not reflect an incoming laser ray towards its sender, thus passively transmitting one bit) and some digital computing equipment, plus extra optionals such as an active transmitter and a receiver (in their absence, the node consumes less power and lasts longer, but it can only talk to a larger entity such as a better equipped dust mote or a base station).

In one example scenario, a cloud of dust motes is dumped on the battlefield from a military aircraft; later a base station with a laser and a high-speed video camera acquires the sensor results from a safe distance, for example to detect the passage of vehicles or the presence of toxic gases. It is also envisaged that the better endowed dust motes might talk to each other in order to route data from motes that don't have direct line of sight to the base station.

---

[6] Since the link from a node to its parent is indeed a representation of a duckling-to-mother relationship, this graph can be viewed as a duck family tree. So each principal has control over all its offspring.

At this early stage in the project, manufacturing the devices and devising the appropriate low-level communications and routing protocols so that they work at all are, quite reasonably, the primary concerns, and the security issues appear not to have been tackled yet. If the White general deploys his dust motes, how can he be sure that the sensor readings he gets are good ones from his own White dust motes and not fake ones from the much more numerous Black dust motes that his adversary has cunningly deployed over the same area? And, for dust motes that have the capability of talking directly to their neighbours, how is the mutual authentication problem solved?

Once we realise that this is, in fact, a low-power ad hoc wireless network, only with some of the numbers off in unexpected directions by a few orders of magnitude, it becomes plausible to think that the Resurrecting Duckling might be of help. But something is still missing. The dust motes are certainly peers, and it would not feel right for one of them to have to become master of another in order to be able to communicate securely with it, especially given that the individual dust motes are neither self-propelled nor cyber-representatives of hypothetical humans that could physically help them perform the initial contact-based bootstrapping phase of imprinting.

2.3 *Mater Semper Certa...*

You always know who the mother is, the Romans used to say in their wisdom, but you can never be sure about the father, where there may be several candidates. In the Duckling model we don't care about the father at all, but we may have got somewhat carried away on the subject of the uniqueness of the mother.

OK, granted: after imprinting there is one and only one very special principal that the duckling will recognise as mother, and obey to the death; but do we really need to forbid the duckling from ever interacting with anybody else? In particular, would it not be possible for the duckling to accept orders (at least *some* kinds of orders) from other principals too? An affirmative answer to these questions leads the way to the announced extension of the Resurrecting Duckling model to peer-to-peer interaction.

There are two distinct ways of being master that we have so far confused and that we shall now distinguish. Firstly, you can be master because the slave is imprinted to you and will be faithful to you for all its life; this is a long-term relationship which might last for years. Secondly, you can be master on a much more temporary basis, just for the duration of a brief transaction: you ask your dining neighbour to pour you some wine and you assume the role of master for a moment, only to become slave later when it's your turn to pass on the vegetables. So far we implied that, in order for one principal to be master of another, the second principal had to be imprinted to the first. We now repudiate this view: the two devices can establish a very temporary master-slave relationship without either being imprinted to the other.

The imprinted duckling is indeed faithful for life to its unique mother duck; but it is happy to talk to others, and even obey their requests, as long as mummy said it was OK to do so.

The germ of this idea was already in our original paper [7], where we proposed

> "to always bootstrap by establishing a shared secret and to use strong cryptography to download more specific policies into the node. The mother can always send the duckling an access control list or whatever in a message protected by the shared secret."

But at the time we had not yet realised that the mother could also delegate her control over the duckling; in fact we said that

> "an imprinted duckling may still *interact* with principals other than its mother — it just cannot be *controlled* by them."

This limitation is unnecessary, so we now remove it. Of course the mother duck is still special, and she does still enjoy some extra control over her duckling, as we shall see.

Let's model the duckling as an object (in the OO sense) with a series of methods, i.e. actions that the duckling can perform on itself, possibly changing its own state. A *policy*[7] for the duckling shall be an arbitrarily complex statement specifying, for each of the available actions, which credentials the principal should exhibit in order to persuade the duckling to perform it. The policy can grant or deny any privileges it wants over the possible actions for the duckling; the only fixed rule, which is in some sense a bootstrapping base, is that if a principal can demonstrate knowledge of the imprinting key of a duckling, then it can upload a new policy into it.

Note that this implication is only one way: we see no reason to also dictate that one can only upload a new policy if one knows that imprinting key. As a matter of fact, for the duckling "downloading a new policy" (and even "committing suicide") are just two of the many possible actions: whether any given principal is allowed to invoke them is something that depends on the specific policy that currently resides in the duckling.

It is conceivable for the original mother duck to upload a policy that would allow other principals to upload a new policy or even kill the duckling. This may effectively be a functional alternative to backing up the imprinting key: it amounts to designating a "godfather" (godmother?) that may at any time take over the role of mother duck.

It should be clear that this power of delegation should be exercised with care, since the designated godmother(s) will be able to kick out the original

---

[7] We appear to be guilty of semantic overloading here, since we previously described the whole Resurrecting Duckling construction as a *security policy model*. We do in fact distinguish the two uses. A "security policy model" is a general security specification that gives overall guidelines for the behaviour of a certain class of systems: a typical example would be Bell-LaPadula [2]. Actual policies (sometimes referred to as "security targets") may be derived from it by specialisation to a particular application and implementation. The reason why we decided to reuse the word "policy" here is to emphasize that this is the same type of entity as those mentioned in trust management systems such as PolicyMaker [5] and KeyNote [4].

mother at will: anyone who can upload a new policy can also kill the duckling (by making that action possible for herself), then re-imprint it and ensure that the old mother is no longer recognised.

Without pursuing the matter in great detail, we hint at the fact that the above problem might be kept under control using a multilevel integrity system, à la Biba [3] — again something that we suggested in the original paper to address a slightly different issue. The various parts of the policy would be ranked at different integrity levels, so that one could allow the low integrity items to be rewritten but not the high integrity ones, which would include the most sensitive actions such as killing the duckling and, recursively, rewriting the high-level portions of the policy.

To sum up the important extension to our model, being mother duck allows one to perform the special action of uploading a new policy in the duckling; but, apart from that, any action can be invoked by any principal who presents the required credentials, as required by the duckling's then-current policy.

This enables peer-to-peer interaction. The remote control will give all the components of the hi-fi system the necessary credentials so that they can ask each other to perform the appropriate operations. The White general will be mother duck to all his dust motes (probably via a cyber-intermediary) and will give them the credentials that allow them to talk to each other — credentials that the dust motes from the Black army won't have, even if they come from the same manufacturer.

2.4   Further Indirection Issues

Interoperability. *If you take me for a ride in your GPS-equipped car, where the GPS is imprinted to you, can my camera obtain the current geographical position from your equipment to stamp the pictures I take while you are driving? More generally, is a duckling limited to only talk to its siblings? If so, there would be no interoperability.*

The interoperability problem is solved by appropriate clauses in the policy.

Firstly, there may be innocuous actions (e.g. giving out the current position for a GPS unit) that a duckling is happy to perform for anyone[8]. This is obtained by not requiring any credentials for the initiators of such actions in the policy of the GPS duckling.

Secondly, my camera still must have some assurance that the positions given out by your GPS unit are trustworthy, otherwise anyone could fool it into stamping the pictures with bogus geographical coordinates. This is obtained by defining your GPS as a valid source of geographical coordinates in the policy of my camera duckling. At the implementation level this may be performed in many ways whose relative advantages will have to be assessed. For example the GPS might be given a "this device can be trusted to give out valid position information" certificate by some standards body, and the camera might recognise and

---

[8] But note the denial of service problem, such as the *sleep deprivation torture* introduced in the original Duckling paper.

accept this[9]. Alternatively, the grandmother duck of the camera might issue such a credential herself for that GPS ("I tell you, my son, that you can believe the coordinates sent to you by this specific GPS unit") and store it in the camera duckling.

Thirdly, there may even be cases where we *want* the duckling to be able to talk only to its siblings, as with the White vs. Black dust motes.

Control interface. *If I go abroad and forget at home my PDA, which is mother duck to all my other gadgets, is it now impossible for me to control them until I get back?*

No. One should not make the mistake (induced by the primary example of the universal remote control) of identifying the mother duck with the control interface for the duckling. As soon as I buy a new gadget, I imprint it to my cyber-representative (which might well be my PDA for illustration purposes), but the policy I upload into it may specify that any other gadget of mine is allowed to control it, as long as it has a user interface that is suitable for issuing the appropriate commands. I may then use any available gadget for controlling any other, and I could conceivably imprint my MP3 player to my PDA but control it from my wristwatch. As a matter of fact I might even keep my cyber-representative in a safe and only ever take it out to imprint my other gadgets.

Tamper resistance. *What happens if the Black general captures a White dust mote, dissects it à la Markus Kuhn [3] and steals its credentials? Can it now impersonate it with all the other White dust motes?*

Yes, unfortunately. If we decide to put credentials inside the ducklings, we must rely on the ducklings being tamper resistant to some extent. The original policy model already stated that breaking the tamper resistance ought to cost more than legitimately acquiring an imprintable duckling. We now add that it also ought to cost more than the value obtained by stealing the duckling's credentials.

The cost to the White general, as well as that of the direct loss of any valuable secrets, would have to include that of revoking those compromised credentials and replacing them by new ones in all the dust motes — a costly operation if they cannot all be easily contacted once deployed.

This in fact highlights a non-trivial conceptual problem: once we introduce delegation like we just did we also reintroduce, in its full glory, the problem of revocation in the absence of an online server. Since we make no a priori guarantees about the connectivity status of the duckling, there may be circumstances where not even the mother duck is contactable. From a theoretical point of view, this is probably just as bad as the original starting point. In practice the problem is somewhat mitigated by the fact that the authority issuing those credentials is now more decentralised.

---

[9] The validity of such a certificate is linked to the tamper resistance of the device, as we discussed in the original paper.

Trust management. *How shall the duckling decide whether the credentials exhibited by another principal are sufficient to grant the principal permission to execute the requested action?*

This is a general problem for which, fortunately, a general solution has already been developed. Ducklings may embed a generic trust management engine such as KeyNote [4]. Policies and credentials shall be expressed in a common language and any duckling will be able to just feed its own policy, the external request and the supplied credentials to its engine which will return a boolean answer as to whether the requested action is allowed or not.

Policy specification. *How will the owner of a device be able to specify a sensible policy for it? It looks as if doing this properly will be a job for a security expert.*

Writing a policy will indeed require competence in security and will be no less complicated than programming. End users will not be expected to write their own policies; instead, devices will come with a portfolio of "sensible policies" (hopefully with explanations), that the user will be able to parameterise. Power users will be able to write their own policies if they wish, or edit the supplied ones, and probably web sites will appear that archive the best of those homebrew variants.

Family feelings. *Wouldn't it be possible to exploit the fraternal love among sibling ducklings as an additional security feature?*

Sure, neat idea! The policy for the ducklings in your home might say that they should stop working when they feel lonely, because in normal operation it is reasonable for them to expect that they will be surrounded by at least n siblings. This is a case in which we make explicit use of the *short range* of our wireless communications, inferring proximity from connectivity. If they are not in range of their siblings, it may be because they were stolen, so they should refuse to work. (Of course this heuristic fails if the thieves steal the whole lot...)

3   Conclusions

The Resurrecting Duckling security policy model regulates secure transient association between devices in an ad hoc wireless network where authentication servers may not be available. In this paper we have extended this model from a strict master-slave situation to a more general case that includes peer-to-peer relationships.

Now the mother duck defines a lower level *policy* for her duckling on imprinting; through this policy, the power to control the duckling can be delegated to any other principal. The important conceptual step is to distinguish the long-lived master-slave relationship of imprinting from the temporary master-slave relationship of asking the duckling to perform one action.

The versatility of the extended model covers a wide range of new uses. We think we have addressed most of the practical scenarios in ad hoc wireless networking, but as this work is still in progress we shall gratefully receive any criticisms about exceptions and omissions.

Acknowledgements

Over the past year I have talked about ducklings to maybe ten different audiences on both sides of the Atlantic and I am indebted to all of them for their stimulating and often very sharp comments which have influenced and fuelled my progress. Space prevents me from acknowledging all the worthy suggestions individually, but I especially thank Jonathan Smith from the University of Pennsylvania and my colleague James Scott from the University of Cambridge for first pointing out cases in which the master-slave relationship was inadequate. Randy Katz's mind-blowing talk on smart dust was very inspirational to me, even though (or perhaps precisely because) it offered no solutions to the security problems. Many colleagues at AT&T Florham Park and Newman Springs, including at least Matt Blaze, Ed Chen, Paul Henry and Ben Lee, provided constructive criticism and encouragement. Ross Anderson, who co-authored the original Duckling paper, was always available for comments and fruitful discussions. Finally, the audience of this Cambridge Security Protocols workshop was very responsive; in particular Virgil Gligor, Markus Kuhn and Pekka Nikander offered interesting insights, some of which have been incorporated in this revision.

These grateful thanks should not however be mistaken as claims of endorsement, and I remain of course fully responsible for defending any ideas and opinions herein expressed.

References

1. Ross Anderson and Markus Kuhn. "Tamper Resistance—A Cautionary Note". In "Proc. 2nd USENIX Workshop on Electronic Commerce", 1996. ISBN 1-880446-83-9. http://www.cl.cam.ac.uk/~mgk25/tamper.pdf.
2. D. Elliot Bell and Leonard J. LaPadula. "Secure Computer Systems: Mathematical Foundations". Mitre Report ESD-TR-73-278 (Vol. I–III), Mitre Corporation, Bedford, MA, Apr 1974.
3. Kenneth J. Biba. "Integrity Considerations for Secure Computer Systems". Tech. Rep. MTR-3153, MITRE Corporation, Apr 1975.
4. Matt Blaze, Joan Feigenbaum, John Ioannidis and Angelos D. Keromytis. "The KeyNote Trust-Management System". RFC 2704, Network Working Group, Sep 1999. http://www.crypto.com/papers/rfc2704.txt.
5. Matt Blaze, Joan Feigenbaum and Jack Lacy. "Decentralized Trust Management". In "Proceedings of the 17 th IEEE Symp. on Security and Privacy", pp. 164–173. IEEE Computer Society, 1996.
   ftp://ftp.research.att.com/dist/mab/policymaker.ps.
6. Joe M. Kahn, Randy H. Katz and Kris S. J. Pister. "Next Century Challenges: Mobile Networking for "Smart Dust"". In "Proceedings of International Conference on Mobile Computing and Networking (MobiCom 99)", Seattle, WA, USA, Aug 1999. http://robotics.eecs.berkeley.edu/~pister/publications/1999/mobicom'99.pdf.

7. Frank Stajano and Ross Anderson. "The Resurrecting Duckling: Security Issues in Ad-Hoc Wireless Networks". In Bruce Christianson, Bruno Crispo and Mike Roe (eds.), "Security Protocols, 7th International Workshop Proceedings", Lecture Notes in Computer Science. Springer-Verlag, 1999. `http://www.cl.cam.ac.uk/~fms27/duckling/`. See also [8]. Also available as AT&T Laboratories Cambridge Technical Report 1999.2.

8. Frank Stajano and Ross Anderson. "The Resurrecting Duckling: Security Issues in Ad-Hoc Wireless Networks". In "Proceedings of 3rd AT&T Software Symposium", Middletown, New Jersey, USA, Oct 1999. `http://www.cl.cam.ac.uk/~fms27/duckling/`. Abridged and revised version of [7]. Also available as AT&T Laboratories Cambridge Technical Report 1999.2b.

The Resurrecting Duckling — What Next?
(Transcript of Discussion)

Frank Stajano

AT&T Laboratories, Cambridge

I'll start with a summary of the resurrecting duckling security policy model for those who haven't seen it. It regulates interactions between wireless gadgets: the scenario is one where you have plenty of items that all have a microprocessor in them, like everything has nowadays. The claim is that what is going to happen next is that they will all have a transceiver in them so that they will be able to talk to each other and they will be able to be peripherals of each other and exchange messages. You won't have situations like your camera having to have a microphone inside to do the voice annotation, because you can use something else that already has a microphone – like your telephone for example, or your tape recorder – and just use the microphone in that to send sound to the things that need the voice annotation, and so on. So everything can use everything else as a peripheral.

This is based on having ad hoc wireless networks, ad hoc meaning you form the network as and when the devices get near each other. One fundamental problem in this type of scenario is that you have the secure transient association case, which is an authentication problem that is not addressed by the traditional protocols because we don't have an on-line server. If you have an on-line server you can authenticate devices by either getting a Kerberos style ticket from the server or, if you're using public key, you can use the server to see if the certificate is fresh, you can use it for revocation, and so on. But if you don't have any of that, how are you going to do the authentication?

And besides, the problem that's of interest here may be slightly different. The example I like to give is that of a universal remote control that controls many gadgets, so at the same time it might control my TV, my hi-fi, my blinds, my heating system and so on. Now what happens when I buy a new television? I would like to be able to unbind my remote control to the old television so that I can give it away to someone else. At the same time I would like it to be difficult for someone who steals my television to bind it to his own remote control. So there should be some security in this association but it would also be transient in that I can also undo it. The proposition for solving this is the resurrecting duckling policy. The duckling part comes from a discovery of Konrad Lorenz who was a Nobel prize winner for his studies on animal behaviour. He was looking at the way ducks and geese behave, and he discovered that when one of these comes out of the egg it will follow the first thing it sees that moves and makes a sound, as if it were its mother, even though it doesn't look like a duck. In the first and foremost case it looked like Dr. Lorenz and this duck was following him around and he had to pet it and put it to sleep making duck sounds and so on.

B. Christianson et al. (Eds.): Security Protocols, LNCS 2133, pp. 215–222, 2001.

So we want our devices to behave like this, the first thing the duckling sees (the duckling being the television for example, or the DVD player, or whatever) becomes its mother. If you think of the device's hardware as the body and the device's software or state or secrets that are inside as the soul, then you have a pretty good model of this and why the resurrecting comes in. You have the soul that's the shared secret that the mother puts in the duck when the duck is imprinted and as long as there is this shared secret, there's this imprinting bond between the mother and the duck. The duck stays faithful to the mother and obeys the mother, the mother can tell the duck to do things and the duck will always obey the mother and nobody else. When I want to sell my television to someone else or just give it away, I want someone else to become the mother of this duck. I, the current mother, will tell my duckling to die and when it dies, it just deletes its soul and the body stays there and you can imprint it again because it's like a rebirth. The metempsychosis is in reverse because in classical metempsychosis, as in many religions, you keep your soul and you visit a number of successive bodies, whereas here you keep your body and you have different souls that inhabit it.

There are various ways in which that can occur. You can die of old age if after a certain time the bond between the mother and duck just dissolves or it could be at the end of a defined transaction, once something has happened then it's no longer necessary to stay together. For example, if we see this model as not between a remote control and a hi-fi item but between an e-wallet and an e-cash machine then we see that as I approach the cash machine, then I become the mother duck of it for the time it takes to complete my transaction and it is securely bound to me for the duration of that transaction. When I complete the transaction and I go away, it can be imprinted to another e-wallet.

Of course another way that we could have the soul dissolving, is by assassination. If someone tries to make the soul dissolve so that they can imprint the thing to themselves, that's what a thief would do, then we want to prevent that so part of the policy has to specify that this has to be sufficiently expensive that there is no advantage in doing so. And then there is the mother-induced suicide, which is what makes the association transient and is something we want, we want to be able to tell the duckling to die. But what about the case in which I break my remote control? Am I going to lose control over all the devices in my home? That would be very embarrassing. So one thing I originally proposed was to have escrowed seppuku. Seppuku being the thing that disgraced samurai have to do, where they have to slit their belly. But this wasn't that good an idea because someone would have to hold a master key somewhere that would tell all the devices that they would now have to commit suicide. I would have to, for example, phone Sony and say, oh I broke my remote control, can you please make my TV commit seppuku so I can re-imprint to the new one, and they would say, yes, but then they would have the power to do that to all the televisions they ever made. So is this a good idea, and do I want to put this centralised trust like this? Maybe not, think of the Pentium 3 and all the other big brother things.

So the solution I advocate now is rather some local escrow. There is nothing bad in escrowing your secrets, but just like you prefer to leave your keys with your neighbours rather than with the police, you should do so with your secrets. It's fine to make backups of these imprinting keys but you shouldn't have a centralised agency to do that.

Mike Roe: You could encrypt on two parents by introducing a father or whatever for the ducklings and then you've got two controllers, one of which is still OK.

Reply: Yes, effectively that would be a local escrow but there is a subtlety there which is, if you call them two parents, then you are implying that they are active simultaneously whereas this means there is one at a time and the other can take over later.

Another point in the fine print is how do you bootstrap all this? We are talking of wireless contexts in this protocol and if you have, this was the example I used last year, a bunch of thermometers which are all potential ducklings and you're a doctor with a PDA that wants to imprint one to the PDA, how do you know that the one you are imprinting to is the one you have picked up and not any other one in the bowl of disinfectant. You don't actually care which one you get as long as it's the one you think it is. So the appropriate way to bootstrap this is to use physical contact before doing all the wireless stuff.

Now these are all old concerns, what comes up after that? One of the themes of this workshop is the boundary of protocols and there's one thing that comes up here which is a classical confusion, and it's basically who is a principal? Is it the object that's the principal, or is it the owner of the object that's the principal that is just being represented by this object and so on. If I have this remote control that controls the DVD, am I the mother duck or is the remote control the mother duck? So that's something I have been thinking of and perhaps there is a perversion like this of saying, well both, which might in some cases be useful. You could say, OK the remote control itself is a mother duck to the DVD player. However I, person, am mother duck to the remote control that I can imprint to myself using a PIN, for example, as the shared secret, or something like that. So you have a cascade of principals, some of which may be objects, some of which may be people.

Virgil Gligor: Is the remote control a master without you? In other words, do you have multiple masters or just a delegation to the remote control? You delegated your authority to the remote control, that's one scenario, in each case there is only one authority, there is only one mother duck and that's delegated to the remote control. Or is it that there are multiple mother ducks, you separately from the remote control?

Reply: In what I am describing here, there is me as mother duck of the remote control and the remote control as a separate mother duck of the peripheral.

Virgil Gligor: Why can't you think of the same problem as – there is only one mother duck who is delegating some of the authority temporarily to the remote control.

Reply: Yes, but the fact is that there are two imprinting chains here, one between the remote control and the device and one between me and the remote control, so that's the distinction. But yes, there is an issue of delegation.

Now I also wanted to explore some cases where the duckling as I proposed it last year doesn't quite work. All these scenarios I described work well when there's some sort of personal owner of something and this owner has a master/slave relationship with the peripheral. So that there is the master actor that orders things to happen and then there is some passive thing that obeys. Now what happens when there isn't an owner, what happens when there isn't a person at all, what happens if the DVD and the television are there talking to each other, and the DVD says, OK this is a wide-screen film so I want you, television, to set the screen up in a wide-screen format instead of the normal format, or something like that. Is it logical for the DVD player to become the mother duck of the television? Not so in my opinion, why would there be such a master/slave relationship between those devices that are essentially peers?

Smart dust is an interesting development that was done at Berkeley; it's one of these nano technology gadgety things where you have little things about this size, which they call dust motes, which contain a battery and a sensor and some wireless means of communication which may be radio or laser or mirrors. Suppose we manufacture these by the millions and, since the military are one of our sponsors, we'll take a military example. We fly with an aircraft over the enemy battlefields and we drop all these things and all this dust settles in the enemy field. Then we can have each one of these sensors report the variations in temperature or whatever, and so we can spot people walking in this field by the variations in the temperature that all these dust motes report to us.

This set me thinking about the security of this thing, how do you control the various dust motes. How do you know that if you are the white army, the black army hasn't set up even more dust motes than you and is not relaying you false information about where these things come from and so on? So I tried to think whether the duckling stuff would apply to that because this is just a gigantic ad hoc wireless network in fact, and so that's how I came up with the next bit.

So I think that the crucial point is we should distinguish two ways of being master in this master/slave relationship. Two possible masters are she who owns your soul and she who orders you to wash the dishes. So this is the mother duck, there is only one who owns your soul, but you can have many girlfriends who order you to wash the dishes. So just asking the peripheral to do something is not being the absolute master of that peripheral. You can ask for a favour without being in control over every aspect of the device and so with this distinction, the mother duck is only what puts into the duckling a policy and some credentials and based on this, the duckling can do things that also involve other principals which are not the mother duck. It's not the case that the duckling can only talk to or obey or whatever, the mother duck that originally imprinted it. The policy says what the duckling can do and the duckling can therefore interact with other principals.

So in our case of the smart dust, the army general is the mother duck of all the dust motes. He buys the dust motes from Berkeley, and all the motes are individual ducklings imprinted to this general. But the general can put in credentials that say, you are a white army dust mote and you can talk to other white army dust motes and so. The black general can also buy dust motes from the same manufacturer and can put in his own policy and his own credentials, and this will not interfere. Of course there are tamper resistance issues in this solution because if the black general goes into the field and takes a white dust mote and can open it à la Marcus Kuhn and find out all the credentials and then put them in his own dust motes, then he can probably tie up the white army completely, so this has to be part of the policy as well.

Now, one can say that this is not a good idea because then the ducklings can only talk to their siblings, to other ducklings that have been imprinted to the same mother, so you have no interoperability. If I buy hi-fi equipment and then you have bought some hi-fi equipment and I visit your home, I cannot have my CD player play on your amplifier when I visit you and things like that, because we are different mother ducks. But this is wrong because, first of all you sometimes want to be able to have these separations so that the things that you imprinted only talk to other things you imprint, in the case of the dust it's fairly obvious. Secondly this objection doesn't quite hold because the white mother can easily say, OK if you want to talk to yellows you can do that as long as you don't talk to blues or browns or blacks. So there's nothing that forces the mother duck to specify a policy where you can only talk to your siblings. You can insert some rules in the policy that say, OK you can also talk to people that I haven't imprinted. And you can even say that some things you can accept from anybody regardless of the credentials they present. There may be cases where an action is sufficiently innocuous that you don't care, you can be ordered to perform this action by anyone.

So that's the stage I'm at with trying to make this duckling model cover more cases than it originally did and I'm trying to have this be a general way to govern the interaction between the devices in a wireless ad hoc network. I hope that you will tell me if I am missing something fundamental, or if there are other cases that I haven't covered.

Tuomas Aura: One thing you might want to cover when you're bringing this policy in is that you also have a policy between the duckling and the mother duck and that policy is now built into the model. It may be that when you are making the rest of the policies more explicit, you might also want to make that policy more explicit.

Reply: The policy that links the mother and the duckling is basically that the mother is the only entity that can tell the duckling to commit suicide and then therefore be re-imprinted to a different mother.

Tuomas Aura: Well in a way you imply that the duckling trusts, whatever that means, the mother completely even when it is asked to commit suicide. There might be situations where you might want the duckling to think that something else is the mother, so I think you might want to consider more complex trust relations.

Virgil Gligor: The associations that you make here are fairly static. In other words, your devices get a soul based on your application and they communicate, and then at some point (when you decide to change your TV set) the association changes and you get a new soul. What about a more dynamic type of solution, do you envisage any situation where you may have devices come into the association, then leave the association, fairly dynamically, without having to lose their souls, without having to imprint?

Reply: Well yes, if I may state this a bit more formally. Basically what I see is that the duckling is something that has a number of actions it can perform. One of these actions would be to kill himself, that's a special one, but there's just a list of actions it can do. This policy is basically some sort of table that says, this action you can do when someone comes in with those credentials and so it's just a special case of this policy that this rule of killing yourself comes in only from the principal that imprinted you. But in theory even this could be changed if you wanted to delegate that power, you could even delegate that. And in terms of the associations, it depends what one means by association. In this model I envisage that the special privilege between the mother and the duck can not be made by anything other that this imprinting. But any other thing that you may want to do in the coalition of ducklings could be specified in theory by this policy, because what's a coalition other than devices that are prepared to do some things together and you could specify this in the policy if you wanted to couldn't you?

Virgil Gligor: Yes, but for example can I take your remote control and use it or can I take your camera and use it in a different coalition? In other words, suppose that you come to the US and you rent a car and you now have a variety of devices around your car including perhaps a GPS station and you want to make that GPS station work with your remote control, and with your digital camera, and so on, but you've brought your own digital camera. Can you make the digital camera work in your new coalition that you find yourself in?

Reply: I would assume that when I rent the car I imprint the devices of the car to me. Is this a bad model?

Virgil Gligor: No, I'm just asking what are the limits of the model.

Geraint Price: There are a number of user interfaces in the model. If you are thinking about the relations between yourself and your remote control, you would be the mother duck. Now let's say you're not selling it but you're only lending it. How do you avoid killing your remote control and just temporarily overwrite some of your credentials or whatever.

Reply: Well we had something in the original paper which was multi level secure souls which could address some of that where we have some deeper soul which is my ownership of the phone which stays there, but there's some more superficial thing which I could kill off and I would only be killing the superficial part of the duckling and giving it out, whereas it would still stay mine in some deeper sense.

Matt Blaze: I can only think that the delegation model which you have would address that problem.

Reply: Yes, well actually we should talk about this off-line, one of my plans was to build a keynote thing inside this.

Marcus Kuhn: I've not yet fully understood how I should decide which of my gadgets is the mother duck and which is the duckling. It is quite obvious in the doctors and thermometers case but in the rental car scenario I've got the of key of the rental car, I have my Walkman, I have a camera, I have a GPS receiver and I want the GPS receiver to work with my camera and things like this and my normal mother duck is my PDA which I have left at home. How can you decide if it's a kind mother or is it an evil mother, or is your camera also able to become a mother for anything else.

Reply: That's a good point. I have thought about this and my view of this may be wrong, but my current view on this is that I am in some sense the mother of the devices I own, and I must have a digital representative. And that's where the cascade comes in so I am represented in the digital domain by my PDA because it's something where I can specify policies more easily and so on. And so the PDA is actually the mother duck of all the devices at the lowest level and there's some sort of tree where all the devices are peers - the GPS, the camera, the car keys, the CD player or whatever, and they are all imprinted to my PDA which is in turn imprinted to me in this object and person type model. So with this scheme if you forget your PDA and leave it at home then you're speechless in the digital world and you're snookered and you just have to look at the map instead of the GPS.

Marcus Kuhn: Is it not possible to build a system such that any device that hasn't sufficiently powerful user systems to be the mother could relay the mother for this purpose. Is it not even possible to develop a direct key on the device so that you just need some backing interface in order to set up a policy that verifies that you are the mother. It doesn't have to have a sufficiently powerful interface to be the mother but is something small like a wrist watch that is attached relatively close to your body and you are less likely to lose it.

Audience: There might not be a need for such a thing as a tree of relationships but instead you could just have your personal gadgets as a pool and let them decide themselves who is their mother. Then if you leave your PDA at home, your camera will take over what there is to do.

Reply: Well what about people trying to claim ownership of this group, you know, malicious intruders.

Audience: If you first imprint all these things to each other then it would be difficult for someone to gain access. Theft prevention should be part of this model.

Reply: Well, I firstly disagree with this because you can use this policy model to model very many different things, one of them could be computers. It depends on what you can consider to be the computer. If you're thinking of the computer just as the bits you buy from Dell then it doesn't quite follow this policy because it has most of the features, but it lacks assassination. Anybody can assassinate my laptop just by reformatting the hard disk and then they have a fresh laptop they can use for themselves. However if you consider as part of the computer also the operating system that's installed, all the applications that are there, and all the state, then in this case it's true that assassination is difficult because you can't get in unless you have the root password.

Audience: What I'd like to do is have the means to transfer information from one system to another and then what I don't want is someone else coming through to join in this information transfer so that, let's say, the tourist next to me was able to download the picture from my camera.

Reply: Exactly.

Tuomas Aura: I think we are talking about two different things. One thing is that we have to set up the security relationships for the first time and then maintain them and break them up and we must have the security policy to do this. The second thing is to use these devices everyday and now we are pretending that we need the mother duck in order to be able to use the devices daily as well, but that's not needed. In a way we can have a mother duck which we can put in a safe once we've used it and we take it out of the safe only when we want to change the security policy or the security relationship. So the everyday user interface is more or less independent of the mother duck.

In that case, you can leave the PDA at home once you have set up your devices.

Reply: That's a good point, you should be able to transfer the interface to something else like Marcus was saying, once you have set up the policy of who can talk to who else.

Mike Roe: I'm wondering if you could use some sort of voting system. If you are worried about one item being stolen, then you can imagine some thing where you imprint on several parents, and the mother is chosen by a simple majority.

Reply: Or you could even sort them, you could sort them beforehand and if there's a conflict you take the highest order.

Markus Kuhn: You could also attach to the device a sort of family feeling that only if at least five of the devices are together one of them gets lost then it apparently has been stolen, because Frank never goes out with only one of these devices.

Matt Blaze: That raises the spectre of these devices developing an adolescence in which they stop listening to their mother.

Stewart Lee: Years of therapy?

Reply: The duckling and the shrink.

Mike Roe: That might be a good point for this to stop.

An Anonymous Auction Protocol
Using "Money Escrow"
(Transcript of Discussion)

George Danezis

Cambridge University Computer Laboratory

I am going to talk today about some results that came about following my final year project. I'm still an undergraduate student, and the project is supervised by Frank Stajano. We call the mechanism I will present, money escrow.

Let me first explain to you the context in which this mechanism arose. In my project, I have been studying the implementation and use of anonymous transactions in e-commerce. I have chosen to implement an auction that should be anonymous and this follows from the cocaine auction as proposed by Anderson and Stajano[1]. In the original proposal of the cocaine auction you have people who do not trust each other, who do not trust the seller, and who would still want to trade anonymously in an auction environment. So the main objectives of this auction were actually to produce a winner and to produce a shared key between the winner of the auction and the seller in order for them to communicate (and find a place to exchange the money and the drugs).

This auction fails under some circumstances, but these failures are not always to be attributed to the cocaine auction protocol specifically, but are a general problem of anonymous auctions as a whole. For example, the seller can bid in the auction which is a very difficult thing to prevent in any kind of anonymous auction, it is not specific to the cocaine auction protocol, so I did not really address this problem.

There is also a general problem in which the auction house fails to give goods to the highest bidder. I tried to address this by having a receipt mechanism: for each bid the bidders receive a receipt and if somebody who considers that he has the highest bid does not receive the goods, he can complain somehow and can prove that the house did not follow the proper auction procedures.

But the interesting problem, which is difficult in many instances of anonymous protocols, was how to prevent dead-beat bidders; these are bidders who just bid and then do not pay, or do not turn up when they have to pay, or just do nothing after the bid, which can be considered to be quite a problem because the auction has to start again from the beginning.

One of the ways to discourage dead-beat bidders is by trying to trace their identity. So the auction is anonymous until somebody cheats and makes a bid that is not honoured later, and therefore in this case we would like to know his identity, we would like to know who he is. This follows from the concept of

---

[1] The Cocaine Auction Protocol: On The Power Of Anonymous Broadcast Frank Stajano, Ross Anderson (Univ. of Cambridge) pp434 – 447 in Proc the 3rd International Workshop on Information Hiding, Dresden, LNCS 1768

B. Christianson et al. (Eds.): Security Protocols, LNCS 2133, pp. 223–233, 2001.

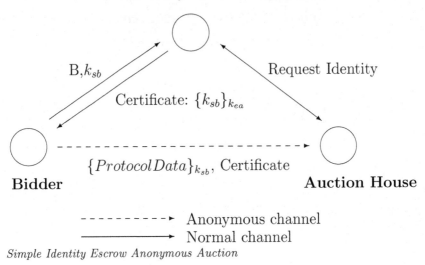

Identity Escrow Agency

B,k_{sb}

Request Identity

Certificate: $\{k_{sb}\}_{k_{ea}}$

$\{ProtocolData\}_{k_{sb}}$, Certificate

Bidder   **Auction House**

------------► Anonymous channel
───────────► Normal channel

Simple Identity Escrow Anonymous Auction

identity escrow introduced by Kilian and Petrank[2]. They describe the fact that in a garage you don't care about who enters and who leaves, you just care that they are authorised to do so, but if there is a crime, for example, one night in the garage, you would like to know who was in there. So there is a two level system, one for normal use and one in case of emergencies and maybe such a system could be useful and helpful for the auction. In order to do that we have the bidder, and we have the auction house, and we will have an identity escrow agency. In order not to rely on only one that could be not trusted, we could split the secrets across many identity escrow agencies in order to be sure that the identities are not going to be revealed without reason.

So, for example, the bidder can give his identity and a signing key, and then the identity escrow agency gives back to the bidder a certificate that asserts it knows the identity of who is behind the signing key. During the auction the protocol data exchanged is authenticated using the signing key and the certificate is sent that certifies that, although the communication is anonymous, the identity escrow agency knows the bidder's identity. So the protocol can go on and if there is something wrong if, for example, the bidder does not honour his bid, then the auction house requires the identity from the identity escrow agency. So this is a general framework of identity escrow. Obviously the mechanisms described by Kilian and Petrank are much more complicated than this very simplistic approach here which is only meant to illustrate the point.

---

[2]   Joe Kilian, Erez Petrank: Identity Escrow. 169-185 in CRYPTO 1998: Santa Barbara, California Hugo Krawczyk (Ed.): Advances in Cryptology – CRYPTO '98, 18th Annual International Cryptology Conference, Santa Barbara, California LNCS 1462, Springer, 1998, ISBN 3-540-64892-5

There are still some problems. The first one is: how does the auction house prove that cheating took place? If we don't have a way to convince the escrow agency that cheating took place, then maybe the identity could be released without reason. So there is a stronger need to prove that cheating actually took place. That can be quite difficult, especially in the context of an auction where cheating could be considered not sending a message.For example if I bid, I win and then I don't reply to the request for a meeting or something like that – so cheating occurs because a message was not sent. We must be careful in solving this problem so that we do not open ourselves to other attacks. Imagine if I bid in an auction, I win and then I'm prevented from replying by a denial of service attack: not only am I denied service but also there are repercussions by the fact that my identity is being traced and things like that. So that's the first problem that we're going to address.

The second problem is, what we do with the identity of the cheater? In case someone cheats, the auction house gets the identity, what can it do? The first solution is to sue them. Well that's quite difficult, especially in the global network – different jurisdictions have different rules, it is expensive to launch an international lawsuit, so for everyday usage that's not very practical. The second thing that could be done is to exclude them from future service which is also quite a difficult thing to do given an identity because the whole service is anonymous by default. There is really a difficulty in denying service to an identity because the service is anonymous and has been designed *not* to make it easy to prevent particular identities being serviced. So maybe a scheme where the escrow agency is used by the auction house to check against a blacklist of excluded identities could be used to accomplish that, but then again you could open yourself to attacks like the auction house trying many different identities from the phone directory until it finds to whom it is talking, therefore defeating the purpose of the anonymous protocol. So we'll try to address this problem as well.

So the first problem is about proving that cheating took place. I tried to do that by merging the payment with the bid action. So now the identity escrow agency has a second rôle, not only does it escrow the identity and a signing key that could authenticate the bidder, but also a private key and some conditions of release (we will see what they are in a second) and then it gives back a certificate with the signing key and the conditions. Then what the bidder does is, he sends the protocol data, a coin (and we will discuss what kind of electronic money this could be) encrypted under a private key that should remain secret, and then he signs these and sends the certificate. The auction house conducts the auction, it sends back a certificate of ownership if the bidder wins, and the bidder sends back the private key that should decrypt the money so that the auction house gets paid. If at some point this fails to be done, then there is a backup mechanism, the escrow mechanism, where the auction house can require the secret key to decrypt the coin from the identity escrow agency. If the coin decrypts to junk and therefore there is no money available, the auction house could require the identity. So in this case the whole protocol is done in one go, therefore, denying

Identity Escrow Agency

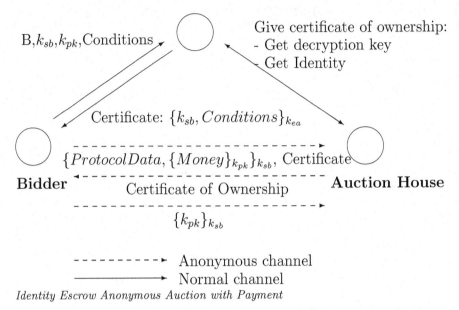

B,k_{sb},k_{pk},Conditions

Give certificate of ownership:
- Get decryption key
- Get Identity

Certificate: $\{k_{sb}, Conditions\}_{k_{ea}}$

$\{ProtocolData, \{Money\}_{k_{pk}}\}_{k_{sb}}$, Certificate

Certificate of Ownership

$\{k_{pk}\}_{k_{sb}}$

Bidder

Auction House

- - - - - - - - - ▸ Anonymous channel
———————▸ Normal channel

Identity Escrow Anonymous Auction with Payment

service is not really a major problem, and then even if the service is denied so the bidder is prevented from giving his secret key to unlock the coin , then the escrow agency can still do it and the transaction can still proceed through the backup route.

We still have some problems so a few remarks on that. The important thing to note here is that the conditions of release agreed between the bidder and the escrow agency, could be in a formal language and therefore the escrow agency would just follow the bidder's instructions. What does that mean? For example, the instructions of release of the private key and the identity could say: if you are presented with a bid signed by me and if you are given a certificate of ownership for my name, then the auction house has the right to have the secret key. This could be put in a very formal way, in such a way that the identity escrow agency knows when to release the secret key. And obviously in the conditions of release you can say, if you see my bid, you have the key so you decrypt the coin, and if it is not valid a valid coin or enough to honour my bid, then you release my identity. And this can be specified by the bidder. Of course the conditions can be known to the auction house and the auction house must have a policy on what are the minimum conditions that it should require to accept a bidder. Therefore the identity escrow just follows these instructions and when the auction house says, I have this bidder, with the key to decrypt my payment, I gave him the ownership but he hasn't replied, then the identity escrow agency knows that it can release the key. So I believe that this is an improvement.

Wenbo Mao: Is the bidder already a winner?

Reply: Oh yes, this happens in case of winning, because when the bidder wins, there is a certificate of ownership for the goods that is being released.

Wenbo Mao: So only the winner is entitled to engage in this protocol, no other body is entitled to use this protocol.

Reply: No, there are many bidders that give such bidding messages to the auction house. In fact in the protocol data, there is a promise of payment for a certain sum. The auction house runs the protocol and finds out which is the highest one and then creates a certificate of ownership of the goods for the highest bidder. So many people are actually running it but only one person receives this kind of certificate and, therefore, for only one person the auction house is entitled to go to the escrow agency. Obviously if there are different escrow agencies there is a possibility of the auction house cheating and issuing more than one certificate in order to get more money, but then you can prove that cheating took place because two people are going to have the certificate for the same goods.

Wenbo Mao: I was thinking about denial of service.

Reply: Yes, in the previous example denial of service could take place if there are not very formal conditions specifying when the identity is going to be released or there are no conditions at all, which could be the case. So what would happen then is that the auction house would say to the identity escrow agency that it hadn't received a message and how would the auction house be able to prove that it hasn't received the message or that the bidder intentionally did not send a message. It's quite a difficult problem, that is why I push the whole thing into one message in my system.

So in case of that happening where the payment is included inside the protocol, the transaction can still happen from the escrowed route because the identity escrow agency knows the private key, and therefore can unlock the money, and if the certificate is given to the identity escrow agency it could be retrieved later by the bidder.

But that could be a problem. The escrow agency can link identities to transactions which defeats the purpose of having an anonymous protocol like that because if I launch a denial of service on the winner, every time the escrow agency can say, ah, this identity has done this transaction. Obviously the auction house does not know that, because the identity is not given to it, but still there is a party, the identity escrow agency, which we should trust to hold this information. And we still have the problem that we don't really know what to do with the identity. If I don't send the right message, the key is requested, the money decrypts to junk and therefore cannot be used, I get an identity, but so what, we still have the same problem of what to do with it.

So, to resolve these problems in certain contexts, we propose a money escrow mechanism. We've seen key escrow, where a third party holds your keys, and this mechanism is used as before. We've seen the identity escrow being proposed where actually you can trace identities. But in the case of cheating what the auction house wants is to get paid. Obviously there is the case for a moral point

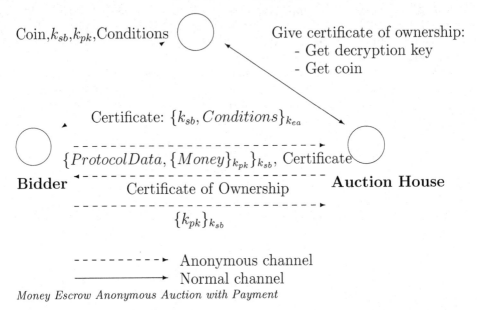

Money Escrow Agency

Coin,k_{sb},k_{pk},Conditions   Give certificate of ownership:
- Get decryption key
- Get coin

Certificate: $\{k_{sb}, Conditions\}_{k_{ea}}$

$\{ProtocolData, \{Money\}_{k_{pk}}\}_{k_{sb}}$, Certificate

Bidder   Certificate of Ownership   **Auction House**

$\{k_{pk}\}_{k_{sb}}$

- - - - - - - - ► Anonymous channel
───────────► Normal channel

Money Escrow Anonymous Auction with Payment

of view that there should not be any cheaters and we should detect them and put them in jail because they are evil people, but really for the auction house the identity is just an indirect way to get some money, to get some compensation. So given that we have already used electronic cash, why not replace the identity itself with an electronic coin of some form (and we will see what form this could have) that is given to the auction house as a compensation if the transaction coin is invalid. We modify the protocol again. So where we had the identity, now we have a compensation coin, that can be split across many escrow agencies to avoid problems. Now it's a money escrow agency, it's not an identity escrow agency. The communication channels are anonymous between the bidder and the money escrow agency, the money escrow agency does not really need to know who the bidders are, it just needs to know that the compensation is valid, the verification key to verify that a bid originates from the bidder, the secret key and the conditions under which these should be released. It can then issue the certificate about what these conditions are, what is the verification key, and what the compensation is so that the auction house knows, although this could obviously also be in the conditions.

So the protocol takes place as before. If there is a problem at any point, the auction house requests the private key to be released, it can prove that it is entitled to get this private key because it has all the signed data by this key. And if this coin decrypts to junk again, what happens is that the backup mechanism takes place and not the identity this time but the compensation coin is released and can be cashed by the auction house. So this is actually a more straightforward way to get the compensation than going through the tribunals.

Geraint Price: Unless I am reading something wrong here, in this example you have the possibility of the money escrow agency being able to out-bid everybody in the auction all the time, because it sees in advance what this compensation coin is and could make some sort of guess as to what the highest bid would be.

Ross Anderson: You can randomise the client shares.

Reply: Yes, you can randomise it but I would think that you don't need to have the compensation equal to your maximum bid. This would be a perfectly valid point in the case of Dutch auctions, that are non-interactive, everybody gives their bids in sealed envelopes and then the envelopes are opened and the second highest bidder pays the value, so there are actually auctions where this is happening. But the compensation does not need to be related in any way to the bid, it can be of high value because it should never be used.

Frank Stajano: Also the bidder does not have to state for which auction he is depositing the money, the money escrow agency could have compensation for plenty of auctions which an auction house is running at the same time.

Reply: Yes, one could think about systems like that. In practice though you need to include at least some information about the auction and the auction house.

John Ioannidis: How does auction house B know that the money that has been escrowed isn't also used in an auction in auction house A?

Reply: Yes, I will address this problem shortly.

There is a case for separating information and signing different kinds of batches here because there are data here that may not need to be communicated to the money escrow agency in order to prove that a bid actually took place. This is just a rough sketch, more thought is obviously needed as to what exactly is needed in order to prove the point without opening yourself to problems.

So there are no more bidder identities involved, from the point of view of setting up an anonymous auction, that's good. Now the question is, what kind of coin should be used for the compensation and also for the bid. I think that the coin used for the bid that is encrypted is less of a problem because if the bidder goes and double spends it, then when you decrypt it and you try to cash it, this pops up, and maybe there could be in this electronic cash scheme ways to trace people who do double spend.

Ross Anderson: The problem is the auction has already finished.

Reply: Yes but if that happens and there is a failure, there is a compensation coming in, so if there is such a problem, the auction house still has the compensation and double spending is actually a big enough problem so it is entitled to get it. Now the problem is what kind of coin should be used for the compensation because if this is invalid, you don't have any backup mechanism anymore. So, it could be a coin, but that can be double spent. It could be a cheque, but that would present a problem because then the winner would not be anonymous given cheques as we know them, which could be a feature – everybody can take part anonymously in the auction, only the winner is named so that tax collectors can know what's going on, but it's not ideal and it is still an open debate.

I have thought about maybe having some money tokens that are named up to a date, and therefore only the auction house can claim them up to that date, and then everybody is open to get them in such a way that you withdraw this kind of coin from the bank by naming the auction house. Then the auction house knows in the conditions that this coin is valid and this certificate is therefore valid up to a date and therefore before that it can be used only by the auction house and then after that date everybody can cash it. Therefore, if the auction took place the bidder can put it back into their account and I doesn't lose the compensation. But it's still a problem. The other problem is that the agency should not be able to use the coin because when you are a big money escrow agency and you have lots and lots of coins, maybe some employees would be really, really tempted to go to Argentina with your data and lead a nice life there, and then you are more prone to an attack if you are known to have huge amounts of money.

So, here are some properties – this is a non exhaustive list because I have many more wishes than these. We need to have in such a context of money escrowing a proof of need for compensation and the availability of the compensation at the end, we should guarantee these things. We should have some resistance to impersonation, by the fact that you are my money escrowing agency, you should not be able to act on my behalf using my guarantee, and this we have attempted to do by having this signing key that is the only one that should be able to unlock the transaction and the conditions should be specified only for transactions done under this key.

And then a point that is raised in identity escrow as well, is the point of separability. We do not want the money escrow agency, or any escrow agency, to take part in everyday life protocols, it's a very expensive thing to always have to rely on third parties for each kind of transaction. And that's a bit more difficult in the context of money escrow than identity escrow because in identity escrow you have the identity, you can release it all the time and it's never invalidated because you are always you. In the case of money escrow, you need to be sure that this compensation has not been used already and therefore it is still an open problem how you can completely separate the worlds of the money escrow agencies and the everyday running, given that the auction house needs to have a guarantee that the compensation is still valid and has not been spent somewhere else. And the mechanism is still quite computationally expensive – many, many signatures, and things like that, especially if we want user compensation not to be for a lot of transactions but only for one transaction. It is also quite expensive because the escrow agency has to do lots of work.

Mike Roe: I have a suggestion as to how you might do the compensation technique. If the compensation names the auction house as payee but is anonymised, you put a serial number in it so that you can make it distinguishable, the auction house can keep a list of bids naming the payee that have been presented in an auction that's running, and do the double spending checking itself.

Ross Anderson: What happens if the vendor himself does a denial of service attack on the purchaser with a view to trowsering the compensation coin?

Reply: The compensation coin is going to be released only in the case when the money in here is not valid.

Ross Anderson: Or in the case of a dead-beat bidder. I consider that the auction house might run a denial of service attack on the bidder.

Reply: A denial of service attack with guns you mean?

Ross Anderson: No not with guns, you SYN-flood the bidder in order for the auction house to get the compensation and keep the cocaine.

Larry Paulson: The money is in the bid.

Reply: Yes. In order for the auction house to claim the compensation it needs to show the data signed by this key, so it cannot change this encrypted message. So the first thing the money escrow agency checks is that the money is valid and only if it is invalid does it release the compensation in such a way that the auction house cannot mess around with that.

Matt Blaze: In this model the auction house is well identified and the bidder is considered to be anonymous.

Reply: Yes, the auction house has to be well identified for more than one reason. We could think of a parallel protocol somehow taking place between the auction house and the actual seller.

Matt Blaze: Right, so the auction house is e-bidding so to speak and may represent multiple sellers.

Reply: In this model we do not make a distinction between the auction house and the seller but this is a crucial point which should be included in future research – to see how there could actually be a parallel protocol happening with the seller and maybe the auction house acting just as an intermediary and this check happening by the seller directly.

Audience: Are time-stamps used in this protocol?

Reply: Yes, given that auctions have a closing date, it is very important actually to time stamp the bids and also to time stamp the lifetime of the auction in such a way that the bidder can claim the compensation back at some point when it is finished. Therefore, in order to convince the money escrow agency that the bid was in time, you actually need to have some time stamps otherwise the auction house says, OK I received this bid but it was not valid because it was too late. So time, especially in the auctions, is quite important. But my aim in presenting the auction as an example is just to illustrate the point of money escrow, and not the implementation details of any auction.

Maybe money escrow (and I have a few ideas that are too rough to present here) could be used in other contexts where you need to have anonymous service, first level assurance and then even higher assurance in case of cheating. I mean maybe this is a model that could be extended to many other protocols where time is not as important as here, so I think that the time stamping should be seen inside the protocol data and conditions.

Wenbo Mao: I'm still not very clear. If this bidder is not a winner, then he hasn't won anything and there is no need for any money transaction. Only a winner is involved in money transactions.

Reply: Yes, this is true. The protocol *could* run in two steps instead of one. The first step is the bid and then there are lots of bids and a winner is drawn and then the second step is the payment. But that then leads to the problem of me, a nice bidder who doesn't want to cheat, making a bid along with lots of other people's bids (and we assume that there is money escrow or identity escrow around us). Then an auction house tells me that I'm the winner and I have to send the money – what if I'm prevented from sending the money? The auction house has no way to know whether I have been prevented or whether I have done it maliciously. But I think the worst part is, the auction house has no way to prove that I haven't sent it. Obviously there could be receipts and a validated receipt mechanism that could be used. But this is why I include both steps inside the same transaction and only the winner is actually going to release the money and the non winners are never going to show the money.

This encrypted money could be considered as a pseudo transaction, because if the auction house does not actually think that this is the winner, it should never require the key.

Frank Stajano: Concerning the dead-beat bidder denial of service attack, if I don't like the auction house and if I don't want to pay but I just want to disrupt the auctions, then every time there is an auction I can bid ten million dollars but never pay. So all the auctions are won by me but I don't pay because I never intended to and so I'm denying service to everybody else who is in the auction.

Bruno Crispo: So it is possible that I deny service to everyone else in the auction even though you may be the winner.

Reply: Yes, I'm sorry these aims were not clear.

Frank Stajano: Basically if the bidder doesn't follow through, the money that's in escrow goes to the auction house and the auction house also keeps the goods. Now ideally if we could, we would like to give support for the transaction to go through so that the auction house receives the payment and the guy gets the goods, whether he wants them or not.

Reply: A necessary condition for the auction house to get the compensation, or even the key, is to give a certificate of ownership. So actually the money escrow agency could (and this is a rough sketch I'm doing here) before actually giving compensation of money, require that the auction house has signed a certificate of ownership for the bidder and this could well be in the conditions of release. So I think this is a question of policy that should be specified.

Tuomas Aura: But wouldn't it be trivial for the auction house to claim two winners?

Reply: Yes, it's true, it could, but then there would be two certificates signed and you'd be able to prove that I have these two certificates. You lose in the short term – you have to go to court I'm afraid to win that one.

John Ioannidis: What if the escrow agency claims an auction denial of service, pays with somebody else's money and gets the goods: you are just moving the problem to a corrupt money escrow from a corrupt auction house.

Reply: Yes, it's true, the escrow agencies have to be trusted in that sense and this is why there is an "s" at the end. Maybe we could distribute, not actually this kind of information, but shares to many escrow agencies with the certificate that they are valid and after that require the auction house to take them from many people, therefore, not attaching so much importance on one agency that could cheat. There is always the problem that the money escrow agency and the auction house could collude to cheat and you would lose, but then you require more and more people to collude and, I hope, it will be less likely that many independent people could act in that way.

Matt Blaze: But if you do that why have the auction house at all, why not just merge the functions of the escrow agency and the auction house, but distribute it?

Geraint Price: Effectively a distributed auction house.

Ross Anderson: I think that the characteristics required to be a successful bank in a small Caribbean country may have something useful to contribute here.

Reply: Yes, given all these mechanisms, I'm not quite sure this could really be used for cocaine! There is this idea of trust that everybody can see differently obviously. The only thing I should think the dealers trust is guns, and I think that this does not really fit into that model.

But yes, in a bit more elaborate proposal, there is actually a bank (that I hope you can trust not to steal from you because otherwise it has no reason to be your bank), that creates many shares that are given to the bidder and the shares are distributed, with the certificates that the shares exist at some point and they are forwarded to the auction house in such a way that no one agency could cheat.

Short Certification of Secure RSA Modulus
(Transcript of Discussion)

Wenbo Mao

HP Laboratories, Bristol

I'm Wenbo Mao, I work for HP Labs at Bristol, and I will be talking about Off-line Public Key Validation (PKV). First I'll introduce: what PKV is, and then Off-line PKV, and the problem with RSA. Then we offer a new solution, and actually the new solution is a protocol. Then that protocol is made into an off-line one, so that just one party must run it, which makes it easier and more efficient. I will not talk about the protocol in detail, that's all in the paper. Here I'll be discussing more the protocol's security properties.

So what is PKV? The purpose of it is to validate some arithmetic properties of the private component, the private key matching a public key, that I think to be important and therefore check with you whether this is true by asking a question. If your answers, or most of your answers, agree then I will carry on, otherwise I shut up and stop talking. [laughter]

Since the use of public key crypto means either to encrypt a message and send it out, or to verify and accept a signature. So my question to you is the following: if you use an invalid public key to do these, is it dangerous? I take it your silence means approval, so I will carry on. [more laughter]

William Harbison: What makes a public key invalid?

Reply: They lose their arithmetic properties. Usually public key crypto is discrete-log based or factorisation based. In the case of discrete-log, there could be a very small group, or a smooth group for which there is no big prime factor group.

Matt Blaze: So an invalid public key is one that's not secure, rather than one for which the private key doesn't work?

Reply: Could be both. In the case of insecure RSA, there could be three prime factors, or maybe some small factors. In the case of invalid RSA, it could be that the owner says, this is my public key, but even he or she doesn't know the private component. Or imagine the smartcard case, the hardware or software had a glitch and so maybe one bit of the private key is flipped.

Markus Kuhn: Is a public key in this case worse than a public key for which the private key has been compromised?

Reply: That could be, yes. It could be easier to compromise the private key.

OK the requirements for secure public key. You have a set of arithmetical requirements for a private key, *e.g.* for RSA, I say, you require two primes and they are of similar size. Yes, this is a requirement. If this requirement isn't met, then the key could be easier to compromise, that is the motivation.

If the owner wants to publish their private key, no-one can stop that. I will not deal with such a problem. However, I'll be talking about a key certification service which is desirable: a server, a CA, can convince an e-commerce provider

B. Christianson et al. (Eds.): Security Protocols, LNCS 2133, pp. 234–237, 2001.

that, yes, this is a good key, a strong key. Then I am pleased, I have a lower liability. So these are desirable properties.

Actually many standard-bodies and groups are doing PKV, so I'm not the only advocate.

One direction of PKV proposed by Don Johnson in several standards bodies is to include the PKV information in a public key certificate. So you only need to do it once. The owner, after generation of his or her public key pair, proves its correctness to the certification authority. And the certification authority verifies it and then signs something within the certificate, thereby moving it off-line. I think of this as a good idea: to include the verification information inside a certificate.

So now we look at some specifics. PKV is easier for discrete logs, regardless of whether the implementation is elliptic curves or the normal way. In the case of elliptic curves, this involves first checking some domain parameter which defines the curve. The check is actually very easy and the standard bodies and groups have already specified how to check these parameters.

After these checks are done then PKV will be very easy, they will just check whether a public key is a point on the curve which is defined by the parameters, and it is a point in the prime order sub group. So this is a desirable feature.

And this can also be seen very clearly in the conventional way of realising discrete logarithms: suppose this is a public key and the X is a private key, here is the generator G and P is a big prime. So we will require that there is a big prime Q which divides P-1, and also G to the Q is 1 while G is not 1, that will guarantee that the group is big. So these are easy to do because all of these are public computations which can be verified by the verifier itself – there is no need for the key owner to help – and so therefore they can be done off-line.

Now something which I say is complicated: a secret thing that I have to verify is that a modulus is a product of two prime factors of roughly equal size. Previously there is not even a way to do this verification. The only known way so far today has at least three steps, and that's a fact of life. So far, if we really want proof of such a statement, you have first to go to using some quadratic residue information to prove that the modulus has two prime factors, but you cannot say that they are not prime powers. So you do this, and then you use some protocol to show that there's no square numbers inside this modulus, which means these powers are one, and then you say, I still don't know, these two proofs don't give you any idea about prime size, so then you have to do this.

Mark Lomas: What do you do if you *want* the key to have three components? This is useful for some purposes.

Michael Roe: Obviously in those protocols you have to make the modulus a little bigger than the RSA setting.

Reply: If you want three components, then you need another set of criteria to do it.

So the last thing that you have to do, you can't verify using only public information, because it's a property of the secret X. I can't verify how many digits a secret has without some help from the key owner. If you really want to say that the public key is in a big group then this can be established, you want to say the prime component is really as large as possible.

So these steps are chronological, which is complicated, and you need three steps, and you need the key owner's help. So it's difficult to make it off-line. Now here I come to solve the problem.

The new method is to show this in one step, saying that about the particular prime. It can be done, although I won't go into the details now; they're in the paper. However we look at some properties here, about efficiency. Since this can be done one step, it is rather easier for us to make it non-interactive. A non-interactive proof or validation is a string of $K log_2 n$ bits, where K is the security parameter which bounds, limits, the probability of error to a very small value. The probability of error is the chance that the RSA key is not valid but the validation passes. So for instance if we look at one embodiment, say for 1024 bit modulus, if you do the proof with $K = 40$ then you have 5KB which I think is small. I even think this verification string, which is totally off-line verifiable, may be included either as a directory in your bigger certificate, or it's easy to go to a URL, it's a block like a PGP key block. So with this parameter you find the error property is one to the one trillion, 2^{-40}. This is quite good.

Although I don't go through the details, I would like to talk about its security, which arises from some condition to allow this off-line validation to happen. This gain does not come from nothing, you have to pay something for this efficiency, namely the owner must disclose two pieces of additional information, each of which is in a big group, of the order n. You disclose $A = g^p \bmod P, B = g^q \bmod P$, two additional constants[1]. These are now public numbers, so the rest of this talk is about the potential security loss due to the disclosure of the additional information.

So what is security? The threat is to find p, q from this mechanism without being able to find them before. Before the problem was to find p, q from n, now it is to find p and q given n and A, B. So I am not allowed to claim this is a factorisation problem, neither I am allowed to claim that it is discrete algorithm problem, this is neither. So the problem is, we need to identify whether it is still a difficult problem, that is the interesting thing.

As usual, we suppose there is an efficient algorithm, efficient meaning polynomial time in the size of n, which given the available data n, g, A, B, P, produces p, q with non-negligible probability. We must know that this algorithm works efficiently only when we have this congruence here, when A and B are related so that $n|XY$ where $X = \log_g A, Y = \log_g B$, so X is congruent to p (mod n), and Y to q (mod n), or vice versa. Otherwise, if they are not so related, the algorithm cannot output $X \bmod n, Y \bmod n$ with non-negligible probability. We assume that factorisation is difficult, so far we cannot find an efficient algorithm to do that, and we say that discrete logarithm is the same, so we can make this assumption. So it's because of this, only because of this, that we can make this assumption about the relationship between A and B.

---

[1] Recall that $n = pq, P = 2\alpha n + 1$ is prime, $g = f^\alpha \bmod P$ where f is random.

Now if we let A', B' be arbitrary elements in the group generated by g then the algorithm will output the exponents with non-negligible probability if and only if n divides $X' \cdot Y'$, in which case X', Y' are permuted from X, Y. So the algorithm actually decides if $(g, A', B', 1)$ is a Diffie-Hellman quadruple, or if A' is in the subgroup generated by A (if B' is in the subgroup generated by B).

So now we come to the conclusion. This is a typical problem here, which is that the algorithm $\mathcal{A}$ decides subgroup membership, and we know that the subgroup membership decision problem is a difficult problem, which hasn't been solved yet, although not frequently used in cryptography. A problem that is frequently used in cryptography, or one equivalent to this, it is to say that the decision problem $\mathcal{A}$ decides whether $(g, A', B', 1)$ is a Diffie-Hellman quadruple. This is a Diffie-Hellman decision problem, which is nowadays very popular in this community to be used as a guarantee of hardness, to prove that something is secure. Here one of the elements is fixed, so it's a special case, and I think because of this, that implies subgroup membership is a difficult. So I leave the talk here.

Authenticating Web-Based Virtual Shops Using Signature-Embedded Marks – A Practical Analysis –

Hiroshi Yoshiura[1], Takaaki Shigematsu[1], Seiichi Susaki[1], Tsukasa Saitoh[1],
Hisashi Toyoshima[1], Chikako Kurita[1], Satoru Tezuka[1], and Ryoichi Sasaki[1]

Systems Development Laboratory, Hitachi, Ltd.,
292 Yoshida-cho, Totsuka-ku, Yokohama, 244-0817 Japan
{last name}@sdl.hitachi.co.jp

Abstract. Authenticating Web-based virtual shops is a critical problem
in establishing electronic commerce as a social infrastructure. One solution is to use guarantee marks pasted on the Web pages of the virtual
shops. However, its effectiveness depends on the reliability of the marks.
This paper proposes a verifiable mark system in which digital signatures
are embedded in the marks. A prototype authentication system based on
this mark system was implemented and evaluated from practical viewpoints. The results show its feasibility.

1 Introduction

Internet-based electronic commerce (EC) is rapidly growing as a social infrastructure. In this type of EC, most consumers communicate with virtual shops
through Web systems. However, since communication thorough the Web is not
face-to-face, but based only on Web page contents and addresses, several problems occur [1,2]:

(1) Impersonation of virtual shops
    Fake virtual shops may trick consumers into doing business with them by
    impersonating established sites. This causes trouble for both the consumers
    and the impersonated virtual shops.
(2) Malicious virtual shops
    Virtual shops may disappear after receiving money without sending the
    goods. They may also sell the consumer's private information. This is trou-
    blesome for consumers.
(3) Unclear service
    Consumers cannot accurately judge the service level of shops. For example,
    the policy on returning goods may be unclear.

One solution to these problems is *virtual shop authentication using marks*,
which has the following procedures [1,2,3]:

– Authorities evaluate virtual shops and, if the shops pass the evaluation, issue
  guarantee or rating marks to them.

B. Christianson et al. (Eds.): Security Protocols, LNCS 2133, pp. 238–248, 2001.

Fig. 1. Example of guarantee.

– These marks are pasted on the Web pages of the shops.
– Consumers trust shops displaying these guarantee marks or can understand their service level via the rating marks.

Fig. 1 shows an example of a guarantee mark.

However, since marks in the cyber world are simply image data and are easy to copy, forge, and tamper with, the following new problems occur:

(1) Virtual shops that have not been given marks might copy marks from the Web pages of other shops or forge them. Then, they could impersonate these other shops or pretend to be guaranteed shops.
(2) Virtual shops might tamper with the designs of marks and thus pretend to have a better rating than they actually do.

These problems will destroy consumer trust in the marks and undermine mark-based authentication. Therefore, mark-based authentication must not only show marks to consumers but also provide consumers with means for confirming their validity. This paper proposes a verifiable mark system and a virtual shop authentication system based on it. Sect. 2 clarifies the requirements for mark systems for Web site authentication and Sect. 3 proposes a mark system that meets these requirements. Sect. 4 describes an implementation and its evaluation. Sect. 5 compares the proposed method with alternatives and Sect. 6 concludes the paper.

2 Requirements for Mark Systems for Virtual Shop Authentication

The following requirements must be met by mark systems in virtual shop authentication.

(1) Validity confirmation
   R1a: The consumer can confirm that a mark on a Web page has been authentically issued to the virtual shop.

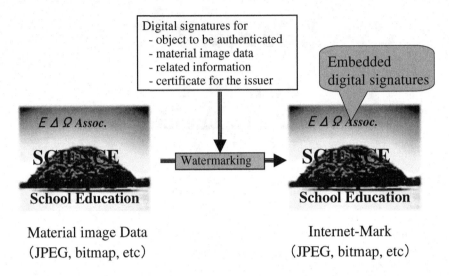

Fig. 2. Basic structure of an Internet-Mark.

R1b: The consumer can confirm the current validity of the marks.

These requirements are essential for keeping trust in the marks.

(2) Operability

R2a: Operations for the validity confirmation are easy for consumers.

R2b: Response time of the validity conformation is short enough, i.e., the confirmation processes do not irritate consumers

These requirements are necessary for practical use.

(3) Low cost

R3a: Setting up and operating costs for consumers are zero or negligible.

R3b: Setting up and operating costs for the evaluation authorities and virtual shops are within acceptable limits.

These requirements are also necessary for practical use.

(4) Extensibility

R4: The confirmation and operation methods are easy to change and extend.

This is necessary for long-term use.

3   Mark System for Virtual Shop Authentication

3.1   Internet-Marks

Our strategy is to use Internet-Marks, the digital marks for authentication, which we have already proposed [4]. As shown in Fig. 2, an Internet-Mark is a digital image into which digital signatures are embedded by digital watermarking. The digital signatures are signatures for the data to be authenticated, for the material image, and for related information such as time.

3.2 Internet-Marks for Virtual Shop Authentication

This section proposes Internet-Marks for virtual shop authentication, as shown in Fig. 3. In the rest of this paper, an Internet-Mark for virtual shop authentication, a digital signature, and a virtual shop are simply called *a mark, a signature, and a shop*, respectively. An evaluation authority is also abbreviated as *an EA*. Signers of signatures are assumed to be evaluation authorities (EAs).

The following items are embedded in a mark:

(1) Signatures for the identifier of the shop to which the mark will be given the URL and IP address of the shop's Web site are used as the identifier. These signatures enable the mark to be detected if it is used by another Web site.
(2) A signature for the material image, which enables tampering with the mark to be detected.
(3) The term of validity of the mark and its signature, which enables the system to detect if the mark has expired.
(4) Names of the EA and virtual shop and their signatures, which enables the system to correctly show these names to consumers.
(5) Certificate of the EA's public key, which has been issued by a Certification Authority and which enables the verification of the signatures mentioned in (1) through (4).

Fig. 4 shows the mark verification method, which extracts the signatures, the certificate, and the additional items (e.g., the term of validity) from the mark and verifies the signatures using the certificate.

3.3 Virtual Shop Authentication Using Internet-Marks

This section describes a virtual shop authentication method consisting of the following steps (Fig. 5):

(1) The certification authority issues a certificate of the EA's public key.
(2) The shop applies for a mark by sending its address (URL and IP address) to the EA.
(3) The EA evaluates the virtual shop and, if the shop passes the evaluation, issues a mark for the Web site by the method mentioned above and sends it to the shop.
(4) The shop pastes the received mark onto its Web page.
(5) The mark is validated when the Web page with the mark is downloaded to the consumer's machine. A validation program installed in the consumer's machine validates the mark by the above-mentioned method. This validation can either guarantee or deny each of the following:
  (a) The mark is on the Web page of the shop to which the EA issued it.
  (b) The mark has not been forged or tampered with.
  (c) The mark has not expired (i.e., it is within its term of validity).
  The names of the EA and the virtual shop are also shown to the consumer.

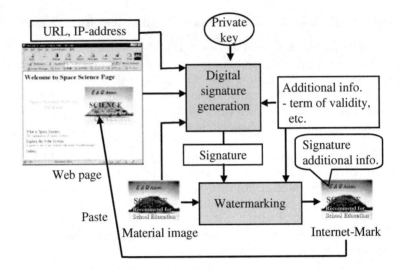

Fig. 3. Internet-Mark for virtual shop authentication (Generation).

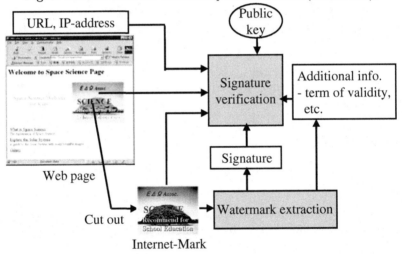

Fig. 4. Internet-Mark for virtual shop authentication (Verification).

4   Implementation and Evaluations

4.1   Implementation

A prototype of this authentication system has already been completed. This prototype has a total program size of 45 kilolines of code in C language and is very close to the final practical system. This section describes this prototype.

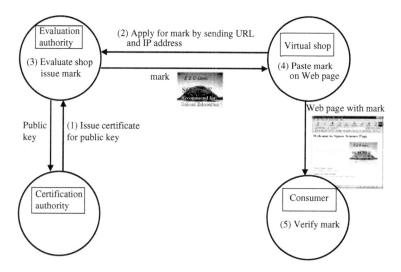

Fig. 5. Protocols of proposed virtual shop authentication.

(1) Mark

The material of a mark is an image with an area of roughly 100x100 pixels that has been JPEG-compressed. A total of 2 Kbytes of data for the signatures, certificate, and additional information are embedded in this image. The mark has noise on it caused by the data embedding, but, as shown in Fig. 6, this noise is weak and thus does not disturb the consumers' recognition of the mark.

(2) Pasting mark to Web page

The link to the mark is described in the HTML definition of the Web page, as a link to an ordinary JPEG image.

(3) Installing the validation program

Installation of the validation program is automated by using Script commands.

These commands download the validation program from the EA site to the consumer's machine if it has not yet been installed. The commands are included in the HTML definition of the Web pages and are activated when the page definition is parsed by the Web browser.

(4) Activating the validation program

An existing function of the Web browser is used, i.e., the browser activates the program when it encounters a link to the mark in the HTML page definition.

(5) Response time of the verification

Total response time (including extracting the signatures from the mark, verifying them, and displaying the results) is less than 1 second on a personal computer having a 266MHz CPU.

(6) Displaying the results

Fig. 7(a) shows an example display of successful authentication. The dis-

Fig. 6. Internet-Mark generated from image in Fig. 1. The image has a little noise but this does not affect image recognition.

played information is enough for consumers to trust the shop. Fig. 7(b) shows the display of an authentication failure, which reveals that the mark has been copied from other Web site.

(7) Upgrading the validation program

The validation program is re-installed when the confirmation and operation methods are changed. This re-installation is automated in the following way:

(a) Each mark has its version embedded in itself.

(b) The validation program first checks the version of the mark and, if the mark is a newer version, downloads the latest version of the program.

4.2   Evaluations

This section evaluates the proposed method in the light of the requirements mentioned in Sect. 2.

(1) Validity confirmation

R1a (Verification): As mentioned in Sect. 3.3(5), success in signature verification can guarantee that a mark has not been copied, forged, or tampered with.

R1b (Current validity): The expiry of a mark can be detected by comparing the embedded term of validity against the current time taken from the clock in the consumer's machine. However, it is not possible to detect that a mark has been revoked within its term of validity, because the EA cannot change the mark after it has been sent out.

(2) Operability

R2a (Ease of operation): Consumers do not need to do anything; installation and activation of the verification programs are automatic.

R2b (Response time): The response time of the mark validation depends only on the performance of the consumer's machine and not on either the network or the EA's machine because the validation is a local process in the consumer's machine. The response time is under 1 second on a

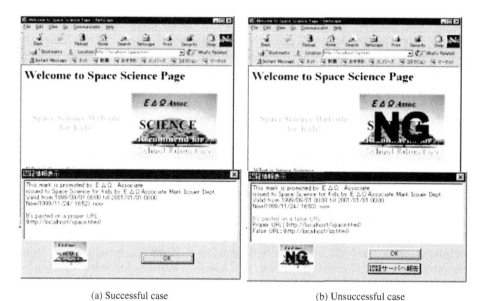

(a) Successful case   (b) Unsuccessful case

Fig. 7. Example display of verification result.

typical personal computer as mentioned in Sect. 4.1(5) so it is acceptable in practice.

The time taken to download the verification program is 1 to 3 minutes. Although this is not short, it seems acceptable because downloading is done only for initial installation and when upgrading.

(3) Low cost

R3a (Cost to consumers): None. Consumers do not require any additional equipment because the verification programs run on their existing computers.

R3b (Cost to EAs and shops): An EA needs a server machine and systems for mark generation, an interface with a Web site (for receiving mark requests and sending marks), database management (for recording the Web sites it has authorized), and downloading validation programs. The labor cost to the EA is small because the reception of mark requests and the generation and transmission of marks can be automated.

A shop needs a server machine, HTML editor, Web server, and an interface system with the EA. However, the additional cost is only for the interface system because the other four systems are already necessary for normal Web services. The labor cost for the Web site is for pasting marks onto its pages, but this is small because the pasting is done as ordinary HTML page definition.

(4) Extensibility

R4: Systems need to be changed in the machines of consumers, shops, and EAs. Changes in consumer machines could be problematic because these machines are widely spread. Changes in the shop machines could be also problematic. Actually, however, changes in the consumer machines are easy because upgrading of the validation programs is automatic, as mentioned in Sect. 4.1(7), by embedding the version IDs in marks. Changes in shops are pasting new marks with new embedded information. This is easy because it is done as an ordinary HTML page definition.

Thus the proposed method is easy to extend.

5   Comparison and Combination with Alternative

5.1   Comparison with Alternatives

Although several institutes and companies have proposed virtual shop authentication using marks and some of the proposed systems are in real operation, details of their methods have not been disclosed. However, we can guess from the literature that these methods can be classified into the following two types:

(1) Off-line authentication

All the information needed for authentication is attached to Web pages by embedding it into marks on the pages or by some other methods and authentication processes are performed locally in consumers' machines. Our proposed method belongs to this type.

(2) On-line authentication

Some information for authentication is located at EA sites and authentication processes involve communication with the EA machines.

The properties of off-line authentication depend on the information attached to the Web pages and the attachment method. Comparison between our proposed method and other off-line methods has already been reported [4]. On-line authentication is totally different from our proposed method. Thus this section compares it with on-line authentication. Table 1 summarizes the comparison.

In online-authentication, the EA maintains a database of information about the virtual shops it has evaluated. The mark confirmation process sends information (e.g., URL) of the virtual shop with which the consumer is communicating. The EA judges whether or not it can guarantee this virtual shop by referring to its database. Although the communications between the consumer and the EA can be attacked, signature-based secure communication such as SSL can be used to resist these attacks. Revocation within the term of validity can be detected by constantly maintaining the database, and this function is an advantage of on-line authentication over the proposed method.

A problem with on-line authentication is that the response time depends on the traffic status because it requires communication between the consumer and the EA machines. In addition, the computational burden on the EA machine is heavy when it communicates with many consumer machines at once. This computational burden can be handled by using a high-performance machine, but this solution imposes a high cost on the EA.

Table 1. Comparison between proposed method and on-line authentication.

| Method | Validity confirmation | | Operability | | Cost | Extensibility |
	Verification	Current validity	Ease of operation	Response time		
On-line authentication	Same as signatures	Revocation not detected	Easy	Constantly small	Low	Good
Proposed method	Same as signatures	Revocation detected	Easy	Depend on environment	High	Good

In summary, our proposed method is inferior to on-line authentication in terms of revocation detection but superior in terms of response time and cost to the EA. It is thus more acceptable for consumers and EAs.

5.2   Combination with On-Line Authentication

Since our method cannot detect mark revocation, while on-line authentication can, one idea is to combine the best features of each.

(1) Use the proposed method in ordinary situations.
(2) Use on-line authentication in critical situations such as when sending money.

This combined method can detect mark revocation in critical situations, and consumers seem willing to accept the long response time of on-line authentication because it only occurs in critical situations. EA machines do not communicate with many consumer at once, so high-cost machines are not needed. Thus on-line authentication can be incorporated into the proposed method to improve security without degrading performance.

6   Conclusion

Virtual shop authentication using marks is becoming widespread. However, its effectiveness depends on the reliability of the marks, i.e., users should be able to confirm that the marks were authentically issued to the virtual shops and have not expired. Moreover, mark confirmation must not disturb consumers, the operation cost must be small, and the system must be extensible.

To meet these requirements, this paper proposed the use of Internet-Marks, the verifiable marks in which digital signatures are embedded. A prototype authentication system based on Internet-Marks was implemented and evaluated from practical viewpoints. Comparison with alternative methods showed its superiority and also suggested that combination with on-line verification could improve security without degrading performance. The proposed method has been tested by real users and will be soon deployed.

References

1. White Paper of the Ministry of Posts and Telecommunications of Japan, 1999, p30.
2. Electronic Commerce Promotion Council of Japan, Proceedings of ECOM Forum'99, 1999.
3. The U.S. Government Working Group on Electronic Commerce,: Toward Digital eQuality - 2nd Annual Report, http://www.doc.gov/ecommerce/ecomrce.pdf, 1999.
4. H. Yoshiura, S Susaki, Y Nagai, T Saitoh, H Toyoshima, R Sasaki and S Tezuka,: INTERNET-MARKs: Clear, Secure, and Portable Visual Marks for the Cyber Worlds, 1999 Cambridge International Workshop on Security Protocols, 1999.

Authentication Web-Based Virtual Shops Using Signature-Embedded Marks – A Practical Analysis – (Transcript of Discussion)

Hiroshi Yoshiura

Systems Development Laboratory, Hitachi Ltd.

I would like to talk about authenticating Web-based virtual shops using Internet-Marks. Last year my colleague Sasaki presented the basic idea[1], so this year I present the methods and system. This system has been adopted by one of the largest economic societies in Japan, to which tens of thousands of companies belong, so this method has a high probability to become the Japanese standard.

This is the content. First, problems with Web-based electric commerce will be detailed. Virtual shop authentication using Internet-Marks will be proposed, and implementation and evaluation will be reported.

Problems. Most users communicate with a virtual shop through the Web, but this communication is not face to face – usually it is based only on the Web page contents. For example, the consumer contacts the virtual shop using Yahoo. This means using only a keyword, so only Web page content is recognised. This causes several problems. Impersonation, for example: a fake virtual shop impersonates an established shop. Criminal action: disappear after receiving money without sending goods. Unclear service policies, for example on returning goods.

Authentication using a video mark or a seal is one effective solution to these problems. In this solution, an authority evaluates the virtual shop according to guidelines and then issues a mark guaranteeing or rating them. These marks are pasted on the Web page of the virtual shop. This is an example Web page and this is a guarantee mark: the consumers trust or know the service level of the virtual shop, due to the mark. Using a mark is a potentially good solution, I think, because complex meaning can be briefly expressed by a mark. For example, this mark may mean that the evaluator guarantees that this shop is suitable for school science education in the way that guidelines require.

After having been repeatedly used, the meaning of the mark will be widely recognised. Similar and confusing marks could be prohibited by trademark laws, and these effects cannot be achieved by other representation means. However, using marks has serious problems. First, it is easy to copy the forged marks, so a virtual shop can still impersonate a guaranteed shop by copying its mark; pretend to be guaranteed by a phoney mark; or pretend to have a better rating by tampering with a mark. So our research purpose is to establish the validity of marks in virtual shop authentication.

---

[1] LNCS 1796, 195–207.

B. Christianson et al. (Eds.): Security Protocols, LNCS 2133, pp. 249–252, 2001.

Now I propose a method. First of all I will clarify the requirements for a mark system for virtual shop authentication. Validity confirmation by consumers is an essential requirement. The consumer should be able to confirm that a mark on a Web page has indeed been issued to this shop by the designated authority, and that the mark is currently valid. The operability is a critical consideration for practical use. Authentication should be easy for the consumer and it have rapid response. Cost is also critical for practical use, it should be negligible for the customer and acceptable to the validation authority and virtual shop. Extensibility is important for long-term operation.

This method is based on the Internet-Mark which we presented last year, so I briefly review the Internet-Mark. Internet-Marks are secure marks, because digital signatures are embedded in them by digital water-marking. Digital signatures are generated for the digital object for which the Internet-Mark will be used, and the material in this data itself, and a generated signature will be embedded into this image to generate an Internet-Mark. So each Internet-Mark has a digital signature embedded in it for virtual shop authentication, which includes the URL and IP addresses of the virtual shop which will be guaranteed by the Internet-Mark, and the corresponding Web page. The signatures are generated for these URL and IP addresses, Web page content and material image, and embedded to generate the Internet-Mark. Additional information, including term of validity, name of issuer and virtual shop, are also embedded within this digital signature. A certificate for the issuer is also embedded. Then this Internet-Mark will be pasted on the Web page.

Verifying an Internet-Mark. We have URL and IP addresses of the virtual shop that the user is currently communicating with, and the corresponding Web page. The Internet-Mark is pasted on the Web page, and so the first step is cut out this Internet-Mark. Then the signature is extracted from the mark and this signature is verified by comparing with the URL, IP address and the Web page content, and the material image data.

Additional information is also verified by signature. A certificate is used to establish the issuer's public key. This is how each information item is used. The URL and IP address are used to detect if the Internet-Mark is copied from elsewhere, from another site. The Web page contents detect altered Web pages, and this image data is used to detect altered Internet-Mark design. The public key protects all the Internet-Mark, and the time of validity detects Internet-Mark expiry. The names are used to correctly show to the user.

This is the protocol. The first step is that the CA issues a certificate for an evaluation authority.

Question: How does my browser know which certificates to accept?

Reply: You are pointing out that everybody can pretend to be an evaluation authority by getting a certificate and issuing Internet-Marks.

Question: At least one issuer of an Internet-Mark can pretend to be another, if their images are similar.

Reply: I have two comments. One is that impersonation of an evaluation authority is rare compared with impersonation of virtual shops. The second comment is that we have several versions of the system, and I think this problem can be solved by . . .

Michael Roe: . . . the water-marking protocol, that can put data into the image in such a way that it's very hard for an attacker to modify that image to take data out. If you've got that then in fact they can't modify an image in such a way as to embed their identity.

Ross Anderson: Why not just use the standard certificate instead of a copyright mark? You can give everybody in Japan a piece of software which displays the logo of the certification authority, and the URL and so on certified, surely that's enough.

Reply: Oh that's a good question. What the consumer will get from the individualised signed mark is better than what they would get from the issuing authority seal of approval.

An evaluation authority has specific knowledge and skills, and validates virtual shops from various points of view, for example evaluating virtual shops from the view point of privacy, and the view point of the service level. This authority has very much greater know-how, including knowledge of the guidelines, a CA is a more general validation organisation.

Matt Blaze: What are the semantics of verifying, or interpreting, a mark that appears inside a frame? A frame being a component of a Web page that's actually on a different server with a different URL. One possible way of getting a mark on my Web page that wasn't actually issued to my Web page would be to display the mark that's on another Web page inside a frame. This is a problem of the discrimination grain. Using only this information, one cannot discriminate two different Web pages.

Frames break quite a few things, because there's no right answer as to what the semantics should be. If you say, use the outer, top-level frame, then nothing on display inside a frame will every verify. If you've got to use the innermost frame, then you have this "this thing is framed in" attack.

Ross Anderson: There's an argument for using a mark instead of a certificate! An alert person can see that . . .

Matt Blaze: . . . if they notice that it's a frame. If the browser sees that it's getting different security indications for different parts of the frame, then it should indicate that to the user somehow, it should say, this is a mixed object and you should be aware of it. Web-site designers who want to use this should make sure that anything covered by the page is somebody else's.

Reply: So. Implementation and evaluation. Downloading and activation. The evaluation authority has a validation program of the size of several hundred gigabits, and Internet-Mark. The virtual shop has a Web page which is defined in html. Linked to the Internet-Mark is a script to download and activate the validation program, described as part of the html definition. The html is downloaded to the consumer, and the consumer system is the Web browser, because we have the labour of undergraduates, and the Web browser first checks that the validation programme exists or not. If yes then activate, and if not download this program, which takes about one minute on a 64 kilobit line, and the downloaded program is saved and activated.

Once the validation programme has been activated, the next step is to check that the versions of the Internet-Mark and the program coincide. If yes, then to validate an Internet-Mark takes less than one second on a PC. If not, reload later version by this program. We have an example of this case, this is a successful case, this is the Web page and this is the Internet-Mark, and this is a dialogue box that the validation program showed to the user. This is the unsuccessful case, the mark is changed and the superimposed "NG" means no good. This may be Japanese English. This dialogue box says that the Internet mark is based on a false site.

Comparing the time of validity of the Internet-Mark and the local clock confirms that the mark is still valid, but the location of an Internet-Mark within its time of validity cannot be detected, because an evaluation authority cannot change an Internet-Mark that has already been sent out. But this problem can be solved by combination with ongoing validation. So consumers need do virtually nothing, because if the situation and activation of the verification programme is automatic, where first time is less than one second. This cost has been has been accepted in real end-users.

Extendability: no consumer operation is needed, because upgrading the verification programme is automated. Few operations are needed at the virtual shop, because pasting new marks to Web pages is ordinary html editing. As for an evaluation authority, considerable work is needed, but that's not a big problem.

So I conclude. Consumers should be able to confirm the validity of authentication marks. Authentication is by using the Internet-Mark proposal, which contains signatures for Web site address and Web page contents, time of validity, names of issuing shops and a Certificate for the issuer. Its feasibility has been shown by implementation and validation. Thank you for your attention.

I Cannot Tell a Lie
(Transcript of Discussion)

Mark Lomas

Goldman Sachs International

This will just be a brief remark, but I'd first like to say what inspired it. At the 12th International Symposium on Economic Crime there was a presentation by the Attorney General of Bermuda where he told about a court case that had happened in the US where a US citizen was served with an order by the court to write to a bank in Bermuda asking them whether he had an account with them, and if he did, to send details of all the transactions that had taken place against that account. So what the court was trying to do was overrule the Bermudan banking secrecy laws. What I asked him at the time was, would it have been legal for a Bermudan bank to have a special form of bank account for American citizens where the contract says, if you wish to request any information about your account, we're happy to give it to you provided you send us a signed affidavit saying you are not subject to any request for that information by any judicial authority anywhere. And his response was, yes that would be perfectly legal and that's a good idea.

This inspired a thought following the discussions on Monday about the RIP bill. The actual text has a few holes in it but this is essentially the idea. Suppose I'm trying to write a corporate security policy. Let's imagine it says, a type A certificate is a signed affidavit requesting some information that is in a foreign jurisdiction, for the sake of argument our US headquarters. It's requesting the information but it ought to assert that this request is not being made at the request of anybody else, in particular, is not at the request of any judicial authority. A type B certificate is very similar, it says I want this information and either I have received a type A certificate, in other words somebody else has given me an affidavit that they're not subject to a judicial warrant, or I've been given a type B certificate. So the type B certificate is to allow you a chaining rule, so that you can have a collection of certificates which together say, all the people who participated in this agree that none of us has been served with a warrant. And then I say, it is my corporate security policy that under no circumstances may anybody return information to the United Kingdom unless they are given one of these certificates.

The idea behind this is that if I wish to retain backups of cryptographic keys, for instance, I should send them to some foreign jurisdiction where they are subject to this security policy. If I were then to be sent an intercept warrant saying, we would like to have a copy of your backup key, I can say, it's impractical for me to give you the key because I don't have it, and I can prove – it's written down in my security policy – that I do not keep backups of my own keys. I keep them offshore and I'm perfectly happy to tell you where I keep them. However,

B. Christianson et al. (Eds.): Security Protocols, LNCS 2133, pp. 253–255, 2001.
© Springer-Verlag Berlin Heidelberg 2001

the people offshore are subject to this rule. So that's the thought I'd like to implant in your mind.

Matt Blaze: My impression (one of the most valuable things I've learned from the amount of time I've spent talking with lawyers) is that, at least in the United States, the law is very much not a computer program. This is not a Turing Machine that will simply operate according to the instructions and rule sets, even though the instructions and rules look very much like programs. The judges tend to be, if not smarter than we think they are, they are at least less patient with what they consider nonsense than we might hope they are. So I can imagine being ordered to commit perjury by a judge, at least in the United States, who believes that he is right.

Reply: Isn't that a conspiracy, if you're requesting somebody to commit an offence?

Matt Blaze: But it's not an offence committed in the United States, so if they ordered you to do it you'd just have to do it.

Ross Anderson: Surely you cannot order somebody to commit perjury, because so much of the legal infrastructure by rests upon sworn statements by lawyers.

Matt Blaze: I think the judge, or the prosecutor, might argue that this was not an operative legal deposition, it's specifically intended to subvert the rule of law. You know, judges have wider latitude, at least in the States and probably here, then externally you might think they do. So one has to be very careful. I wouldn't want to be the first person to appear before a court ...

Michael Roe: ... to be found in contempt of court for having said nothing in the first place!

Ross Anderson: Well the perjury attack can be very simple. Just modify logon, so it asks you each logon: is the password that you're about to enter being entered under any compulsion, under any jurisdiction that follows you, and under the use of any penalty for perjury? And if you answer "yes" then your hard disk will crash. How would that run with H.M. Customs I wonder?

Reply: There's another thought that comes to mind, although it is slightly facetious. Would it be legal for you to attach a lie detector to your computer?

Ross Anderson: To use computer evidence in a criminal trial you've currently got to have a statement by the operator of the computer saying that the evidence was produced by the system. Now unfortunately the Law Commission has recommended that this be removed. Maybe the industry should block the removal of that, so if you're placed under compulsion, certainly if you're forced to commit perjury, you can simply decline to issue the certificate.

John Ioannidis: My argument on whether we can come up with technology to preserve the last few rights we have left, is that if they're really out to get us then they can always change other rules and get us anyway. Maybe I'm being extremely pessimistic about the ability of the system to defend itself or us, but if a judge wants to throw me in jail, he will find a way to throw me in jail whatever I do, however long a statement I may give. And frankly if I try to be too clever, he will probably put me in a deeper jail and in a colder cell.

Frank Stajano: I think that if you view the law as a sort of system, then when the law is changed you have to find another way through it, and so on.

Reply: Actually in my particular case I think the judge would probably say, yes I agree with all that argument, but I also think that anybody who thinks the way you do is inappropriate to hold a banking licence.

Afterward

Larry Paulson: I've always wanted to know why these RFCs are created as plain ASCII text files with figures drawn in ASCII art as if this were 1975.

Matt Blaze: You can still read them. Would you rather have them formatted for a printer that was discontinued in 1979?

Larry Paulson: I'm quite serious, it's no wonder that people make mistakes when the documents are so hard to follow.

Roger Needham: I think the serious point is that the documents that specify these protocols tend to be so repulsive that ... [laughter]

John Ioannidis: I don't think that they're repulsive. I don't even think that this should be discussed here.

Matt Blaze: That won't stop us!

John Ioannidis: Do you think that the repulsion of the documents would be reduced if they had jumping frogs, like some Web homepages?

Roger Needham: It's an intellectual problem not a typographic one.

Bruce Christianson: Ribbit ... Ribbit ...

Roger Needham: I think we should move on.

Michael Roe: Well there isn't actually an official drinks reception, but we could just go down the pub and see what happens[1] ...

---

[1] Nothing happened. The frog remained a frog.

B. Christianson et al. (Eds.): Security Protocols, LNCS 2133, p. 256, 2001.
© Springer-Verlag Berlin Heidelberg 2001

Author Index

Lecture Notes in Computer Science

For information about Vols. 1–2086
please contact your bookseller or Springer-Verlag